The Pit

Written by Vlad Vorgal

Inspired by true events.

Self publishing

Chapter 1

Very early in the morning, a Grand Cherokee was meandering graciously along the road running through the rocky massifs of the Bucegi Mountains, which are among the most impressive and majestic mountains of Romania. As the sun was rising behind the wooded crests of the Carpathians, the last ghosts of the night were slowly gliding over the old fir trees that clad these legendary Transylvanian mountains, one of the last truly wild landscapes left in Europe.

The jeep's driver was steering in apparent relaxation, taking in deep breaths of the fresh mountain air of the wonderful November morning through the half-open window. He had woken up in a very good mood; this was the day he had been waiting for and for which he had been making preparations over the last months. This was the moment of truth, as he would call it.

On the back seat, his eyes staring at the road unfurling in front of him and breathing almost imperceptibly but very quickly, his mouth half open, was the protagonist of that morning, whose name was on more and more people's lips in certain circles. Some would say he had supernatural powers, which they would put down to external additives, while others would speculate it was pure luck and that he hadn't met the right opponent. There were others yet, those who had a well-trained eye for it and who had been in the field for many years, who would find in him a paragon of all the qualities they had been looking for all these years. He had all that and something extra. His name was Bronco.

He was a superb specimen of American pit bull terrier, aged one year and four months, the gladiator of the canine world, deemed by the lovers of this legendary fighter the uncrowned king of all dog breeds ever. His fur was dark russet, except for the chest, which was covered with a symmetrical white spot. His dark yellow vigilant eyes seemed to transfix you, a clear sign of this animal's psychical power. His muscular body sat still, as if thrust on the back seat of the SUV, knowing exactly from the energy transmitted by his master what would come next. And he could hardly wait. He had been bred for it, because he had been training every day, and because all his genes told him he was the best. Born to fight.

His master, Radu Voicu, though he might have seemed completely relaxed to those who did not know him, was actually totally focused on what was going to happen, projecting the victory and letting his feelings of love, pride, and trust in his dog run like waves of energy through every fiber of his body and turn into goose pimples. Ever since he could remember, dogs were what he had liked and what he had always fallen for in this world. As he had grown up in communist Romania, where people could hardly afford semi-decent food for their family, his parents had not allowed him to have a dog, but they would take him to the dog exhibition organized by the Party every year. This was the moment he'd wait for the whole year; he would try to pat and play with every dog there, and they would answer him with the same affection. Dogs had always loved him and were attracted to him like a magnet.

When he grew older and could afford, at last, to buy himself one, he bought a Boxer, but shortly after that, since the communist wall fell and the first pit bull specimens appeared in Romania, he had a crush. He knew that dog was made for him. Nothing ever impressed him more than this breed and he never felt the same respect and love for other breeds as he felt for them. Ever since then, he only reared pit bulls, dozens of them. He kept a small number of those he looked after but those were top class specimens. That was Bronco's case;

he was one of the six pit bulls Radu owned now, and his greatest hope.

Bronco came from a pack of four males and two females, who had been fighting since they were two months old. Their mother, Cindy, was an absolutely exquisite specimen, a chocolate babe, four years old. Now retired from the world of fighting, she had won all eight matches she had participated in. Cindy was also Radu's dog, he had bought her in Serbia when she was seven weeks old from a stock farm there, and she had an old lineage of champions. He had paid $1500 for her, which was an awful lot of money back then, but since the moment he bought her, this lovely dog had been his pride and joy. Her affectionate temperament, her sharp intelligence, and her fierceness in battle while fighting other female dogs in the ring had won her Radu's love and respect entirely.

The puppies' father was Romania's champion, a tawny red-nosed male, who had also been imported from Serbia and had not only been undefeated on Romanian territory, but also won the fight with Attila the Iron Kid, Hungary's absolute champion. The stake of that contest had been $20,000 among the dogs' owners only; the total sum gambled reached hundreds of thousands. Radu had to go to Bucharest in order to mate his bitch, for which he had paid $1000, but the investment had been worth the money. He got the dog he had always wanted, the perfect pit bull.

Bronco's qualities were clearly superior to all the fighters he had seen before, and he had seen hundreds of ring dogs. He had kept the four male dogs until they were six months old because he knew that, even if both parents had exceptional qualities, not all the puppies would inherit them; on the contrary, in most situations, not even one puppy of a real champion matches the parents' value. However, this was not Bronco's case. Since he was three months old, whenever he engaged in serious fights, longer than ten minutes, with his siblings, he would always be the best. Since he was about four months old, Radu allowed him to fight his siblings in one-to-one competitions. After fifteen or twenty minutes, the opponent would show that it was tired, and it would be replaced with another one, which was ready to start. Bronco would win the new battle every time, irrespective of the order Radu chose for the remaining three dogs.

He developed mentally, knowing that it was not enough for him to defeat one opponent. Odds were that another one would replace it, for which he had to be prepared. Radu knew that Bronco was a champion. And that morning, he was certain that Bronco would do justice to the trust he had in him. In the contest for the category of twenty-five kilos, he would meet Voodoo, a black male of one year and a half, which came from the south of the country and had not been defeated in the three contests he had fought.

The road along which Radu was driving was crossed by a by-road, which Radu took, a road that led deep into the mountains. After approximately twenty minutes of driving along the gravel road, which went deeper and deeper into the forest darkness, the sunbeams efficiently filtered by tall fir trees that grew just a few meters from one another, Radu reached a wooden barrier. A few acquaintances of his were there chatting; among them was Viorel, his host.

His house, which stood in the middle of the forest, used to be a woodsman's house; he had bought it a few years before as a party house, though what he had built behind it was the most important asset. In his huge yard, which looked more like a glade, there was a fighting pit. It was made from girders, thoroughly tied with ropes, and had a diameter of twenty square meters. It wasn't exactly a professional pit, but it definitely served its purpose.

Radu greeted the guys fleetingly while they were lifting the barrier for him to pass, after which he entered and parked his car as remotely as possible from the pit in order to be as far as he could from the crowd. As always, he wanted to spend a few more seconds of peace with his gladiator before the fight started. He let him free and allowed him to mark the trees in the area for a few minutes then he called him and, while affectionately caressing his head, he whispered reassuring words in his ear. Bronco, his ears turned backwards, could feel the trust and love imparted by his master and fully enjoyed these moments of calm before the storm, which he knew was near. Then the two of them, dog and master, headed for the crowd gathered around the pit, sharing the same focus and giving out the same energy.

Radu was holding the bottle he had prepared for the contest in his hand and, in his pocket, he had a thin piece of hard wood, which he might need to slip into the dog's mouth in case the two opponents had to be separated. There had already been two matches, one for female dogs and one for two heavy males of over thirty kilos, but Radu was not curious to know the results. He asked, out of courtesy, a guy he knew how his female dog had done; unfortunately, she had lost, and her master was caressing and encouraging her while they were heading for the car. Radu's eyes met those of Voodoo's owner. Both nodded, which meant they could wash their dogs. He handed Bronco over to Lorin, his best friend, who would never miss a contest featuring any of his dogs, and made for Voodoo, which was now held on a leash by a friend of his owner. Radu knelt and started to wash Voodoo with the water from the bottle, while Voodoo's owner did the same thing for Bronco. This was to prevent either of the breeders from cheating by anointing his dog with various substances that might harm the opponent during the fight. Once this was done, Radu headed for Lorin and took Bronco back. He took him in his arms and they entered the pit. In the opposite corner, Voodoo was taken into the pit by his master. It was the moment of truth.

Chapter 2

Radu came from Galati, an average city in terms of size in Romania, with an intense economy. A city on the Danube, it was the second largest port in the country. In the last many years, the city had been mainly supported by an iron and steel plant that had been built during Ceausescu's Communist regime, which continued to work after the fall of the Iron Curtain. However, as on any other level and in any other field in post-communist Romania, the chaos unleashed by the lack of prohibitions, which the people who had lived under the communist yoke for so many years started to feel in the first hours of the revolution, made itself felt in the people's approach to the plant. Thus, hundreds of kilos of tin left the plant daily without being recorded anywhere, and between the hundreds of thousands of dollars which lined the pockets of the people in power and the petty thieves who would sneak into the plant through the sewers during the night to steal and then load the wheelbarrows waiting for them outside with the stolen stuff, the plant was eventually depleted.

Radu grew up on the outskirts of the city. He had a happy childhood, even if largely deprived of the comforts enjoyed by the children in neighboring countries. In the last years of communism, electric power was cut off between 4 p.m. and 9 p.m. for the whole city, a reason for joy as Radu and his school mates could play in front of the block of flats without being disturbed by their mothers, who would yell at their children and tell them to come home and do their homework as soon as the power was on again. That would be the saddest moment of the evening for them.

In the winter, the children would play in pitch darkness, with only the moon casting its light on the thick layer of snow where the kids were rolling over, sleighing, or snowball fighting. It was terrific. He could also remember how, in the winter, his mother would put two bricks in the oven to get hot, and then wrap them up in thick towels and put them under the blanket to keep their feet warm during the night. There were almost no TV programs; during the week, the only spectacle to watch was Ceausescu, who would enthusiastically announce that production records had been broken again, while food store windows were always empty, and the queues for fresh bread and milk endlessly long; that was their everyday life. At weekends they would occasionally broadcast a Romanian film advertising the same lofty ideas.

There were no computers or video games nor were there video players, so the kids' only activity was playing outdoors. And there were so many opportunities! When Radu and his friends in the neighborhood were not playing football, they would improvise a catch-me-if-you-can after tree climbing; when they were not playing hide-and-seek or some other game, they would be engaged in playing two-camps-at-war, Radu's favorite game. Once in a while, they would make a raid on the water tank in the neighborhood to steal ball bearings, which they would use in the most imaginative ways.

Whenever he visited his parents, who still lived where he had grown up, he felt sad to see how kids of this generation would play in the park in front of the blocks of flats, just banging the ball against the wire fence of the park, without any sense of organizing a game. In the same park twenty years before, he and his friends would spend most of their afternoons and holidays either playing football, provided they had gathered in a sufficient number to form two teams, or other games that could be played by only three participants; or "heads," as they had called it, a game where two participants were enough. "Heads" was a game in which each boy would choose a spot on one side of the fence as a gate, and then they would pass the ball to each other, being allowed to touch it only with their heads while trying to score goals. Or they would play foot tennis on the even-sized tiles in front of the flats, or draw on other playgrounds, either with a piece of chalk or with chips from broken bricks.

Kids of the new generation only take turns banging the fence with the ball, producing an extremely annoying and monotonous noise, and that was only once in a blue moon when they played outdoors because their parents insisted they should. That's sad. Radu smiled a melancholy smile when he remembered how they would throw bags full of water from the balconies or from the roof at the passers-by, and the bags would break against their heads and they would get soaked; or how his father would spank him when, coming back home from work, he would find the potato boxes on the balcony empty and all the potatoes scattered on the pavement as they had been used as bombshells by Radu and his friends.

They would also organize real ambushes for innocent passers-by. They would hide behind the bushes with plastic tubes filled with pin-tipped paper twists, and people passing by them would find themselves showered with devilish twists that would thrust into anything, including skin. The kids would make slings from anything using stones or twisted pins or brackets, as they would call them, for weapons.

Radu also had a less pleasant memory from that period when, at least for a while, bows and arrows were fashionable in the neighborhood and all kids had made bows from tree branches. Well, there was this boy who had a genuine Reghin bow, bought by his father, a strong bow that released an arrow that thrust into Radu's eye from ten meters away. He pulled it out at once. He couldn't see with that eye so his parents took him to the emergency room, where the doctor, after a quick exam, told them he was exceptionally lucky. If the arrow had hit him within a hair's width above, the eye would have been pierced but as it was, the arrow hit below the eye. A few days after the accident, he regained his sight, and the first thing he did when he returned from the hospital was to take the bow he had so carefully crafted; unpeeling the branch, painting it red, and even adding a pirates' flag to it; and tear it to pieces.

Ever since they were children, fighting had been very important as it settled the hierarchy and established the role each boy would play in the small groups they formed. Radu's best friends had always been Lorin and Stefan, who were his age; they grew up together as neighbors living on the same street. Ever since they were very little, the three boys were inseparable and they would always plead for each other's innocence in front of the other kids, never allowing anyone, even older boys, to patronize or offend them in any way. Those who tried suffered. As the years went by, the fierceness of the three boys became legendary in the neighborhood, and, later, in the entire city. The older they grew, the deeper they went into the underground circles of Galati, and the profits they gained from their small businesses started to grow.

After some troubled years, with many arrests and street fighting, mainly with the gypsy clans in the city, who enjoyed power and whose authority would be contested by few people, the three friends started to turn to other places where life would be easier and would bring them more satisfaction. Radu was already deep into the pit fights, which, even if they had only been a hobby in the beginning, started to be a source of good money because people had started to gamble. And he knew that in order to focus completely upon the dogs and their training, he had to leave the city.

Lorin also had a pit male he would occasionally take to contests, but he didn't have the skills of a champion breeder Radu had. Most of his income came from various dealings: he knew some guys from the Republic of Moldova who brought weed from Kishinev, and he would double its price to sell it in Galati. After dealing locally for a while, Lorin made some contacts in Bucharest; the guys there were into the same kind of business but in the capital, the price was much better. He started to sell less and less by the gram in his own city, which was too risky and failed to give him a substantial income, in favor selling it by the kilo to his friends in Bucharest.

On one of his trips to the capital, he met a girl in a club and fell in love there and then. After a few months of sending her three love letters a week when he could not spend time with his beautiful girlfriend in her flat, Lorin decided that he should move to the capital. His business was mainly there anyway, and besides, he felt that he could not live without that woman. He was head over heels in love and he was sure that she was the future mother of his children. They spent most of their time in bed or walking hand in hand through the parks of Bucharest, sharing their most intimate secrets or telling each other interesting events in their lives or whatever had impressed them during their journey through life.

Cristina was a law student in her last year and, after realizing how Lorin made his money, even if that was not exactly the job she had imagined for her man when thinking about her future soul mate, she had nothing against his way of managing it. In the first place, she saw he knew exactly what he was doing, and secondly, she knew that he would have had to work half a year to make the money he made in one month. And that really turned her on. When Lorin was in prison for three of the seven years he had been sentenced to in Germany for breaking into a bank, she waited for him, even though their relationship was still in its early stages. She did not cheat on him even once and she stoically took all the reproaches of her parents and friends. However, when he came back, she made him promise he wouldn't leave her alone again. With tears in his eyes, Lorin swore he would always be by her side and he took an oath to himself that he would never again get himself into that kind of mess.

Stefan, his other childhood friend, had gotten into porn. Everything had started in Amsterdam, where he had lived for a few months in a building inhabited by just one man and fifty girls. It was the head office of an international videochat, which had branches all over the world, and recruited the most beautiful girls to work for them in Amsterdam. The girls lived and worked there, sharing bedrooms for four; they took turns working in the computer rooms, and the whole three-story building was full of cameras, which kept them under uninterrupted surveillance. They would allow only two couples in the building, and when Stefan got there in the company of a girl from his town, who had mortgaged her house to join him in Europe, there was one more Hungarian couple there.

After he, easily, overcame the only inconvenience, that of having to pee under the incessant surveillance of the cameras, Stefan found himself in paradise. He was surrounded by beautiful women, half or completely naked, all of them very interested in him. And that was not only due to his good looks and the personal charm few girls could or at least would resist, but also because during the three months while they worked there on a contract basis, the girls were completely forbidden to meet anybody who wasn't a tenant. The firm had had some problems in the past with models who had dated clients they met online, who then raped them, and some hands had to be greased for the issue to be smothered.

Their orgies and parties attracted a film production company, the first of its kind in Romania. They also had the local videochat owned by the Dutch company, so when they heard that a good-looking, charming Romanian made a lot of money in a videochat in Amsterdam, they contacted him and invited him to an interview. That was the very opportunity Stefan had been waiting for. The idea of becoming a porno star had dawned on him a long time before, especially since he had been talked into the videochat job by most of the women he had slept with. After a trip to Bucharest and a brief meeting with the producers, in which they settled the details of the subject, they decided that Stefan would star in the next film, their second film shot by them. The shooting had to start in four months, and the only thing the producers suggested was that, in the few months before the shooting, he should hit the gym and maybe take some proteins and creatine in order to be as fit as possible for the kind of job in which good looks are of utmost importance. That is how Stefan's pornostar career started.

Chapter 3

Radu lived in a house that had belonged to his family for many years. It stood in the heart of the Bucegi Mountains in a place called Poiana Tapului. A village rather than a town, Poiana Tapului is one of the most breathtaking spots in the Bucegi. It is far away from any highway and the citizens built their houses on both sides of a gravel road running through the village. Radu's house was the last one in the line of houses, and where his yard ended, the forest began. Although the house had been built several decades before by members of his family, Radu wouldn't have changed a thing if he had had to build it again from scratch. He had fallen in love with the place the very first time he went there with his parents, when he was only about five years old. The unspoiled landscape and the sense of freedom and communion with nature he felt while being there had impressed him so much that he always knew it perfectly matched his rebellious and, somehow, antisocial soul, which was, nevertheless, so keen on animals and nature.

The house had been built in the 1970s by two of his aunts, both of whom had been incarcerated in the communist prisons for more than twenty years without being even slightly guilty of anything, apart from a desire to live in a free world, free from the oppression of the communist regime which had taken everything from them before throwing them into jail. The main reason for this misfortune was that one of the sisters was married to one of Radu's grandmother's brothers, who had been the leader of the legionary movement in post-war Romania. When the communists came to power after World War

II, one of the first measures they took was to confiscate the lands of all the old families who had some fortune. Radu's family was a very old one, his genealogical tree being recorded in many writings since the middle of the 16th century, and their fortune was considerable. Owning many mansions, hundreds of hectares of land, and employing people to work for them, his family was one of the first victims of the communist regime. Their entire fortune was confiscated and most of their members were imprisoned, be they men or women, and treated diabolically.

Lucian, who then became the leader of the legionary movement, was left with only one option; arming himself, together with other people who were in the same situation. Deprived of home and family, they fought the regime from the shelter of the woods. Unfortunately, their brave action didn't last long. The communists hunted them down as they would animals in the mountains, and those who were not shot dead on the spot were transported to a special jail from which there was no return. Radu remembered rather sadly that, right after the fall of communism, there was a TV broadcast called "The Memorial of Pain," in which old people of over eighty, former members of the legionary movement, talked about their ordeals. He would never forget the streams of tears falling down his grandmother's cheek when several legionaries talked about the screams coming incessantly from the room next to Lucian's, their leader and Radu's grandmother's brother, who died after being tortured by the communists. They injected him with epinephrine in order to keep him alive, and took turns using the most sadistic methods ever invented to torture him. And that was not because they wanted information, all the legionary members having already been caught, but simply because they wanted to scare away anybody who might have thought they could plot against the regime.

The hatred Radu nurtured for the communist system and for any form of oppression or domination ever since he was little, was fierce, and very often he would show it, even when the odds were against him and no good would come of it. However, his own good always counted less than the hatred he felt for oppressors, hypocrites, cowards, petty bastards, or any people displaying the traits he loathed. And he would have felt like a coward and ashamed of himself, which he would never let happen, had he ever allowed anybody who might have fallen into any of those categories to go unpunished, even if that meant a broken jaw or a few fractured ribs. He always felt that the punishment hadn't been harsh enough to meet the hatred he felt for those he hurt. Most people were intimidated by him and his attitude, since he always seemed ready to fight, looking for a reason to hurt those who got on his nerves one way or another.

As far as he was concerned, Radu stirred one of two reactions: the one which prevailed was intimidation and fear, and he detested everybody who feared him because that was the most obvious proof of their weak character. The other kind of reaction from people was one of worship. Those who took him as he was and saw his true value and qualities would immediately fall for him and would be impressed not only by his physical strength, but also his psychic resilience and intelligence. That must have been why he had fallen so much in love with pit bulls, the main characteristics of this breed being very close to his own character. The features he appreciated most – courage, loyalty, tenacity, strength – were the qualities of this breed. This, and the love he had always felt for animals, caused the intimate and strong bond between him and the pit bulls.

When his two aunts, after twenty years of prison, were eventually set free, more dead than alive but with their moral philosophy and principles intact, the first thing they did was put as much distance as they could between the communist civilization and their life, so they looked for a place that was as isolated and as picturesque as possible; and they found it at Poiana Tapului. With the little money left from the huge fortune they once had, they bought a piece of land as remote as possible from the roadway, verging on the forest, and they built the whole house with their own hands there. Two women, one of them a doctor and the other a university professor, after two decades of incarceration in tough conditions, which were hard to imagine for those who had never been in the prisons built by the communists to silence anybody who opposed them, had the physical and psychic strength to carry in their wheelbarrows stones they splintered in the mountains and carve the wood cut in the forest, and then build, without any help, a wonderful house in which they lived until they passed away. Now the house belonged to Radu.

Since he had no close relatives who might have wished to claim the place, he had no problem becoming its legal heir and moving into his dream house. He had never felt as good in a place as he felt there. It had taken the two sisters about seven years, but their achievement was exquisite. The house was a true work of art, built on the mountainside, and, like all the other neighboring houses, surrounded by woods. There was a smaller courtyard in front of the house where Radu would park his car, and there was also a backyard of approximately two thousand square meters, where the kennels stood. The kennels were built along two sides of the yard, right behind the two-meter high wooden fence. On one of the sides of the yard, there were four kennels of the same size, and along the same line, on the perpendicular wall, there were four more, all of them with heating. Radu had built them two years before, when he had moved in.

There was just one story to the house, with the kitchen, living room, and a bedroom on the ground floor and two rooms and an attic on the first floor; the latter being the room where he spent most of his time when he was there. The attic was framed with large windows on the two sides overlooking the yard, and the view it offered was like a fairy tale pictures of dragons and knights in shiny armor Radu had seen in the books he read when he was little. The house stood against the background of the mountains rising majestically above the clouds and covering the horizon on all sides. Near the double bed in the attic there was a small bookcase where Radu kept his collection of a few hundred books, and opposite the bookcase, there was a small table where his TV set stood, which was always connected to the PlayStation console underneath. When he did not read, he would play games or watch TV, lying on the bed and smoking weed while gazing meditatively at the forested crests or listening to the rain that sometimes fell incessantly for days in a row in this wilderness and gave him so much inner peace and joy.

Underneath the house there was a cellar that covered the underground surface of almost the entire house, where his aunts had kept their pickles in jars, a few wine barrels, the vegetables, most of which had grown in their own garden, and a few more chests and tools for which they found no better storage place than this basement. However, Radu had completely transformed it. Now, most of his income came from what was stored in the cellar. Only two other people knew its secret, and they were his childhood friends, his best companions all these years, Lorin and Stephen.

Apart from being a pit bull breeder, Radu also grew weed. He had built a professional marijuana greenhouse in the cellar, all the tools having been purchased from the Czech Republic. He had ten special high-power lamps connected to an electric panel where he set the times. The panel was equipped with a timer, and around its clock face there were some plastic flipping clamps, one for every five-minute interval. When the clamps were flipped, the power was on, and when they were not, the power was off. Only the time and temperature had to be set, the heat and light were adjusted automatically. There were two engines at the cellar entrance, one which drove the air in, and another which drove the air inside the plantation out through the smoke chimney, after a complicated gadget had cleaned it. Hooked to the ceiling and anchored with heavy chains, there was a two-meter long and an about one-hundred-kilo heavy roller connected to one of the engines through a thick aluminum-coated hose. This gadget, wrapped up in a thick layer of cotton, was designed to draw in the air inside the plantation and then send it to the cleaning system.

Apart from that, there was a big two-hundred-liter barrel that Radu would fill daily from the cellar sink, and inside the barrel, there was a water hoover connected to a long hose with a hand-held watering head. Every day, Radu would carefully mix the chemicals needed by the plants in this barrel, following the schedule he had received when he had purchased the respective solutions from Prague, which informed him about the compost he had to use, when to use it and the quantities needed. These alternated, depending on the evolution cycle of the plants, since they became more and more complex as they grew. He had five hundred plants, which gave him around seven kilos of buds every two and a half months. The pots were close to one another, and before the plants were cut, the cellar turned into a real jungle since the plants reached a height of one meter and a half. Every day when he watered them, Radu had to drag the pots in the middle of the cellar aside, and after he finished watering them, he had to walk backwards from the end opposite the entrance along the path, putting the pots back in their initial position and blocking the path so that all the plants received the same amount of light and air, thus the buds growing on the lower parts of the plants did not suffer from a lack of light. Except for one hundred grams which he kept for his own consumption from one harvest to the next, Radu would give all the weed to his childhood friend, Lorin, who got rid of it in Bucharest. And with each harvest, the quality of the weed became better and better, as Radu learnt through experience the little tricks a grower of indoor weed needed to know.

Chapter 4

When Radu entered the pit, holding Bronco in his arms, the referee was already there and, after a brief inspection of the animal's teeth, he invited Vodoo's owner into the pit. Sometimes the breeders sharpened the dogs' teeth or covered them in iron, which is forbidden in contests of this kind. What people who have nothing to do with pit fights don't know is that, everywhere in the world, there are two kinds of contests, although one of them can hardly be called a 'competition.'

On the one hand, there are those who love and respect this breed more than anything in the world and who treat their dogs as their own children. These people created this breed of super-dogs and developed it along the years until it became what it is now, a dog whose qualities are undeniably superior to any other breed's. They know that in order to get a good pit fighting dog, one has to invest one's entire time and energy, and that the animal has to be treated exactly as a sportsman is. Diet, training, sleep, and as little stress as possible are essential for a pit fighting dog's performance. Apart from this, the dog's genes are also determining factors for the dog's behavior in the pit. These breeders are fully committed to the dogs they breed and they invest huge amounts of money in their animals along the years, knowing they don't always get their money back from fights or from mating. These are the real pit bull breeders, those who love and understand this absolutely special breed and who always value their dogs' safety and health, irrespective of the results at the pit or of the money won or lost.

Unfortunately, there is also the second category of so-called pit bull breeders, those who give the qualities of this canine athlete a bad name by their attitude to the animal and by the actions they take. It is a shame indeed that it is their actions that are highlighted in the press or on TV, as the brutality and lack of respect their deeds imply defy the imagination. They are those who, having no love for the dogs, see pit fights as a business and the poor innocent animals as the pawns of their wicked plans. These so-called breeders invest almost nothing in the process of animal breeding, pay modest prices and thus lower the quality of the dogs, mate the animals among themselves and ignore selection criteria, which explains the reduced quality of their pets. The only thing these dogs need is an antibiotic injection after the fight and maybe a stitch or two in case their skin, which is three times thicker than any other breed's and with fewer nerve ends, was pierced by the opponent's fangs. However, these people, who have no soul or respect for the animal that would give its life for them, let them recover, tied to their kennel, with no assistance whatsoever.

The worst part of the way in which they treat their pit bulls is the way in which they let them fight. There are no rules, of course, since they don't care about their dogs, and that's why the animals are allowed to fight until they lose all their strength. This never happens when the fights are organized by the true breeders, who see to it that there's a referee in the pit, especially to ensure the dogs' safety, and vets close to the pit for the small interventions they need after the fights. More often than not, these people fail even to watch the fights, the only reason they organize them being the little money they can afford to bet. Sometimes the bastards lock the dogs in trucks or other closed spaces and let them fight without any supervision, releasing them one hour later to see who won the money, which often goes to cover the price of the next heroin dose.

It's sad that, very often, out of indifference or the way in which these fights are organized, plus the lack of consideration for the anonymity of these kind of activities, the dogs are deprived of appropriate living conditions in, often, public places, and the TV channels compete in showing how tough these traitors are on their pets. Nobody, apart from the true breeders, knows that, in fact, the pit bull fights and the entire process of breeding, training, and fighting have nothing to do with the way in which these individuals degrade the most amazing animal ever created by humans and everything this animal stands for. The differences between a true champion dog and a dog used in fights by these lousy bastards are the same as those between a boxing champion and a beggar. The genuine fights are organized in strict secrecy, with very few witnesses, and those who attend are very reliable; they are never covered by the press, while the actions of the other category have made the whole world fear this superb breed, and even hate it most of the times.

Radu made Bronco sit in the pit corner; the dog, as tense as an arrow ready to fly from the stretched bow, facing his opponent in the opposite corner of the pit, sharing the desire to fight. Anybody who ever attended a pit bull fight noticed not only the extraordinary desire these dogs feel to fight but also the pleasure they take in the confrontation, constantly wagging their tail and doing their best to defeat their enemy. If these dogs didn't like fighting, they wouldn't be as good as they are at it. Just like the people who take to contact sports, they are really motivated or satisfied only when they fight. As a Labrador is happiest carrying the duck shot by its owner in its mouth, and a German shepherd feels most at home guarding the sheep and goading them as its genetic code dictates, so the pit bull is most satisfied when it is in the pit with an opponent it tries to dominate, because this is dictated by every gene of its body.

Contrary to popular belief, the pit bull doesn't need training to be aggressive to the other dogs because it has these traits in its genetic code. The training sessions are meant to keep these dogs fit and not to teach them how to fight. Each pit bull has its own fighting style, and this is hardly ever influenced by training. The differences between a better-trained dog and a less well-trained dog can be seen only after the first twenty minutes or half an hour of fighting, when the bites of one of them start losing their grip, or the way it shakes its opponent using only the strength of its neck and not of its entire body, or the strength of the body, which is pushing the opponent less vigorously or fails to rise as swiftly as in the first ten minutes. The only things a breeder can do in order to improve the dog's chances of winning is to train and feed it as well as possible; the difference between a winner and a loser lies in the genetic background of each animal. That's why the price for a dog born to a line of champions is more often than not exorbitant. For the same reason, and many others, somebody who invested this amount of money in a dog would always see to it that the animal gets the best care and food.

The referee told the two breeders the same words they heard at every contest: "When I count three, release your dogs." And then he counted "one, two, three," at which both Radu and his opponent released their dogs. The animals dashed at each other, gripping each other's faces and starting to shake.

The first ten minutes of the pit contests usually looked the same, both dogs being the same size and weight and, of course, very well trained. During these first ten minutes, the dogs are very energetic, alternatively gripping the opponent's head and neck and continuously shaking in order to tear as deeply as possible at its skin. The difference between the dogs may be seen only in the latter half of the fight, when the qualities of one of the dogs prevail over the qualities of the other. In ninety-five percent of the cases, the genetically-superior and better-trained dog wins, but occasionally, as in contact sports between people, the inferior dog may happen to win.

One of the dogs may slit the enemy's jugular vein, this vital part going from the neck down to both sides of the chest in the dog's anatomy, and, because of the effort, it can be a bit swollen, which makes the slitting easier. In this case, the contest is always terminated at once, in order to stop the bleeding, which occurs in the first two or three minutes due to the extraordinary healing capacities of this dog. However, if the fight is interrupted, the dog that needs medical care loses, and this doesn't always happen to the dog that would have normally lost the fight. Fortunately, this occurs very rarely, once in one hundred contests, let's say, but when it does, the contest must be terminated instantly.

Another way in which a dog that is not as good as its opponent may win the fight is the nose grip. Although most of the times it is not a long-lasting grip, and it doesn't have any consequences on the result of the contest, one of the dogs may grip the opponent's nose so strongly that the bleeding is serious, and if that happens, the fight must also be stopped. Neither of these incidents is ever fatal, the bleeding being stopped in a minute or two, but the question is who saves the dogs that fight without any witnesses? Who stops the fight when one of the dogs is in danger if there are no owners watching or referees, and without the vets who are always there in professional fights to give first aid to these gladiators?

The difference in quality between Bronco and Vodoo started to show in about the twentieth minute of the fight, when Radu's dog shook even more energetically than during the first five minutes, while his black opponent was starting to lose its grip on Bronco more and more often, and rose with more difficulty when the gingery dog applied his "judo style," as Radu liked to call it jokingly. This style described Bronco's approach to the fight; Bronco would place himself in a parallel position and, while gripping the opponent's head or neck strongly, he would push him in the opposite direction with his shoulder in order to make him lose his balance. Once that happened and the opponent was knocked down, Bronco was himself more than ever, thrusting his feet in the carpet covering the pit and thoroughly shaking any bit of his enemy he may have targeted. That's what happened in this contest; after half an hour, Vodoo was exhausted and could hardly rise, while Bronco looked as if he had just entered the pit.

The referee told the two breeders to separate them, and the hard wood bits were slid through the dogs' fangs. Each of them was taken to his corner and, after the referee counted to three, Vodoo's owner released him while Radu was still holding Bronco lest he should dash at his opponent. This method is used to see if the losing dog is "game," which means whether he can be used to mate or not. If he stops attacking, the contest is terminated at once. If he, even though the loser, attacks his opponent, the dog is considered "game" and able to mate. Vodoo, although he could hardly stand on his feet, ran towards Bronco and gripped him, which is when Radu released him, and Bronco knocked his opponent down from the first impact and continued his series of shaking movements on his front paws. Two minutes later, the referee terminated the contest. It was obvious that Vodoo stood no chance of winning that fight. Radu slid the wood through Bronco's teeth again, unclenched his jaws from the terribly strong grip he still had on one of his opponent's paws and, to the cheers of everybody who attended, raised him above his head. The feelings of love, pride, and communion with his pet were never so well-articulated in his soul as they were in these moments when, to the crowd's cheers, his dog had won another fight. With tears in his eyes, he kissed his dog that, in his turn, licked his face. Radu whispered words of victory in his ears: "Well done, boy, well dooooone, boy, we've done it again, well dooone."

He took Bronco to the car, where he washed away the blood on his body, mainly his opponent's. Bronco was wagging his tail in satisfaction as if he knew as well as any person there that the victory in the fight had been his from start to finish and that Vodoo had stood no chance, compared to his undeniably better qualities. The doctor came towards them to see Bronco. He asked Radu if everything was okay, and then he turned to Vodoo, who needed a bit more attention from him. The referee also came, and, handing him the money he had earned that day, congratulated them before returning to the pit to settle the criteria for the next fight.

The feeling that had taken hold of Radu was the reason why he had fallen in love with these dogs from the very beginning, that love, pride, and infinite respect he felt for them. Bronco jumped on the back seat without his help and he thrust there with an expression of satisfaction on his face, which was still smeared with blood and full of scars, whose number had started to grow.

Chapter 5

Lorin, or The Nose as close friends called him, who was never absent from any of Radu's pit bull fights and wouldn't miss the opportunity to watch Bronco in action for the world, came near the car.

"Bro, told ya he'd do a number on Blacky-boy! I've seen that dog fight before, he's pretty good, but he has nothin' on this one!"

Then he turned to the dog: "Yeah, daddy, you're our champ, there ain't nothing these pooches can do to you."

Bronco was wagging his tail in satisfaction, holding his ears backwards, the way he always did whenever he was complimented or cuddled.

Radu, still a bit tense because of the fight but displaying an omniscient smirk, got behind the wheel and started the engine.

"Where are you up to? Wanna come by ma' place or are you gonna hit the road straight to Bucharest?"

"No, I'll drop by, I've got something to talk to you about."

"Okay, follow me, but I have to stop by Alex's for half an hour to get this one stitched."

Alex was a local vet to whom most of the pit bull breeders in the area turned for medical care after the fights. He himself had a pit bull, and the owners of the breed were his main clients.

"No problem, go ahead, I'll be there later! First I gotta go see what those guys from the Ploiesti clan wanna talk to me about."

"What the fuck do those gits want?"

"Dunno, man, I think they have another trip proposition. I'll go see what the word is."

"Okay, dude, but don't give them the time of day, you know how they are. You'll never be able to get them off your back! I'll wait for you to drop by my place later then!"

Lorin closed the jeep's door and went off to the Ploiesti clan; three related gypsies who were part of one of the most powerful gypsy clans in Ploiesti. They were involved in a wide range of illegal activities, most of them outside the Romanian borders. They controlled a few dozen pickpockets or "kids" who stole only for them, a couple of dozen beggars, consisting of gypsy women and their broods, and over a hundred girls, exploited both for prostitution and in strip clubs. All in all, the clan's profit was a few tens of thousands of dollars a month, and even hundreds of thousands during the productive months. What had always amazed Radu and his friends was the discrepancy between the sometimes extravagant sums of money these people were capable of making and the arrant lack of intelligence they displayed. Although they never cared for this type of people, business often made their paths cross. They had had previous encounters before and they knew exactly what they could and couldn't expect from them. Honesty and character were a big no-no.

Seeing Lorin approach, one of the gypsies, short, with a wide back and a deep scar seaming his face, one of the clan's chiefs, started talking to him. "What's up, boss? I haven't seen you in ages! Man, your mate's dog is a hit. I also saw him fightin' against our champion, Yankee; this Bronco mopped the floor with him. Where did he bring him from, bro?"

"He didn't bring him from anywhere; he's his bitch's pup. But I don't think there's any dog in the country now that could match him. He's a hell of a dog, even untrained, and he eats them alive. Did you see how he clasps and rustles?"

"Yeah, dude, it's a killer dog! And he's so handsome, such a fine color, I've never seen one like this. Maybe I'll buy me one of his pups when the time comes."

Lorin chuckled in his mind: You wouldn't know what to do with a dog like this, even in a thousand years, you bitch! But his answer was: "Talk to Radu, see what he thinks. But he ain't humping for another half a year, at least."

"Well...maybe you can talk to him sometime, he's your buddy. Lorin, dude, look, there's somethin' I wanted to tell ya'..."

"Well, spit it up then!"

"Got some of my boys crossing over in 'bout a month. They wanna do Austria, Germany, and France. They have good spots to breach the border, routes we found and already used, they have berths to stay there, you know, we have a big family. Problem is these boys is only snatchers, they break any locks or alarm systems, but don't know banks. And we wanna move to bank robbery, man, there's more greens in one hit than those "kids" make in half a year. Thought you maybe wanna go with them, bro, show them what's what, guys gives you a cut. You know ma' family always greases the hand that helps."

"Thanks for counting me in but I'll pass, mate. Promised my woman I won't do it again, after those three years in the joint in Germany. Plus, everything's goin' smoothly, I don't need any headaches. I can still do something 'cause we've known each other for a long time. You can send me your boys and I'll tell them a thing or two. But as for going with them, no way."

"How did they nail you that time, bro?"

"Someone spilled the beans. I was travelling with a guy I didn't know, the dudes from Suceava brought him, said he's handy. But after a week there, we'd broken into two Sparkasse banks, the retard was pickpocketing in the subway and got caught. The dumb-ass was wearing the same jacket as in the footage on the surveillance camera, so the cops held him for being present at the scene and as he was lookin' at 15 years in prison, he ratted us all out, the cunt! But

I put my hands on the bastard in Dresden, before he got out after only two years, the fucker. I worked on him for about a week."

"Yeah, I've heard the story. A guy from Bacau, right? So, what, have you grown soft in the knees, now or what?"

"My knees are fine, don't you worry! But I earn enough money now, no need for all that kamikaze bullshit like in the old days, you know?"

The gypsies were obviously disappointed, they knew that having Lorin among them would have been a huge advantage for their group but they hadn't really had their hopes high concerning his cooperation to begin with. They also knew there was no way of making him change his mind so they decided to drop the matter altogether.

"Okay, Lorin, mate, I give my boys your phone number and tell them to call you, and you'll meet with them in your spare time. They gonna bring you a package and you're in for a treat. Don't worry, they're well-mannered chaps."

"Okay, man. Tell them to give me a call next week and I'll meet with them for a couple of hours if they come to Bucharest."

"Cool, boss, much appreciated! And tell Radu I want a pup from him, when he's gonna have them."

"I'll tell him. Cheers."

He shook hands with the three shady guys and went to his car. He had a black Audi A6 he had brought from Germany one year before being arrested there. He started the car engine, covering the ecstatic voices of the breeders whose dogs were fighting in the ring right at that moment.

Half an hour later, Lorin was driving along the gravel pathway that goes through Poiana Tapului, the small picturesque village lost in the wilderness of the Carpathian Mountains that had become Radu's home a few years before. With the thick forest on one side and the Bucegi peaks on the other, few places offered Lorin such views and such delight, and even though he passed by once almost every month for a couple of years now, the grandeur of the landscape always struck his sensitive chords buried deep inside his hard-as-a-rock self.

Radu's house was the last one along the gravel pathway that continued winding through the heart of the mountains. Lorin parked his car in front of the house and went inside the courtyard. The jeep was already there, meaning Radu had finished his job at the vet, which was to be expected since he had seen at the end of the fight that Bronco only had a few minor wounds. They probably didn't even need stitches, only disinfecting, plus an antibiotic shot to prevent swelling.

He rang his childhood friend's doorbell, and Radu opened the door with a smile on his face. It was obvious that the tension that had been hovering over him at the end of the fight had been replaced by a slight euphoria, thanks to the success. The hero of that morning, Bronco, was lying on his couch, slowly wagging his tail when he saw Lorin. Only two of the wounds he got in the fight had required stitches.

A strong scent of weed was floating through the room, released by the thick joint between Radu's lips. He passed the reefer to his friend and inquired about the talk with the clan representatives.

"What did those bastards want?"

"Bullshit. They wanted me to go robbing banks in Germany and France with some of their men. They're fuckin' insane; don't know what got into them. When did I ever do such business with them?"

"Yeah, fuck the goddamn mudskins! They bark at any tree available to see if something falls down."

Lorin started feeling the effect of the blunt. Everything became a bit fuzzy and a feeling of joy and relaxation flooded his senses. He passed Radu the joint.

"Tell me, Lorin, ma' mate, what did you wanna talk about?"

"Yeah, man. Do you remember Tasos, father of all malakas?"

Tasos was a Greek student who, together with another few thousand Greeks, came to study in Romania because the education prices were lower compared to other nearby countries and the diplomas could be earned pretty easily.

The majority of the Hellenic students were drug consumers; most of the money their parents sent for their studies would end up in Lorin's or other top Bucharest dealers' pockets. The rest of the money sent from Greece covered the bribes so that the Romanian university professors would pass them.

The problem was that, upon their return to Greece, they were asked to take a validation exam, which most of them failed, the five years spent in Romania having been nothing more than a continuous party. As a result, not so many Greeks sent their children to study in Romania anymore.

Tasos, being more intelligent and resourceful than his colleagues, and having lived in Bucharest for more than seven years, had gone into business with the local dealers for an extra buck, or at least to cover his own drug needs.

He usually bought reasonable quantities at lower prices than those on the market and then resold it to his Greek colleagues with his own mark-up. This business was going well, especially with the newcomers who didn't know where to get their narcotics or were afraid to contact the Romanians directly. One of the Greeks' favorite drugs was ketamine or Special K, an injectable animal tranquilizer with powerful psychedelic and hallucinogenic effects when turned into powder and snorted.

The colorless liquid had to be held over a small flame for several minutes to crystallize; after that, the crystals turned into powder and could be snorted, just like cocaine for example. The best way to procure this drug in its pure state is directly from the source, the vets. But for that you need to have contacts, for no doctor would sell you ketamine without gaining a substantial profit or without knowing you very well.

"Tasos wants to import ketamine into Greece, he says it's very rare and expensive there. He claims he has people there who would buy wholesale if they could find a direct supplier for the liquid, and they will process it themselves."

"So, the Greek wants to get involved in exports..." Radu smirked while passing Lorin the reefer. "How much did he say he wants?"

"Two, three liters to start with, and if it proves to be a good deal, more after that."

"And how does he figure out getting it across?"

"He said he's gonna put it in water bottles. K's odorless and colorless ...like water."

"This malaka of yours may not be that stupid after all!"

"I know, mate. I told you he's a capitalist, his mind is set on making money. He said he'd give us a thousand dollars per liter."

Radu made a quick estimation, deducing how much he'd spend on the bottles he'd get from the doctor to make a liter; from a thousand dollars, there was a good few hundred profit.

Then he made an estimation of how many grams of powder could be made from a bottle, then multiplied it by the number of bottles necessary to have a liter of liquid, and realized the Greek's profit would be way bigger than theirs.

"Damn, this malaka of yours is some piece of work, trying to get all the loot for himself. We should be happy to gain a few hundred per liter while he gets thousands? No, bro, tell him that if he wants the deal, he should pay us two thousand per liter. He's got a huge profit as it is. If he's not satisfied, let him find some other scoop with a better price, but I can guarantee you no one he's got access to could get him such a large quantity. Do you realize that for three liters, I have to talk to more people 'cause nobody has such a quantity in stock. I don't imagine they anesthetize ten horses a day. Tell him that if he wants us in, he should give us six thousand upfront, two thousand a liter and he should buy at least three liters 'cause I don't wanna vouch for a few pennies. We're gonna pay around two grand for them, and we'll split the bread in two."

Which meant they'd earn around two thousand dollars each, a pretty good profit for quite a small effort. Radu, being well connected with the vets because of the pit fights, knew exactly who he could talk to and about what quantities when it came to ketamine.

Every time Lorin came to him asking for a few tens of grams, he helped him, especially because of the substantial profit in it, but this was the first time such quantities, more than a liter, were involved. Radu loved the feeling that he was making progress, that he was moving to the next level every time business and profits escalated.

The moment he passed him the joint, Lorin saw the complacent smile ingrained on his face and the wheels of the money-making machine in his head, the way he imagined them, were turning with the speed of a turbo power engine revved to the max, its sole purpose being to produce the most expensive type of energy: satisfaction.

Chapter 6

Stefan, Radu's other childhood friend, had become, in the last few years, one of the most successful porn movie actors in Romania. After some productions filmed in his country and in Hungary, Stefan met the woman that would influence his future in the most positive way possible.

Her name was Jana Konevova, a splendid 28-year-old girl from the Czech Republic, owner of an adult movie-modeling agency. Stefan and Jana first met on the movie set for an Italian production in Prague. The Milanese agency had hired Stefan as the protagonist in that movie; the other two male characters being played by Italian actors, while Jana's agency provided the feminine presence, eight beautiful girls, all of them from the Czech Republic.

The moment they first laid eyes on each other, there was an irresistible attraction. Stefan couldn't take his eyes off her the entire shooting period, while she was smitten with his charms every time she set her eyes on this perfect male specimen from Romania.

His prominent muscles, moving like serpents under his bronze skin covered in tattoos, and his aquiline look that seemed to pierce her actually made her knees weak and the general sense of strength and confidence Stefan emitted made her fall madly in love with him the first day they met.

After they finished shooting the movie, Stefan remained in Prague for another couple of days, spending most of this time in Jana's mansion, where they spent some unforgettable moments. Stefan had never truly been in love, even if he would have needed a notebook the size of a phonebook to write down the names of all the women he'd been with.

But this stunning Czech girl had changed something inside him; for the first time, he felt something more than an animal attraction for a woman. This longing to be with her when they were apart, as well as the intense joy that being together stirred in him, made Stefan wish for a serious commitment for the first time in his life.

One September evening, while they were walking down the narrow causeways of the old town center, a genuine time machine that transports you a few centuries back, Jana proposed that he moved to Prague. "Why do you like living in Romania when life in Prague is way more beautiful…how about moving in here, with me?"

She tightened her grip on his hefty arm and looked into his pitch black eyes, smiling with hope. Jana went on with the same ease so typical of her people, especially the women.

"I really dig you. I've never met a man who could impress me as you do…I'd very much like us to be together. Money wouldn't be an issue, you could get more contracts here than in your own country. You've seen yourself that Prague is slowly becoming the European porn capital. How about it?"

Stefan had already considered this alternative a few days before. He was very pleasantly impressed by this astonishing city, with its Gothic turrets that decorated most of the centuries-old buildings, as well as its dark causeways, lit only by lampposts, and its multi-centenary bridges, decorated with angel statues, that cross the Vltava river, joining together the two parts of this medieval city.

He never expected Prague to be as beautiful or, especially, as liberal as it was. He had lived in Amsterdam for a while and until then he thought no other city could offer such freedom and tolerance, but he was wrong. In Prague, he found the same coffee shops, head shops, and display window prostitutes as in Amsterdam.

The only difference was that the Czech city lacked the hordes of Arabs and Africans that invite you to buy drugs every step of the way in the Red Light District; nor did they have the type of tourist that only wanted to get high and have sex with prostitutes, vomiting at every turn and making an unimaginable racket day and night. Prague was a quieter place while offering the same degree of freedom and cultural diversity. Moreover, Stefan liked it more as a city, from its Gothic architecture to the energy this gorgeous European capital inspired.

Most of all, Stefan felt that he was falling deeper and deeper in love with the Czech girl and that he could no longer live without her. After three months of corresponding and visiting each other a few times, Stefan moved to Prague. Just as Jana predicted, the job offers were plenty, primarily because the Czech Republic didn't have porn actors of a remarkable quality, though they had the biggest number of actresses in the industry. Also, due to the low taxes for filming the Czech government imposed, Prague had become one of the most frequently-used locations for adult film producers.

The countless casting agencies here were sources for producers, not only when it came to extremely pretty girls at reasonable prices, but also the charming filming locations. Stefan was not employed by a particular agency, he was a freelancer, and producers contacted him personally. Jana suggested he should work for her agency, as a joke, and they both copiously mocked the idea of him being her employee.

Apart from the porn model agency, Jana ran a high-class escort agency. She used to be a call girl herself a few years before, thus she had all the business contacts that later permitted her to open her own agency. The whole business was online; there was a site with pictures of all the girls, a short description of each of them, and their availability.

The girls would go on a one-week trip to one of Europe's capital cities; they'd have accommodation at high-class hotels near airports, or even in airport hotels. The clients were businessmen who wanted to spend their time between flights in the most pleasant way possible.

Everything was discreet and problems rarely occurred, due to the confidential nature of the business and, especially, the social position of the people who used these services. Each girl usually had two to six clients a day. Jana and her assistants organized their schedule and were contacted telephonically by the clients, most of whom she knew personally from her days as a call girl.

They paid the girls in cash and Jana knew exactly how much money each of them had made by the time she waited for their return flight. Her agency had a commission of 50%, and it rarely happened that a girl wouldn't return with the money, or tried not to pay, because through Jana's agency, and because of her business contacts, the girls made a lot more money than they could make on their own, plus they had the safety it offered. The difference between the two businesses the Czech owned was that while for the porn movies she could send girls who didn't look perfect to casting, for the escort services she could only use girls who looked like top models. Some of her employees worked for both agencies. A lot of them bought or were given luxury cars, even from their first year of work.

That morning, Stefan had film shoots in a high-class mansion outside Prague. It was the third and last day he would go to that location. The agency that had hired him was French, and its owner was a Parisian ex-porn star, maybe the most successful actor in the business to come from France. Stefan burst into laughter when they first met because the French man was the protagonist of the first porn film he had ever owned, a videotape he had purchased a few months after the revolution, when Western products started to appear in the Romanian market. The mansion had two floors with a total of eight rooms, out of which two were equipped with a Jacuzzi. Stefan had to shoot two scenes that day, one with a brunette from the Czech Republic in one of the Jacuzzis and the other one with two girls, one from Slovakia and the other one from Belarus, in one of the bedrooms.

As usual, the shoot was going by slowly, most of the time being taken by setting the decor, the audio and video equipment, and makeup. Although he had been on the set since about nine, the shoot only started around lunchtime. The Jacuzzi scene went on for approximately one hour, with short breaks for changing the positions of the cameras, but everything went smoothly. The fact that the actress from the Czech Republic was very beautiful and uninhibited had helped Stefan perform at the highest level.

The girl had had three orgasms throughout that shoot; this was another reason why Stefan was very appreciated by the producers. The girls who acted with him would always reach repeated orgasms. In time, this became his signature; any porn movie amateur knew that in the scenes he was in, the girls would reach climax.

This was mostly due to a technique he had learnt from a partner many years before, more specifically, hitting the woman's G spot and the specific moves that had to be made simultaneously, with pressure applied to the clitoris, to cause an extremely strong orgasm. The women would often end up squirting.

In time, Stefan had become an expert in using these moves and he took pride in making any woman come in less than two minutes. With few exceptions, all his partners could confirm this to be true.

The second scene he shot that day, with the two girls in the bedroom, lasted longer than the first. Even if he was a little exhausted after shooting the first scene, when the two girls started having a lesbian moment, which lasted for about ten minutes, Stefan could hardly wait to get in the middle of the action! And neither could the girls, who, even while being busy pleasing each other, cast him lascivious glances from time to time. When he got into the action, it was beyond even his wildest expectations. The scene lasted more than an hour straight and was very intense the whole time, being classified by the French boss as one of the best porn scenes he had ever seen.

As it was the last day of shooting for that production, the whole team got invited that evening to celebrate together. They had a copious dinner in a luxury restaurant situated in the Zizkov tower of Prague, over two hundred meters high. It was an eccentric building from the Communist era, with some gigantic children made of metal climbing up and down the tower, with barcodes instead of faces, which made them look more like toasters than human beings.

From his table, Stefan could admire the whole city in all its splendor, with its red roofs and Gothic turrets placed on every building that decks the City of Gold. After dinner, they popped in to a pub where, to the surprise of the French team, most of the people were smoking joints, passing them around to all the customers in the bar; their table had their share, even though they knew nobody there.

After a few glasses of absinth, of over seventy degrees, and a few smokes from the shared joints, the porn gang, much more jovial now and seeking fun, decided to move on to a club, to get a taste of the city's night life that had made quite an unexpected and exciting impression on the French. They entered one of the largest, most successful clubs in Europe, Pavilion, whose owner was a former star singer from the 80s in Germany.

Klara had moved to Prague over ten years before and, with part of the money she made in her singing career, opened this high-class club that proved to be a real financial success. The initial investment paid off in two years after the opening. Stefan and Klara knew each other; they had met a few months back. She was a friend of his girlfriend, Jana.

As soon as they entered the club, they were welcomed by two girls who knew the Romanian and led him and his friends to the VIP section of the club, where they offered them a table for ten. The French team was very impressed by the way their leading actor was being treated, and felt privileged to be in the VIP section of one of the most well-known clubs in Europe on their very first visit there. After a few glasses, the French producer spoke into Stefan's ear:

"Stephan (that's how his name sounded on his lips), do you think it would be possible to score some coke in this club? It would hit the spot right now! What do you think?"

"Sure thing, I'm on it. How much d'you want?"

"I don't know. I was thinking about five gs, enough for all of us. How much for it here?"

"I'll go find out, wait a sec!"

Stefan went to one of the girls that had led them to the table and asked her where he could find Klara.

"I think she's in her office; if not, she's in the bar upstairs, that's where she usually sits. Do you want me to give her a message or something?"

"Yes, please, tell her I want to have a word with her, okay?"

"Sure. I'll tell her to come to your table when she has a minute, all right?"

"Yes, thanks, you're a doll!"

In less than ten minutes, the former German pop star showed up in the VIP section and headed towards their table with a wide smile on her face. "Stefan, it's such an honor to have you here again!" And she leaned over to kiss him on both cheeks. "What's up, are you having fun? Do you need anything?"

Stefan whispered in her ear: "I could use some coke for my friends. Can you help me?"

"Sure, no problem, I've got some guys dealin' in the club, I'll send one over, okay?"

"That would be perfect! Is it any good?"

"Well, it's not Colombia good, but it will do. If we're talking large quantities, there's a different deal."

"No, no, just for tonight, to have some here at the table."

"Sure. The only request I have is that you don't snort here, at the table, do it in the bathroom. I don't want any trouble here!"

"OK, Klara, no problem. Thanks a lot!"

"Don't mention it. If you want to talk to me again, I'll be in my office, you know where it is. Kisses, see you later!"

She cast him a meaningful glance, and then turned around and left, shrouded in the air typical of those who have made it in life and who are exactly where they want to be, full of confidence and self-satisfaction. Less than two minutes later, a stranger walked up to Stefan. They got acquainted and he told him he was sent by Klara to talk some business.

Ten minutes later, the atmosphere at the table had become more vivid. Everyone was talking louder and faster, they were laughing more, and the waitresses were called more often to bring bottles of alcohol to their table.

Stefan had noticed something upon his arrival in this country, and every time he went to a club, this conviction got stronger. Unlike other countries he had visited, in the Czech Republic, the drug of choice, consumed almost exclusively in clubs, was coke.

He remembered when he first asked for Ecstasy in Prague, the Czechs gazed at him in surprise and asked him if he liked "gaypills." At first he thought that was strange, but then he understood why the Czechs called it that.

Indeed, in Prague's clubs, most of the lovers of speed were gay, the rest of the people were on coke. When he asked why people didn't take XTC, which was the favorite drug of the clubbers in Romania, he got an answer that, unexpectedly, made sense:

"Pills are for fags, they take them and are full of love after that, they feel like kissing everybody. We're not like that. I don't wanna take somethin' and then start kissin' people. I like to snort and then feel good, get filled with strength and energy, exactly what coke does."

Every time he went out, Stefan noticed that aside from the weed that almost everybody smoked, and that was grown by many here in a highly professional manner, many people snorted cocaine but its quality was far lower than that found in town.

This was due to the fact that the wacky dust had to pass through many hands before reaching central Europe, and every handler added some substances to increase the quantity, thus lowering its quality. On the other hand, because for the Czech's drug consumption meant doing coke, this made the city a very good market for the dope.

What had become obvious to the Romanian was that here, with a mid-quality product at a reasonable price and a few distribution contacts, which he already had, one could make a fortune. In addition, there was a very liberal and relaxed way of looking upon drug consumption in this country. For instance, as long as you didn't cause any trouble or stand out with fabulous quantities, you would be left alone and considered as rendering useful services for the community. At least that's how he liked to see things, and his day-to-day experiences were reinforcing this belief.

Stefan was convinced that something had to be done in this respect, even if he didn't know what exactly. But this was surely a subject he would tackle when he met his childhood friends, Radu and Lorin, for the New Year's celebration. And suddenly he remembered: Radu's pit bull Bronco had had a fight just a week ago, and he had forgotten to call him and ask him how it went.

Chapter 7

Stefan took his cell phone and dialed Radu's number. Radu answered in a jovial and relaxed voice, and the actor drew the conclusion that Bronco must have won the fight.

"How are things? Prague's stolen you, man, you've forgotten us...and I was thinking maybe you've been kidnapped by those porn producers or something. Are you okay?"

"Yeah, bro, everything's fine on this front. I've been busy like hell, you know. So...how did Bronco manage?"

"He won, that's how he managed. The black devil was knocked out after half an hour."

"Wow, congrats! And who's the next opponent?"

"Don't know, man, I'll just let him take his time now. Holidays are near, and I won't be chasing the dogs up and down the hills. We'll find him an opponent next year. Are you coming over for New Year's Eve?"

"I think I might, are you planning something? Is Lorin coming?"

"You bet! I've invited him and Cristina, the Siamese, who said they'd come, and Irinel and his girlfriend, and you. Oh, and the Dutch woman."

"What? Are you barmy? Is she coming home for Christmas?"

"Yeah, she called me and said she's coming with some friends for New Year's Eve, and I've invited them, too. It'll be cool, you know the Dutch know how to party, and they'll have some stuff on them. Are you bringing your Czech girlfriend or what?"

"Yeah, I'm bringing Jana with me, she can converse in English with the Dutch guys. You know, she was a bit worried we'd talk

Romanian all night and she'd miss the point. Does Irinel have a girlfriend?"

Irinel was one of Radu's neighbors, a 19-year-old guy, born and brought up in Poiana, Tapului. The kid knew his manners and at the same time, he was very smart. These qualities, and the fact that he had a passion for dogs, made Radu take him on to assist him in his pit bull training, especially as he often needed a hand when he trained two dogs at once.

Irinel was very pleased by his friendship with Radu because he had earned another status in Poiana among the kids who were the same age as he was. They looked up at him now that he was in Radu's company. He was also fascinated by these dogs, which could not compare to any other dogs he'd seen before, given their physical and psychic strength and the fierceness and stoicism they had in battles. For more than two years, Irinel had accompanied Radu in most of the training and he wouldn't have missed a fight of any of Radu's dogs for the world. Radu had promised he'd give him one of Bronco's puppies when the dog mated, and the dream of his own champion was the boy's shadow.

"And the Siamese'll show up, too? I haven't seen them for ages, how are they doing?"

"Well, you know them…they're having arguments with folks in Galati, now over a fine, now when they take somebody to the forest…they opened their own restaurant a few months ago, you know."

"Have they? I had no idea. They've started doing it legally now, huh?"

"Well, they've grown up. They're party company, we'll have a good laugh with them the entire night. I can't wait to see the tramps they'll bring in tow."

The Siamese were twin brothers from Galati who had lived in the same district as Radu, and together they had turned the city streets into their playground. Physically, the twins were almost identical, only those who knew them well could tell which was which. They weighed over one hundred kilos and were one meter and ninety centimeters tall, and people in the city feared their violent behavior and the excessively brutal manner in which they sorted out their problems. In Galati, when somebody wanted their money back or somebody punished, they would ask the Siamese to do it.

"Okay, Radu old boy, it's settled then; see you on New Year's. Do you want me to bring something from here? Maybe some winter tires, I don't know how the weather's treating you there, whether it has snowed or I should bring some field equipment."

"Tires" were slang for XTC pills, and "snow" for cocaine. There were many other names for them; they used every type of slang according to a specific situation, in order for it to make sense in the respective context, in case someone unwanted was eavesdropping.

"No, man, I already changed the tires. It's been snowing heavily here, the Nose took care of the snow removal. Don't worry about a thing. You just come here with your partner, we've got it all covered."

"Okay, then, Radu boy, it's a deal. I'll get there in the afternoon, I've got a plane to Bucharest at noon and then I'll take a train to Poiana. I'll be there by evening."

"All right, Stefan, mate. Kisses and take care of yourself, play it safe with your model chicks."

"Sure, bro, kisses on my part, too. See you at New Year's."

The few weeks before New Year's went by without any major events. Radu was at the eleventh hour with his marijuana production, that cycle's plants had to be cropped on December the 15th, but he cut them and hung them upside down to dry on the 20th. He spent most of the last two days of the year in the cellar, where he cut the buds off the plants and then pruned them of their leaves. This was the process that required the most work in the entire cycle, the cutting off and pruning of the dried plants. During his first years of activity in this field, he had pruned the buds with a pair of scissors, which proved to be an extraordinarily niggling and time-consuming job. If each plant had dozens of buds, and Radu had a couple of hundred plants, almost a thousand, you can imagine the effort this work required. Two years before, he had bought a machine from Belgium; it pruned the buds of leaves and it worked like a ventilator with metal paddles; each plant would go through this machine to have its leaves pruned, after which the buds could finally be cut off. He saved the biggest, most beautiful buds for the New Year's Eve party. He was very pleased with the result of his work; from one cycle to the next, the buds were getting fluffier and smelled nicer. They were covered with a white fuzz that seemed to turn into crystals when put under a bright light, and the red and orange pubescences that enwrapped the greenness of the bud were more and more protuberant. Radu felt his mouth wet when he smelled those little buds; besides the satisfaction of having a high quality weed with a fine smell, he felt proud to have created such a high standard product that would be highly appreciated.

Lorin also had a quiet month. He had already received the money for the ketamine from Greece; he was going to give Radu his half on New Year's Eve. He spent most of December in Bucharest, either in clubs with his friends or taking Christine out to a restaurant or the cinema. He kept his weed buried in a forest outside Bucharest, where he had dug a hole in a hidden but accessible spot for depositing his kilograms of buds. Every time he went to the hiding place, he would wait for a couple of minutes in the car before getting out, to make sure he hadn't been followed and nobody was around. He only had one more kilogram, which he knew he would sell very quickly because of the upcoming holidays, but he wasn't worried that he might be left with empty pockets because Radu was about to crop his plants before the year came to an end.

He could hardly wait for the New Year's Eve party. He missed being with both of his childhood friends. Although he was surrounded by his new friends from the capital most of the time, nothing compared to the way he felt when he was with his homeys, the way they understood each other, the way they could relate to the exact same experiences and the similar way in which they viewed the world and their attitudes in different situations.

Stefan had two shoots that month, both of them Czech productions. The only problem he'd been having more and more often lately was Jana's attitude towards his work. His girlfriend had become increasingly jealous and upset by the fact that he spent a lot of time having sex with other women, even though this had been his job since before she met him. Jana was making waspish hints about the nature of his work, even though she was part of the same industry. The difference was that she didn't have to perform any services; the girls who worked for her were doing that instead. Their situation had become a little tense for the first time since they were together. Stefan was a bit irritated by this, but, on the other hand, it turned him on. This attitude of Jana's and her jealousy proved to him that the woman loved him and that she wasn't with him just because of an excess of pheromones.

On December 31st, they took the plane to Bucharest and then the train to Poiana Tapului. The voyage by train through Transylvania's mountains, covered in a thick layer of snow, was dream-like. The Czech woman, although she had visited most of the globe, had never been so impressed by the spectacular grandeur of the mountains and had never felt such a strong communion with nature as she did in these spots of fairy-like wilderness.

Chapter 8

Radu opened the wooden garden gates to let the first-comers in. It was Irinel and his girlfriend, who came a little earlier on purpose to help with the preparations. Irinel's girlfriend, Alina, was a petite brunette, pretty and always smiling. The boy was head over heels in love with her, and one could see in his face, from the way his eyes followed the girl's every move and the way he always positioned himself close to her, that he was spellbound. Radu wasn't sure whether he'd had any other girlfriends before Alina, but he was inclined to think he hadn't. The girl worked as a shop assistant for a local mini-market, and Irinel visited her there every day to see her and make sure nobody was causing her any trouble. Radu liked her and the way she was treating his friend, except for an aspect that bothered him a little and he didn't know how to react to it: the girl was a bit too friendly with him, many times openly flirting with him. He had seen the way this troubled Irinel, who would look down in discomfort whenever that happened, trying not to seem offended, but to Radu it was obvious. The last thing he wanted was to see his friend, towards whom he also felt a big brother's sort of responsibility, hurt, especially in a situation in which he had some kind of involvement. He knew he would have to have a private discussion with the girl.

As the young couple was arranging the tableware, the garden bell buzzed again. It was Lorin and Cristina, both of them dressed up but, Radu noticed, as he opened the gates for them, that Lorin's Audi had its hood scraped and one of the mirrors broken.

"What the hell happened to your ride, you crazy dog?" Radu asked him, smiling while the couple from Bucharest was getting out of the car and into the snow-bound yard.

"I had some bloke on the hood, bro. Isn't this goddamn mental, man? The fuckers are waiting on Prahova Valley, passed Predeal, all of them masked and armed with clubs, and if you stop, you're toast. They put boulders past a curve and if you hit the brakes, you're done. I passed like five cars that were pulled over and the fuckin' carolers were beating the shit out of two guys. The others were lined up and the dickheads were taking everything they had in their cars."

The New Year and Christmas Romanian custom, many centuries old, is that those who go caroling and bidding the best for the year that is about to begin, with bullroarers or Little Plough poems, the goat sketch, Sorcova (a sort of enchantment, old and heathen, spoken on the first morning of the year) and Steaua, referring to the "star in the east" (said to have led the three wise men to where Christ was born) reenactment tradition, wear masks and are organized into bands. The boors that had attacked Lorin, on the other hand, were nothing but drunks who were using the door to door caroling traditions as an excuse to get money for booze. Since before Christmas, they had put on colored masks they had crafted themselves and started caroling. Most people didn't have money to pay them for their "services," so they gave them wine and palinca to drink. Thus, after a few days and nights of non-stop drinking, the carolers decided it would be a good idea to hijack the cars driving along Prahova Valley and to buy themselves more booze and keep the party going with the stolen money and goods.

Fortunately, during the last decade, this type of activity has virtually disappeared; on the one hand, because the police have increasingly enforced fighting against such crimes, and on the other hand, because the new generation is more civilized under the influence of the West. But during those first years of freedom, after more than half a century of communist brutalization, things were completely different.

A look of utter astonishment appeared on Radu's face when he heard Lorin's story, and when he gazed in Cristina's direction, he saw that she was still shaking after the shock she had just been through. A vein started throbbing near his temple.

"This is fuckin' insane, man, I can't believe it! How many of them are there, dude?"

"Many, at least twenty or so. All of them masked and shot in the head."

"Damn those thralls... they're in need of some serious waxing! And what did you do?"

'Well, I already told you. The suckers jumped my car and when they saw I wouldn't slow down, one of them got hold of my hood, one hand clinging on to my mirror like grim death and the other trying to break my window with a jimmy. I'm lucky the bastard was wasted otherwise I could have kissed my windshield goodbye! I poured on the coal. The bozos were kicking my car, screaming like devils in hell. About a hundred meters after losing the goofballs, I suddenly hit the brakes and the twat fell. I ripped his face off, but I think I must have pushed one wrong, because my dickbeater's swollen. I spazzed out for not having my Roscoe with me, but I was coming here to party with my buddies, bro. How could I know they were gonna go apeshit on my car?"

Looking at Lorin's right hand, he saw that it was swollen and a little bruised. Black clouds of anger blanketed Radu, and in a few seconds, everything else had disappeared, replaced by an awful hatred and a heinous wish for revenge. He was already visualizing what was about to happen and the violent thoughts that were going through his cortex with dizzying speed took over him entirely, less than one minute after letting his friend drive through the gates.

"We're goin' to knock the dust out of 'em, Lorin, mate. Wait 'til the Siamese twins and Stefan get here and we'll give those guys hell. Fuck 'em and their bad blood ancestors. I'll show them what terror means, stinkin' cocksuckers!"

Cristina, Lorin's girlfriend, got over the initial shock just in time to feel the cold claws of fear take over her being. She saw Radu's expression, distorted by hatred, and felt the apocalyptic energy he generated. She knew him very well, almost as well as she knew her boyfriend, and she was aware of the way he reacted whenever he lost his temper. In all the years she had spent with Lorin, she had witnessed some scenes of such violence that it made her stomach turn every time she recalled them. But, at the same time, it had given her a strange feeling of pride and security because her man and his friends weren't the type of people who would be used as doormats by anyone, ever, no matter how scary or powerful the enemy. She knew exactly what was about to happen and wouldn't stop it even if she could, especially since she still had the vivid images of those innocent people being robbed and abused by the masked gang.

It wasn't what she had in mind for New Year's Eve, but living with Lorin all these years, she had learned not to interfere when the boys had a problem to solve, even if she didn't always agree with their decisions. Anyway, she loved her man for exactly who he was and wouldn't even dream of trying to change that. Coming from a family of intellectuals, where her father, although a professor at the university and very intelligent, had a passive personality and was permanently dominated by her mother, Christine fully appreciated Lorin's wild and independent way of being, even though, time and again, it was too much for her to handle.

In the next hour, Stefan and Jana showed up, as well as the twins, Nelu and Cristi, each in his own car, with their girlfriends. They were updated on the situation and started preparing for the attack.

"Here's the plan!" Radu said to his friends. "When we get there, two cars will go first, it's better if it's my jeep and Nelu's.

We'll let those losers jump us without shooting, keep driving for another fifty meters, and then stop. Lorin's car and Cristi's are gonna come from behind us and you guys will start firing your handguns. The fuckers are gonna start running towards us 'cause they have nowhere else to go; there are mountains on one side and a chasm on the other. When they approach us, we'll catch them in the middle. Be careful not to shoot any of them and get into trouble, but if there's no other way, aim for their legs. We'll get them lying on the ground and beat them with our bats. How does this plan sound?"

Stefan said to Radu, "Bro, I ain't got a gun. I didn't know there was gonna be such a rush. Have you got any spare?"

"We'll find you a pistol, don't worry. The Nose doesn't have his either. You guys have 'em, right?" The twins nodded. "Okay, brothers, let's go get 'em! D'you have bats in your car, or should I give you some?"

Nelu smiled and the scar that marked his face, from a knife wound he got years ago, gave him a ghoulish look that matched the rest of his features perfectly. "Come on, Radu boy, the new year will have started by the time we finish preparing. How the fuck could we not have everything we need in the car? Let's cook 'em before they leave, or some guy with a cell gets away and calls the cops, and we need that like a hole in the head!"

His brother Cristi reinforced his words. "I agree, it's now or never, or the pigs will come fo'shizzle!"

"Don't worry, guys!" Radu replied. "By the time the cops come all the way from Ploiesti, we'll have them eat dirt, and the local cops won't interfere when it comes to so many people. They don't have as many cherry-tops as there are peasants in the streets. Let's go. Nicu, you follow me in your jeep, you guys keep a safe distance of two hundred meters or so. When you see the dickheads, shoot in their direction, make them run towards us, okay? Just be careful how you shoot, it would be great if you could shoot in the air. They'll just panic and run towards us, damn cocksuckers! If they get you, aim for their legs."

Irinel was approaching Radu's car. "And where do you think you're going? Stay here and take care of the women, you didn't think we were gonna leave them here alone, did you?"

"But, why? They're okay, you're the ones who need help!"

Radu raced the engine and cast him a look that cut off any attempt to try to get any further than that.

"Come on, get inside and take care of the girls! See you soon!"

The guys got in their cars; first was Radu's jeep, followed by Nicu's, and a minute later, Lorin's scratched car took off with Stefan in it as well. At the end of the convoy was Cristi's Mercedes.

The closer they got to the curve where the ruffians were waiting, the more the world was disappearing from Radu's universe, being replaced by his focus on what was about to happen. His heart was racing way faster than usual and waves of adrenaline were running through his body, as it always did before action that involved violence. In those moments, Radu felt transformed, as if he were lifted above his normal operational level by an angel of war that gave him powers he never dreamed of, sharpened his senses, and turned him into the absolute prowler.

And suddenly they appeared in front of him. The spectacle was macabre: more than ten peasants, all of them masked and armed with bats, were standing on the roadside, fumbling through cars that had been pulled over. Their owners were trembling, crazed with fear, in the middle of the road. At the center of the causeway between the mountains were more boors, who were stopping the drivers that had the bad idea to use that road on the last day of the year. The location chosen by the highwaymen served them fairly well, because, at least in one direction, the road was going upward right before the curve. Controlling the car on the thick layer of snow was difficult, and the ice beneath made the wheels slip despite the snow chains that the drivers had thought to use.

Radu stepped on it and almost hit one of the boors; they all dodged at the last second, seeing that the jeep wasn't going to stop, and then they tried clinging to it. The same happened with Nelu's jeep, but, both cars being very solid, they passed through the wall of masked people without any difficulties.

As he was moving away from the scene of the robbery, Radu looked in his rear-view mirror to judge the optimal distance at which he should stop. He slowed down, turned off his engine, and got out of the car with the pistol in his hand. Nelu did the same thing. The baseball bats had been placed on the front seats so they would be handy when needed.

Suddenly, they heard the first gunshots and they could see Lorin's and Cristi's cars in the distance, driving very slowly. After the first three or four gunshots were fired, the thugs came running towards Radu and Nelu, screaming their heads off. They could already see the expressions of terror on their faces as they were moving faster than they had ever done. When they got less than twenty meters away, Radu told his friend: "Now, bro!"

He aimed over the masked figures and started shooting. "Where the hell are you running so fast, you fuckin' roughnecks? I thought you were scaring the shit out of people, you dickheads. What's wrong, lost your balls?"

Most of them got down on the ground. "Wait, don't shoot! Don't shoot and I swear on my children's life, I'm not gonna do it again! Don't kill me!"

Their chorus was even more forceful than earlier, when they were yelling at people to give them all their valuables. Only three or four of them were still on their feet, and one of them addressed Radu. "You think you're big shots 'cause you have guns or what? Without 'em, you wouldn't have had the guts!"

Before he even had the chance to finish the sentence, Radu grabbed the baseball bat from the seat behind him and, in a single continuous movement, jumped over to him and smashed his face with the bat. He fell on the ground instantly, his jaw hanging on one side. Before they could come to their senses, the other thugs found themselves under the attack. Meanwhile, Lorin, Stefan, and Cristi had jumped out of their cars and started batting the boor mass; in less than a minute, the snow on the mountain causeway had become red.

Of all of them, Lorin was hitting the hardest, even though he was only using his left arm, because he had been the closest to being a victim of the muggers. While he was bashing them, he addressed them, drooling without realizing it. “You’re not badasses anymore, are you, cocksuckers? How many people have you been bullying, hmmm? Take this, you fuck, I’ll teach you to pick on people for no reason!”

The carolers’ screams waned as they were losing consciousness, turning into agonizing groans.

“Stop, bro, they’ve had enough! Let’s bail before the cops come. Now that there were gunshots, I’m sure someone’s gonna call them!” Radu said to his friends, hardly able to draw breath after all the effort and the adrenaline infusion galloping through his body.

The five guys got in their cars quickly and went back the same way they had come towards Radu’s cottage, where the women were worried and waiting for them. Not more than three quarters of an hour had passed, out of which the operation itself took less than five minutes. Now, the party could begin.

Chapter 9

When they opened the gates to the yard, the women stormed out of the house to find out what had happened and whether their men were all in one piece. Of all the women, Jana was the most confused because she had never seen Stefan react like that before and she wasn't used to such a degree of violence. In the last half an hour, her feelings of love and admiration for her boyfriend had turned into a sense of being intimidated and lacking trust. Being raised in the Czech Republic, one of the countries with the lowest crime rates in Europe, it was hard for her to comprehend how Stefan and his friends changed from a relaxed and leisurely disposition into murderers' shoes, just like that. Now that they were back, she couldn't understand how, although their clothes had bloodstains on them, and she could only imagine how their incursion into "boorland" went, the boys were completely relaxed again, all of them smiling and laughing as if nothing unusual had happened.

Another peculiar thing to her was the way the Romanian women had reacted; not only did they not seem worried when their men left them and went fighting, it seemed to turn them on. For the first time, the Czech girl realized that Stefan's savage spirit, which had attracted her so much, and even the untamed spirit of the land he came from, had their roots in something she perceived as dark, and now felt frightening.

Stefan came towards her smiling and hugged her tightly.

"What's up, baby, is everything okay? How did you get along with the girls?"

Without realizing it, Jana started to relax, hugged him back, and kissed him on the neck. "Yes, baby, everything's okay. I was worried about you, but the girls told me to relax because you knew what you're doing. They are really nice. Cristina speaks English very well, the others can speak the language a little too. How are you, is everything okay?"

"Yeah, my little girl. There were some bandits who attacked Lorin and Cristina on their way here, but we took care of them, don't worry!"

She felt his look piercing through her and that the Romanian could not only see inside her but that he also had the power to manipulate her feelings and thoughts. Besides his black eyes, which burned when they were focused upon her, the hefty arms around her waist, slightly trembling under their pressure, the perfect smile, and the self-confidence generated by this man, made all the lack of trust and the confusion that had taken over her entire being until just a few moments earlier disappear completely, to be replaced by the animal magnetism she felt for Stefan the moment she first laid eyes on him.

With a large satisfied smile ingrained on his austere face, Radu shut the gates and invited everybody in.

One of the girls who came with the twins was the first one to inquire about their commando raid. "How was it, did you fuck them up? Did they hit you too? Do you need any medical attention? How many were there?"

Nelu grimaced a smile, seamed by the old sword cut he got from a bar fight in Galati, and cuddled her to his strong-as-a-bull chest. "You sure ask a lot of questions, woman! We're all okay; relax! There were some hoods but we softened their bones all right. It was a warm up for the party."

He laughed throatily as they all entered Radu's almost one-hundred-square-meter living room, where two big tables were brimming with all sorts of starters, snacks, bottles of alcohol and sodas.

With a warm smile and teary eyes, Cristina asked Lorin while she was caressing his back: “Did you hobble those fuckers good? Did you teach them not to do that to innocent people again?”

“Yeah, baby girl, I knocked them out bad. I don’t think any of them is gonna pull one of these things again. Eh, fuck their redneck ancestors. How’ve you been? What did you girls do while we were away?”

“Well, nothing much. We rearranged Radu’s entrées a bit, ‘cause he tried to make ‘em look nice but they looked like they’d been chopped with an ax. But don’t tell him or I don’t know what I’m gonna do to you!”

They all sat down, some of them on the three leather sofas, others on the chairs around the tables. Radu and the twins started filling their plates with some of the entrees the girls had prepared.

“Oh, I see you’ve arranged them here nicely, thanks girls! I thought I did a good job, but everything looks much better now. Come on, guys, let’s all eat so that we can start drinking afterwards. Oh, and I have a surprise for all of you, but after we finish scoffing!”

Lorin smiled and said to Radu, “I say you bring that surprise now so that we can start rolling before everyone finishes eating.”

“What, Lorin? What kind of a surprise is this now? Okie dokie, wait here a sec, I’ll fetch it right away.”

He went to his bedroom and came back with an old silver tray he had found there when he moved in, it was probably part of one of his aunt’s dowries. On the tray, there were three big buds, each weighing about twenty grams. These were the buds from the top of two of his plants, their proximity to the lamps meant they grew bigger than those on the lower part of the plants. Many growers preferred to keep their pots further apart so that the light from the lamps shone on the plant evenly, but this means fewer plants, which, even if they have bigger buds, are less fruitful all in all than if they're arranged one right next to another.

But there are as many growing methods as there are growers. They usually differ from one another depending on the available space of the plantation, accessibility to the chemicals these plants need and, last but not least, the teacher that each grower had, to which we may also add the personal experience. Nobody had shown Radu how to set up a plantation and nobody helped him with the growing process. He just consulted some brochures he found at the shop in Prague, the same shop he bought all his equipment from, and followed the instructions, step by step. From one harvest to the next, he tried small experiments, adding tiny tricks he learned along the way, and the quality of his weed was getting better and better every time.

He hadn't smoked from this crop yet. He had let the plants dry and just cut the buds, and he was very curious to see the result of his three months' worth of work. Judging by the way it looked and smelled, this crop promised to be an excellent one. Except for Lorin and Stefan, no one in that room or, actually, anywhere else, knew about the existence of the plantation in the basement. When Radu appeared carrying the tray with the buds, everyone assumed Lorin had brought the stuff from Bucharest for the New Year's Eve party. And this was exactly what they were supposed to think. Lorin, Irinel and Lili, one of the girls the twins had brought along, started rolling. By the time the joints were ready, most of the people had finished eating so they made a circle around the three of them to pass the joint more easily.

"Wow, good weed, bro, it has such a great taste!" Nelu said, after puffing from the reefer Irinel had rolled.

"Good, good, smell the pipe. Let's see now how it whispers!"

"It looks like a killer, smells like a killer, so it must be a killer. Tell me, Radu boy, I heard Bronco knocked out another one, is that so? There were rumors in Galati that he has no rival. Is your dog that good, bro?"

"I let him go for Voodoo, who had scored three victories before that fight, and he wiped the floor with him. You would have thought he was a stray."

"And who do you plan on letting him fight next, man?"

"I wanna see him against his dad, Joker. Apart from him, there's no other dog to match mine right now. Voodoo was supposed to be the great hope for those guys in Bucharest. But with Joker, it will be a different story. I saw the tape with the fight he had in Hungary, against Attila. Boy, that dog is really, really good! Do you know how he goes for the flippers? He's got a style where he goes underneath the dog and searches for the paws. I'll have to train mine specially to defend his paws or this one will rip them off."

"Well, Joker ain't a champ for no reason, bro. He's had six fights so far and he's won all of them!" Lorin replied. "Bronco-boy is gonna have some work to do against this one, but he'll take him, you'll see! Did you see how he gripped and jogged Voodoo? Your dog's getting better and better with every fight. I've watched him fight since he was a puppy and I can honestly tell you he learns something from every match. He's improving. But you're right, he'll need super training for this one. It's gonna be a bit thick, he's never had an opponent of Joker's caliber."

"Well, don't sweat about it, guys!" Radu said. "Joker may be a good dog but he don't have Bronco's mojo and rhythm. Didn't you see how he jolted that black dog after half an hour of fighting? You could swear the fight had just started. Plus, I'll seriously train him for this fight, but we first have to see if they'll let Joker fight. When I got Joker to ride Cindy, he was bragging about him having no rival, and that no dog goes for the paws like he does. We'll see what happens, but I think Bronco's going to go through him like a fuckin' freight train. Mine has got too much energy and he jolts too wicked for that one to be able to beat him. Did you see the damn holes he opened on the black dog, how they looked like sword wounds? Now, there is the money issue; this dude doesn't let his dog fight without serious bread. But we'll raise it. I'll use all the money he has won with Voodoo and I'll add some more if necessary."

"How much do you think he'll want them fighting on?" Cristi asked.

"I don't know, man, but it can go up to twenty thousand. Especially now that he knows Bronco has won against Voodoo, he might push it to discourage me. The sucker's got a serious bank! But it's fine by me, the more money the better!"

"Bro, if you need any money, you can come ask for it anytime! We won't even charge you high interest for it; after all, we've known each other since we were kids!"

Nelu started laughing throatily after making this joke, his hoarse laugh sounding more like a flooded engine than a human laughing.

"Shut up, Nelu, or I'll give you a kick in the teeth for kidding like this!"

Even though Radu had spoken those words in a half-joking tone, the atmosphere grew cold instantly, and they all smiled uneasily. This was because they all knew Radu couldn't stand being made fun of, not even by his friends, and they didn't know exactly what to expect from him in such situations. All the more so as, in all these years, his friends had had the opportunity to see him react to various jokes different people made about him or those close to him, and Radu's fake smile, followed immediately by an action of extreme ferocity, had made everyone who knew him choose their words and attitude around him carefully. The only men who didn't fall in that category were Lorin and Stefan; they were the only ones who could afford to say or do anything in Radu's company. He loved and respected them completely.

Nelu knew as well as the next guy in that room that, even though he and his brother each weighed thirty kilograms more than Radu, he could silence him with the same readiness he would roll a joint. And this was because, growing up together, the guys had had several occasions to fight with other groups of boys in Galati, and the speed, precision, strength, and especially the ferocity with which Radu hit during a fight were absolutely overwhelming. He seemed to have an angel, or maybe a demon, which animated him when he fought, giving him unusual powers and reflexes.

Radu realized he had ruined the atmosphere a bit with his acidic line so he tried to fix things when he passed Nelu the joint.

"There you go, Nelu mate, take a hit from the reefer, but you should know that I'm writing everything down and in the end I'll ask you to pay for it, if you put it like that!"

Everyone laughed, not necessarily because the joke was good, but because the atmosphere was relaxed again after the few moments of tension that had hovered in the air. Radu knew he crossed the line sometimes and he blamed himself every time something like this happened, especially with people close to him. Most of the times he realized he made people uncomfortable too late, after the deed was already done, his alpha male instinct being his spur of the moment driver in almost every situation.

Chapter 10

While the joints were being passed around the room, the boys opened some bottles of rum to officially start the party. Rum had always been their favorite drink; from when they were fourteen years old and tasting alcohol for the first time, this pirate's booze had been a perfect match.

Radu poured everyone a glass and made a small toast:

"My dear brothers, I'm glad we're here together. There's no place I'd rather be and nobody I'd rather be with, for better or worse! Thank you all for coming. May the Lord bring us many joys and satisfactions in the year to come, more than He has given us in the past years, and, thank God, those years were not bad at all! Cheers, everyone!"

They all clanged their glasses of rum and drank with teary eyes from Radu's mini-toast. He rarely opened his soul and showed his appreciation, and the fact that he did that now had moved everybody. They all felt flattered by the fact that this man they admired and respected had love in his heart for every single one of them.

After that, he addressed Lorin: "Lorin, mate, how about you show us that snort we've all been talking about. Let's see if it's any good!"

"Yeah, bro, I was thinking about proposing that. Go get a larger mirror, if you have one!"

He got a bag with several white stones from his pocket, weighing about ten grams altogether. He got the coke from Bucharest and, unfortunately, it wasn't high quality, having been cut several times before reaching the capital city of Romania. But for guys who weren't used to high quality when it came to coke, having a thirty percent purity was enough for an excellent party.

Radu took down the mirror from the vestibule wall; its wooden frame had been ingeniously carved with different flowers by his aunts. He brought the mirror to the living room and put it on one of the tables, after the girls had taken the plates off them. They were already cleaning them in the kitchen. He took one of the biggest rocks from his friend's bag and cut it with a knife he produced from the back pocket of his pants. Then, with a plastic card, he started pressing the white pebbles in order to turn them into powder. After it had all turned into powder, he prepared a line large enough for every person at the party.

"I made a line for every one of us. At first we'll each do one, and then it's by request, okay?"

"Oh my, Radu, if your aunts knew what you're using their mirror for, they'd turn in their graves!" one of the girls that came with the twins tried to joke.

"I don't think so. The old women were open-minded, I doubt they would mind. On the contrary, they'd be glad to know their mirror is being used and their work appreciated, rather than having it thrown somewhere in the attic, for instance."

Lorin cut the next lines, then Cristi; meanwhile, the first two bottles of rum they had opened were empty and Radu brought new supplies. Less than an hour after their action in the mountains, they were all in an advanced state of exhilaration, laughing and talking loudly, more communicative and with more will to live than usual. Of course, the alcohol and the drugs had softened the rough edges, but, essentially, what gave them the feeling of satisfaction and fulfillment was the camaraderie between everyone present and the fact that everyone knew they could not only count on the people around them, but also, together, they represented a redoubtable force few people could cope with. And this gave them a comforting feeling, strengthening the bonds they had created all those years before.

Stefan had spent most of the time with Jana so she would not feel excluded, being the only person who was not Romanian. But after seeing that she was getting along great with the rest of the girls, he left her chatting with them and sat down at the table with the mirror and the lines.

"When's your girl from the Netherlands coming, Radu, mate?"

"I don't know, dude. She should get here, she said she'd be in Poiana before midnight. There's two more hours till then, she'll be here. She wrote to me and told me she would bring along two other girlfriends."

The girl from the Netherlands was a young twenty-five-year-old from Den Haag, who had bought a mansion close to Radu's two years before. She had purchased the house because of the beauty and wilderness of the landscape, and also because the prices of the properties in the area were accessible; purchasing the house plus the yard had cost her less than she earned in a year working at a firm in the Netherlands. Initially coming to visit the place only during vacations, Sophia had fallen madly in love with the Carpathians and their breathtaking scenery. At first, her parents were against it, being of the opinion that Romania was a dangerous, not very developed, country, and quite far from her own. There was no one to take care of the place while she was away, which was most of the time. But seeing her determination to buy the house in those legendary mountains, they stopped trying to talk her out of it.

She had met Radu in the forest surrounding Poiana Tapului when his dogs, which were there with him training, scared her. Radu addressed her in Romanian at first, but, seeing that she didn't understand, he started talking to her in English. He calmed her down, telling her she had no reason to be afraid of his dogs because they were never aggressive towards humans, and he even let her pat Cindy and Samson. Since then, they'd kept in touch with each other; she would call him from the Netherlands from time to time to catch up with the news in her new community, and Radu had promised to take care of her house while she was out of the country. That meant trimming the weeds in her yard and making sure nobody robbed her. Radu asked Irinel to trim the weeds and to let everyone in the village know that they would be better to keep a distance from the girl's house or else they would be in trouble. The inhabitants of Poiana had already seen how Radu could behave several times and understood that he wasn't the kind of man one should mess with.

Less than half an hour after Stefan inquired about them, the three Dutch girls were ringing Radu's doorbell. He went to the yard and opened the gates for them, but not before pointing out to the others that they should treat them nicely, especially since Sophie's two friends were in Romania for the first time. Radu made the acquaintance of Agnes and Bo, who were very pleased to be there. With Dutch nonchalance, they hugged him and kissed him on both of his cheeks, thanking him for inviting them to such a beautiful place and for welcoming them to his group, even though he didn't know them.

Sophie was the prettiest of the three, her brown hair falling in curls on her milk white shoulders, and her dark green blouse showed a pair of perky breasts. Agnes was a brunette, with fine features, but she was a bit chubby, and Bo was the kid of the group. She didn't weigh more than fifty kilograms, had short hair and her coquettish behavior resembled that of a child, nevertheless, the general impression was a pleasant one.

Radu invited them in the house, introduced them to his friends, poured them a glass of rum, and asked Nelu, who was just snorting a line, to make three more for the newcomers. The girls quickly felt at home. At first, they had been scared of these Romanians because they hadn't heard much about them other than the fact that they were from the country of Dracula, one of the most dangerous in Eastern Europe. But, after seeing the way they behaved and reacted, they realized their fears were unfounded. If someone were to show them a videotape of the boys' action two hours earlier, however, they would probably have left the party immediately. Fortunately, this was unlikely to happen.

In the girls' group, English was used almost exclusively. The three girls from the Netherlands, the one from Czech Republic, and Cristina chatted non-stop, while Irinel's girlfriend, Alina, and the twin's dates formed a separate group, speaking Romanian which Cristina translated.

By midnight, four liters of rum had been consumed, and half of the coke Lorin had brought was already finished. Feeling that they were starting to get a little tipsy, Stefan decided it was time to talk to his friends about the subject that had been on his mind for more than a month.

"Radu, mate, Lorin, come here, I've got to talk to you guys about something!"

"You do? Okay, Stef, wait a sec till we snort the lines the Nose is making now, and then we'll go talk!"

When the three men got up, left the table, and went to one of the rooms upstairs, nobody thought it was weird because they all knew about the strong bond between the three boys. As they always had some business to talk about, it wasn't considered rude when they retreated to talk in private. When they got into Radu's "office," the attic where he spent most of his time when he was at home, the three guys sat down on the couches that encircled the round table.

"Tell us, Stefanel, what did you wanna talk about, buddy?"

"Yo, guys, I think there's room to make a lot of money in Prague, but I don't exactly know how to approach it!"

"Dude, what exactly are you talking about?" Radu asked, his eyes already starting to glitter upon hearing about a possibility to make money.

"Man, everyone's snorting there! And I mean heavily. There are clubs with dealers who sell hundreds of grams a night, and everything's safe, man. The cops don't poke their noses in your affairs as long as you don't make a mess. And the thing is, it's not even that good, it's something like this stuff we're snorting tonight. I'm already in business with people there. I know two big dealers who only sell upwards of half a kilo, they don't do bargain sales. If we had a better product than the one on the streets, and that's not so hard to do, we can make a lot of money!"

"What's the price there, bro?" Lorin inquired.

"Sixty to eighty dollars a gram, and if you buy a larger amount, it's around fifty."

"Okay, so for us to have a cash inflow and sell all of it at once, we should sell it at, like, thirty, right?" asked Radu.

"Yeah, thirty. We'll get rid of all of it at that price. But where the fuck do we get it so cheap to be able to sell it at thirty?"

"Well, let's think it through!" Radu retorted. "So it gets to Europe through Africa, right? We're not counting the synthetic one, they make tons of that in the Netherlands but it's shit. We're talking about natural coke from coca leaves. It usually enters Spain through Morocco. It gets to Africa from South America, so imagine that it's cut once by those from, let's say, Bolivia; then it's cut a lot by the Africans, then the Europeans cut it even more when it gets on the continent. Then it's cut again by all those handlers before it reaches those who snort it. If we wanna make money out of it, there's no use buying it from Europe, the profit is too low. And even if we find someone in Spain who gets it directly, someone from Morocco, for instance, by the time it gets to him, it's already been cut three times, and he won't sell it at a low price 'cause it's already in Europe. He won't sell it for less than twenty, and even if he does, that's ten dollars per gram profit. That means ten bucks a gram, so only ten grand a kilo, and that's not productive enough. The only way to make money is to buy it directly from South America."

Stefan and Lorin stared at him in amazement. Not only did they not expect Radu to suggest something like that but they never really imagined themselves going so far from home.

"Radu, bro, are you mental? Do you really expect us to go to Bolivia? It would be a suicide mission without any connections."

"You don't need no connections, dude. You'll see exactly how it goes, then and there. None of us has ever been there before so there's no use in making plans 'cause we don't know what to expect from them. What's certain is that we can find the cheapest merchandise at the best quality. The problem is…how the fuck do we transport it?"

"Well, I know, that's exactly the problem. You can't get it through the airport 'cause they even search you in the ass now. The only alternative would be water transport. Maybe we should pay someone to bring it…"

"You're barking! Who the hell can we trust with it? Have you lost your marbles? It's not even about the money, there's also a huge risk. Someone might catch on, rat us out, and this is not weed, bro. You can easily get yourself at least ten years in the joint for this!"

Lorin, who had been relatively quiet till then, joined in the conversation. "Man, if we wanna do this, we have to do it ourselves, we cannot get anyone else involved. There are too many variables; to count on other people would be stupid. But, on the other hand, we cannot get involved 'cause we look suspicious enough for these guys to search us until they find it. We have to use someone who doesn't look like a felon and whom we can trust."

"Do you know someone who fits this description? I don't!"

"Oh yes you do, bro! Irinel."

Radu's first reaction was to dismiss it categorically. "You must be crazy to think I would let Irinel be a snort trafficker. I mean, this boy hasn't done such a thing in his life, how could I ask him to travel on a ship with the hink. Are you barking mad?"

"Well, that's exactly why he's the best candidate, 'cause he's never done such things before. With his childish, innocent face, the little boy that he is, he won't raise any suspicion. Plus, he's a cocky devil, I bet he'd want in."

"Of course he'd want in. He's been fuckin' my ears till they started bleeding to let him in on something other than training the dogs. He wants to make money, but I've always talked him out of it, told him he's got some more growing to do."

"Man, are you nuts? How old is he, bro, nineteen, right? Remember what we were doing when we were nineteen? Dude, those were the days, we were fuckin' ruling the whole city of Galati. Why not let him make some money, especially since he's asking you? He's a loyal motherfucker, he's got balls, he'd never spill the beans. He's perfect for this job!"

"He's perfect for you 'cause you don't give a fuck about him, that's why he's perfect! But if, God forbid, he gets caught because of me, what will I do then, hmm?"

"Let's ask him and see what he wants."

"What the fuck do you think he's gonna say? He'd be delighted, of course, that's not what cracks my skull."

"Coome oon, bro, he's not gonna get caught!" Stefan intervened. "We'll only buy a small quantity, let's say half a kilo. That's a small package you can hide anywhere. I have a chemist in Prague who will cut it, and if we buy it from Latin America, pure, we can cut it two or three times. Plus we can sell it for ten times more than we buy it and we get a big profit. Bro', you can't say it's not worth it!"

"I know it's worth it, man, but I really don't wanna get this little fucker involved. I don't want him in any trouble. But it's true that I wouldn't trust anyone else with this trip."

Weighing all the pros and cons, the risks and the profit, Radu decided that this was a business worth putting in motion. "Look, guys, here's how we're gonna do this. If we start this dodge, we won't do it just once. We start this only if you, Stefan, are sure that you can push it there and sell it in large quantities and get rid of it all at once. First time we do it with Irinel, if he wants in, and I'm sure he will, and when we get there, we gotta find someone to come and bring it to us next time, even if it's gonna be more expensive. We'll save some money with the transport and, most importantly, the risk is lower.

"We'll go there with the kid and put him on a ship, but not a cruise ship, a cargo ship. His name mustn't be registered anywhere, we'll bribe the captain to take him and that's it. We won't return with him. We'll make sure he gets on and then we take a plane and wait for him somewhere in Europe. God forbid they find more of us with Romanian passports. They'll start suspecting something if we're together on the same ship."

Lorin and, especially, Stefan, were ecstatic, not only because there was the prospect of a considerable financial gain involved, maybe a higher amount than any of them had ever seen, but also because a new adventure beckoned. Their adventurous spirits were howling like a pack of hungry wolves in the emotional forests and wildwoods that lived inside of their tameless beings.

Chapter 11

Radu called Irinel to the attic. Before the latter climbed the stairs, Lorin gave Radu his share of the ketamine money. "There you are, Radu, mate, before I forget!"

"Did everything go as planned?"

"Yeah, he said next month he wants in again."

"Very well. Give me a call when he drops the bread and we'll sort this out too."

Meanwhile, Irinel had climbed the stairs that led to the attic and came in. On the one hand, he was very excited that the guys had called him in to discuss something, but on the other hand, he was a bit nervous, not knowing what they wanted from him.

"What's up, Irinel, all fine and dandy?" Radu asked the kid after motioning him to take a seat on one of the armchairs.

"Yes, Radu, everything's okay. Alina is enjoying the party a lot."

"That's great, I'm glad! How are you getting on with her, is she the right sort?"

"Yeah, she's good people. She isn't drawing a red herring across the track. She's straightforward, I really like her. Plus, she's a great cook. She prepares some meals that would sweep you off your feet."

"Attaboy, little devil, take care of her, she's a good girl! Listen, here's what I wanted to talk to you about...me and the boys have a proposition for you, but before you give us an answer, I would ask you to, please, think it through carefully before deciding whether you want to get involved or not, okay?"

Irinel's eyes were shining with joy. No matter what Radu was about to propose, he was sure it was going to be something interesting and something that could bring him some money. The boy would do anything to break from the daily routine in the heart of the mountains, even though he knew that he was privileged and that other people had to pay to see, briefly, the landscapes where he had spent his whole life. He wanted to see the outlands, to meet new people, and have as many interesting experiences as possible in order to polish his mountain man way of being.

"Listen, here's what this is all about!" Radu continued. "We want to take a trip to South America, to Bolivia probably, and bring back some coke. We need someone to bring it across because we look suspicious and they're gonna search through our bags. You have the face of an innocent kid. If you want in, we'll go there together, but you have to return alone on a ship, and we'll wait for you somewhere in Europe. We won't buy a considerably big piece, maybe half a kilo, which can be easily hidden somewhere on the ship. The risk appears once you get off. They could search your luggage, but we'll try to find you a cargo boat where the suckers search the containers and not the sailors' luggage as they get off.

"If this goes as planned, there's serious money to be made but you shouldn't forget that it's risky. You can easily get ten years for transporting snort, and clink ain't easy on you in those countries. Think it through before you answer. Maybe you should ask your girlfriend as well, but only if you trust her not to spill the beans in case you have a fight or something, okay?"

"Radu, there's nothing to think about. I want in, absolutely! You know how long I've been waiting for you to get me involved in such a business. I've asked you several times. The risk is no problem for me, honestly. I'm more excited about the adventure in this than the money we're gonna make. As for Alina, I think it's better if I don't tell her and freak her out. I'll just say I'm going to Craiova for a while, to my dying grandmother. If, God forbid, I get caught, you'll see to it that Alina has everything she needs, okay, Radu?"

Radu and his friends were moved by Irinel's attitude, which proved to Radu, once again, that he had decided well when he recruited the boy as his right hand. Radu continued, trying to hide the emotion in his voice. Normally, that wasn't an issue for him, but every time he snorted coke, he became more sensitive, making him feel like tear creek was pushed closer to the surface by the white powder.

"Well, it's settled then! I'll be needing Irinel for another two months for Bronco's training if I wanna challenge the champion, but after that, you can take him with you. I'll stay here because I have to train the dogs, plus you don't need me on this trip, although I'd love to come. We'll arrange the details then. Stef, you talk to your connections in Prague, make sure we can get rid of it as soon as we bring it, and we'll see how it goes. If it proves to be a good deal, we'll do it a couple of times more after this. But I'm sure it will be fine. Let's get back downstairs before the others start to become suspicious!"

"Let's first settle another detail!" said Lorin. "Concerning the percentages. I think me and Stefan should each get thirty percent, and you and Irinel should split the rest, an even twenty-twenty."

"No, bro, I mean, Irinel does all the work and I get the same money as him? You guys take thirty percent each, I'll give the kiddo thirty as well, and I'll take ten 'cause I'm the least involved. And the three of us give the investment money evenly; you don't expect us to make Irinel pay!"

They all agreed that the version Radu proposed was the best way of splitting the profit. This was valid in case everything went according to the plan.

Back in the living room, where the party had toned down a little without their presence, the four guys sat down wherever they found room and poured rum in the glasses.

"Hey you mystery guys, we were starting to think the New Year would come and you'd stay hidden!" Nelu, who was already in a euphoric state, said, "There are a few minutes left before midnight, brothers!"

"How' bout we go up the hill at midnight and uncork a few bottles of champagne? There's an awesome view of the entire Prahova Valley from up there, plus everybody will set off fireworks."

They all agreed and started getting equipped for the snow outside with only a few minutes left of that year. The twins drew out a bag full of fireworks, to everyone's pleasant surprise. When they reached the top of the hill in front of Radu's house, those who hadn't been there before were taken aback. The view was fairy-tale like, with the snowy, wooded peaks of the Bucegi in the background, and Prahova Valley lit up by thousands of fireworks at the foot of the mountains. They uncorked the bottles of champagne, set off the fireworks and lit up the three big joints that the girls had rolled. They hugged each other, kissed each other on the cheeks, and felt they were starting the new year glowing with positive energy.

Back in the house, the party continued.

"Cristinel mate, I heard that you guys opened a restaurant in Galati, is that true?" Stefan asked.

Of the two brothers, Cristi was the quiet one; even so, most people preferred him to his loud brother.

"Yes, Stefan mate, we had some serious cash flow coming in at once so we decided to open a business and use it as a cover in case of an IRS check. We had to at least have some documents to justify the money, or the fuckers would confiscate everything once again, like they always do. And I can't complain, bro, it's going well, people are coming in. Most of them are colleagues of ours, but still that's better than no one. How 'bout you, Radu, still with your pit bulls? That's all you've been doing since I met you, aren't you getting tired of it?"

"Well, to tell you the truth, I was thinking it's about time I started doing something else. I'm tired of running with the dogs on the hills all day long, plus I work them up all the time. Fighting and training is all these dogs know. What I always wanted was to have a champion, and now I do. If he gives it to his father too, he becomes grand champ, what more could I want from the dog, bro? I was thinking I'd use him in some fights, only him, for another two or three years and then I'll let him retire. No more fights. Let others do that, I've been doing it for a long time!"

Everyone who heard what he said looked at him in wonder. They had never heard Radu talk about retiring from the dog fighting business before, and they couldn't believe their ears, knowing that pit bulls were his whole life.

"Dude, are you serious? Do you really wanna quit breeding pit bulls?" Lorin asked in astonishment. "You won't breed any dogs after this?"

"Why, bro, of course I will, I'm seriously considering Staffordshire Bull Terrier breeding. They're the British version of pit bulls. They come from Bull and Terrier, or Half and Half, an extinct breed, but all these fighting devils come from it. Staffie looks like a pit bull, but they are smaller and less aggressive. They have a wonderful character, very playful. Plus, they're very fond of people. In Great Britain, they're called baby-sitter dogs 'cause they're very good with kids and take great care of them.

"There aren't any in our country, but everywhere else is full of them, it's one of the most loved breeds. I think they're gonna be very popular here too. I could sell them for big bucks. So I was thinkin' I'd buy two females and a male from different bloodlines, and start breeding them."

"And what are you gonna do about the pit bulls, man? Sell them?" asked Stefan.

"Well, I'll give some of them away. I'll keep Bronco, his mum, Cindy, and Samson. That dog's the apple of my eye and he's old, anyway, he's almost thirteen. I'll sell Bronco's brother, Leeroy, in

Bucharest, the Franka guy said he wants to buy him and have the two of them mate. He's a guy who takes good care of his dogs too, and the other two bitches I'm gonna give away, one here, and one in Galati. I'm not gonna sell them, I'm giving them away for free on the understanding that if I see that they're not being taken good care of, I'll take them back. And no fights, 'cause these devils don't know how to handle such things and I don't want my girls tarnished.

"I'll give Tanaka to Irinel's cousin, the bloke's mad about dogs and he'll take care of her. He has already started building her a pound 'cause I told him I'm not giving him the dog unless he does so, and I'll give Scarlett to my cousin in Galati. He's totally against dog fighting anyway so I know he won't exhaust her with that. Plus, they both had some fights, they've had it.

"That Tanaka is a killer, she's moving great in the ring and she's very keen on training, that's why I wanted to keep her. I meant to train her and Bronco together, given their top class qualities. She's a better runner than Cindy; the princess has gotten old too. I've pensioned her; she had her last fight last year. She never lost. She's insane, that one, I'll be damned if I've ever seen a better bitch than her."

The guys agreed; they had all seen Bronco's mother in the ring and the barker was indeed phenomenal, winning all of the eight fights Radu organized for her. She was the absolute female champion.

"So, you'll have matches only with Bronco, right, since Cindy and Samson are both retired?"

"Yeah, dude, it's easier to just train one dog, plus, why would I need to raise other pups, bro, when I have my own champion now? I'll have another two or three years' worth of fights with him and I'm done, that's enough. I wanna have my peace and quiet, go walk the dogs through the woods, without having to always run with them and take them to the vet to patch them up."

Even though Radu's explanation made sense to everybody present, nobody truly believed that he would actually give up breeding and training pit bulls, it being not only his biggest passion but also his main occupation.

As the hours went by and the bottles of rum were emptied, the guys became more and more open to one another, putting their arms around each other's shoulders, hugging, kissing each other on the cheeks and promising each other eternal friendship more and more often. At a certain point, Radu told them something that, even though they were all in an advanced state of intoxication, moved his friends deeply.

"We're all fine now, we're among friends, we can't ask for anything more, but tomorrow we may be in jail or passed away. This life is exactly like a ring for fights, brothers, and we're the dogs who give their best to survive and to win. And you often win and have the impression that you're someone, but then life hits you so hard that it puts you in a tight corner, and it takes you way longer to get up than to fall down. On the other hand, there are times when you're down on the ground and you're so angry, you feel like killing everyone and suddenly you see a weakness in your opponent and that twinkle of hope gives you the strength to get up and fight harder than you did at the beginning. We're nothing more than dogs fighting for every inch won in this ring that is life, where there can only be winners and losers. Draws are not accepted, brothers, not while you have a pair of balls!"

While the boys were having these types of conversations, the women were having their share of fun. The main subject was men, with their good sides and their bad sides, the sufferings they caused and the moments of ecstasy as well. Some of the girls were inquiring whether or not there was something going on between Radu and Sophie and if they had already had sex. Upon finding out that wasn't the case, they were curious to know when they were planning on doing it. Jana, Cristina, and the other girls kept encouraging her to sleep with him, maybe because every one of them wished to do so themselves had they not been bound by their obligations towards their boyfriends. Bo and Agnes, the two girls from the Netherlands, were crazy about Stefan, especially when they heard that he was a porn actor, but they couldn't express their opinions about it too much given the fact that Jana was present. The Czech girl was aware of their intentions nevertheless, and, being also strongly attracted to women, she decided that the idea of an orgy with her boyfriend and the two girls from the Netherlands wasn't such a bad one.

Urged by the other girls, Sophie went to Radu, hugged him, and asked him whether he was having fun, then thanked him again for inviting her and her friends. After that, she whispered in his ear: "I'd love it if we could screw each other."

Radu smiled, turned towards her, took her by the waist and put her on one of his knees. He whispered back in her ear: "I've wanted to do that since I first laid eyes on you. Let's spend some more time with our friends and then vanish to my room, okay?"

He started quivering when he imagined what was about to happen. He'd been attracted to this beautiful girl from the Netherlands since the first moment they met in the heart of the woods.

"Wow, Radu, mate, seems like you're a veritable Casanova tonight, you devil! Way to go, your girl's a fox, I really like her!" Lorin told him.

"Yeah, bro, you go take care of the business. We can manage here without you!" Stefan said, endorsing the idea.

"Don't you worry, guys, I'll give it to her, but I'm not gonna run to my room like some obsessed guy now. I'll go later, when the action's over. I'm in the mood for some more partying for now, anyway."

Near dawn, the girls were feeling tired and asked about the rooms they'd be given. The twins and their girlfriends were put into one of the room upstairs with the biggest bed, Lorin and Cristina took the neighboring room. Irinel and Alina bid them farewell and left, since the boy lived within a five-minute walk. Radu and Sophie, together with Stefan and Jana, Agnes and Bo, decided to remain together in Radu's room for a while to continue the party, the goal of every person in that room being to have the wildest kind of sex possible.

Less than five minutes later, the orgy started, the girls from the Netherlands being the ones who started everything, undressing and starting to kiss lasciviously. Jana joined their lesbian foreplay then the boys plunged right amongst them. The orgy went on for a few hours, every party enjoying multiple orgasms. The one who actively participated the least in the shared activity was little Bo; nevertheless, she was the one who had the most orgasms. During the whole orgy, with some exceptions when she helped the others finish, the petite Dutch girl had stayed in a corner of the bed, watching the bodies entangling and wriggling with convulsions of pleasure while masturbating frantically.

Chapter 12

Radu entered the new year training Bronco. He had talked to the champion's owner, the champion being Joker, Bronco's father, and they set the date of the fight for the beginning of May. Each of the owners sent an amount of five thousand dollars to a referee they both knew very well. In case either of the breeders changed his mind about the match, the money would be given to the other. This way, the time and money invested in training the dogs was not wasted in the case of one of the owners getting cold feet before the fight and cancelling.

In the first week of the year, Radu started light training with Bronco, taking him to the snowy woods of the Bucegi Mountains, driving the ATV he had bought especially for dog training when he moved to the mountains. A few hours a day, Radu would drive in the mountain valleys, on the forest roads and, sometimes, right through the heart of the woods, on hilly terrain, closely followed by his favorite four-legged animal.

From the second week of training, he attached the special training collar around his neck, which would only be taken off right before the fight. It was almost as long as the dog's neck and had twenty-five mini-pockets on each side. Once every three days, Radu added a piece of lead on each side of the collar, making it heavier and heavier. In the last month of training before the match, all the pockets of the collar contained a piece of lead; by that time, it weighed ten kilograms. Whether he was running, pulling, hanging, or shaking, the dog was wearing the collar, thus increasing his muscle power and resistance to effort. After carrying this weight with him for a few months of training, the dog moved with the same ease and freedom as before having the collar attached; and when the moment of the fight came and the collar was removed, the dog felt light as a feather, overflowing with force and energy.

In the first week of training with the collar attached, Radu introduced just two pieces of lead to get Bronco used to the sensation of wearing it again and continued making him run after the ATV. From the third week of training, besides cardio, he started working on his gladiator's bite force. He hung thick rubber circles, without any strands inside, from the stout branches of the Carpathian firs. The circle was tied with a thick rope and passed round one of the branches thus making a pulley. It hung a little higher than Bronco, which meant Bronco's front paws weren't touching the ground when he was hanging on to the rubber circle. Radu pulled the opposite end of the rope, sometimes lifting the dog completely off the ground. After about an hour, he tied the rope to the tree trunk at the appropriate distance so that Bronco could continue training on his own. During the first month of training, the rubber was raised just so that the dog couldn't touch the ground with his front paws; in the last month of training, the circle was lifted much higher. Bronco, having to jump more than a meter in the air to be able to grab the rubber circle, remained suspended in the air, hanging from it, for about twenty minutes at first. By the end, Bronco would hang for more than an hour, the strength of his bite depending not only on his own weight but also the collar, now filled with pieces of lead. All this time, Bronco wriggled in the air, making a sort of whistle that was not like the usual noises made by dogs at all. It arose from his frustration that the circle wouldn't break and his stubborn refusal to let go, even though his muscles were dictating otherwise.

The grimness with which Bronco trained often brought tears to Radu's eyes; such nature, a true gladiator, couldn't be found elsewhere in the animal kingdom, not even in lions, which, after pit bulls, of course, were Radu's favorite animals.

Bronco's diet throughout the training period varied, from cheese and sour cream to pasta and boiled rice with huge chunks of meat, beef, and pork bones, and big hunks of raw meat. During off-season, Radu fed the dogs once a day, but during training, twice a day as they expended much more effort.

As for nutritional supplements during the training period, Radu put his dogs on various vitamin diets, having complete faith in his veterinarian's prescriptions as they had yielded excellent results. These diets were similar to those of professional athletes or, more accurately, those practicing contact sports. Their wrestling bodies assimilated all these supplements as quickly as a turbo engine revved to the max consumes fuel, the resulting energy being similar to the one generated by a sports engine.

Apart from the nutritional supplements and vitamins, Radu administered a two-week intravenous calcium cure during training; he did this once a year to all the dogs he used in the ring in order to keep them in the best physical shape.

While during the first weeks, the training lasted only two to three hours a day, plus a long evening walk, during the last two months before the fight, Radu stayed in the mountains with Bronco for as long as six to seven hours each day, occasionally longer. For training of this duration, he needed Irinel's help because it required a lot of effort and coordination from the breeder. One of the special drills they had in these months was for guarding the paws, because Radu knew that his opponent became a champion primarily due to his combat style, which consisted of him going underneath the opponent's chest and trying to grab his front paws. He had also, several times, taken hold of the rear paws, which was even more dangerous because the opponent lost his balance and could be taken down to the ground a lot easier. It was then harder for him to get up if one of the rear paws had been grabbed as those paws are used for pushing and keeping the balance when the animal is bitten by his opponent.

Radu had had the chance to observe the power of Joker's bite in the three fights he had attended, and the dog was impressive indeed. After going underneath his opponent's chest and grabbing one of his paws, he started shaking it powerfully, giving the impression he was about to pull off the limb from its joint. Likewise, the strength that Romania's and Hungary's champion generated while biting was impressive, he never let go in less than five minutes, and when he did so, just to relax his under-jaw muscles, he reoriented his hold on a different part of the opponent. Joker was, indeed, an impressive dog and a real champion and Radu knew it from the first time he saw him in the ring. It was why he decided to let his Cindy mate with him, and this was before he became a champion. It was quite clear to him that Bronco had never encountered a dog of his father's caliber before, and that it was going to be his hardest fight ever but, at the same time, he knew that Joker hadn't fought an opponent close to his son's caliber either.

Bronco, besides the qualities inherited from his father, had a huge advantage, namely the genetic baggage his mother had passed on him. Cindy was, without a doubt, the best bitch ever used in any of the Romanian rings up to that point and Bronco was more like his mother in his fighting style than Joker, and that pleased Radu very much. This gave his dog a complex combat style, not only aiming for the chest and the paws, like his father, but mastering the "judo style," as Radu called it, inherited from his mother, and the same ferocity in the ring, speed, and resistance to effort as hers.

In order to teach him how to guard his paws, Radu let Irinel hold the rubber circle, but this time at the dog's level, not higher, and pull in his direction. Normally, Radu did this type of training to develop his dog's balance, with he and Irinel taking turns pulling the circle in every direction, trying to get Bronco fall. Irinel propped himself as best as he could, straining his well-worked muscles to maintain his balance but in the last six months, it became impossible to bring Bronco to the ground that way. Even though Radu did this training with him every day after finishing the cardio and the exercise for enhancing the force of his bite, this dog's balance was one Radu had never seen in any of the pit bulls he had ever trained.

He made one addition to the exercise, especially for the fight against Joker. While Irinel did his best to get Bronco down, pulling the rubber circle with all his might, Radu would stroke over one of his rear paws gently with a twig, each time saying the word "guard." Thus, a month before the fight, Radu didn't need the twig anymore; whenever he uttered "guard," Bronco pulled his front paws under himself, without letting go of the rubber circle of course.

Radu used the same words and expressions during the fight as he did during the drills; when the dog was hanging in the air or shaking the rubber circle, he told him, "Shake, boy, shake that." When, at the end of the training day, he felt that Bronco was close to exhaustion, he told him, "Take it, boy, take it there", and when he pulled the rubber circle at his level, "Guard, boy, guard the paws." Also, every time he was impressed by the resistance and the way in which Bronco reacted, he complimented the dog. "Way to go, boy, that's it, Bronco, good boy." It was very important for the dog to hear these words in the ring. During training, Radu never touched his dogs, because in the ring it's forbidden to touch your quadruped, except for when you break him up from his opponent. Another thing Radu never did during trainings was to let his dogs sit; they had to be moving continuously. Even during the short breaks between exercises, the dogs were walked at a slow pace so as they did not get used to relaxing in the middle of the effort, which was something that could make the difference between winning and losing in the ring. If a dog is used to relaxing in the middle of the training and, implicitly, the fights, while he's trying to catch his breath, his opponent can inflict such wounds on him that might actually deter him from continuing. This is why Radu kept his dogs in a continuous state of physical and mental concentration throughout the sessions.

The only type of training he couldn't do with Bronco this time of the year was swimming. During summer, he went with the dogs he trained to one of the lakes in that area of the Carpathians. He would get into the water chest-deep, and fix a sharp pole about two meters long. Then he'd bring the dog in the water and attach the collar to the pole. The dog swam for about half an hour during the first few weeks of training, and then longer each time until he was swimming for up to three hours a day. Immediately after getting the dog out of the water, Radu started fighting with him using the rubber circle, in order to improve his balance even when his muscles were tired.

In April, four months after the New Year's Eve party, Sophie took a week off from work to visit Radu. They'd kept in touch the whole period, calling and texting each other almost daily. She told her friends Bo and Agnes, part seriously, part jokingly, that she would not be taking them to Romania again because she wanted to spend some time alone with Count Dracula, as the Dutch girls had called him.

Radu was waiting for her at the airport in Bucharest and two hours later, they were wallowing naked on the bearskin in front of the living room fireplace. The next day, she accompanied him to the heart of the Carpathian woods for Bronco's training. She didn't know much about pit bulls but she liked dogs and she was very impressed by Bronco's strength, his resistance, and his tenacity. She was tired just watching this superb animal move continuously throughout the day. What's more, the close relationship between the man who, during the last few months, had made her pulse rise rapidly each time she thought about him, and his quadruped impressed her. The gentle manner with which Radu addressed the dog, the way in which he praised his efforts, and Bronco's intense reactions, looking in his master's eyes from every angle and following all his instructions with complete dedication, struck a chord in the Dutch girl's heart, one every woman feels when the man she's attracted to proves he'd make a good father.

That evening, while smoking a joint with Radu in front of the fireplace, her favorite spot, their sweaty bodies still quivering after the orgasms that seemed to her more intense than ever because of the wilderness surrounding the place and the tempestuousness of the man that had caused them, she asked him a question that had been on her mind for some time. That day, after feeling the strength of the connection between him and his quadruped, she was even more confused.

"Please tell me something I don't understand at all: how is it possible to love your dog so much, and I saw exactly how much you care about him and, probably, about all of your dogs, and then let him fight to death? Aren't you afraid of losing him, aren't you compassionate about him being ripped apart by another dog? Sorry I'm asking but it really bugs me and I don't get it!"

"No, Sophie, first of all, the dogs never die during fights. It's true that there are idiots who have nothing to do with professional fights and destroy their animals, but this has nothing to do with real pit bull fights. These people are our sworn enemies. They give dog fights a bad name and that's why the general impression is like yours, that these dogs are kept in abject conditions and left to fight to death. There's no way these people could ever get close to the rings and each time we find out about someone abusing his dog, we confiscate it and give it to someone trustworthy.

"Do you actually think that, when it comes to real fights, someone who pays thousands of dollars and invests another couple of thousand in special nourishment, and spends most of his time training that dog, would be okay with letting his dog die? And that's not even taking into account his attachment towards the dog and speaking from a strictly financial point of view. That's why all the fights in the ring are organized, with a referee at the center and veterinarians on the sides, to guarantee the dogs' safety.

"Even if you lose a fight, you train him harder and let him try again, but there's no way you let the dog die in the ring. Anyway, in every match, there's a point where it's obvious that one of the dogs doesn't have the energy to fight anymore and the match is stopped. So this story with pit bulls dying during fights is as true as, let's say, the one that says their jaws lock and they can't let go, or that they were created in a lab, or other myths that circulate about this breed. These stories are perpetuated by those who have no idea what they're talking about, but they like touching taboo subjects in the hope that someone gives them some attention."

"Wow, you're very convincing and you defend your point of view very passionately. I hope my question didn't offend you but it's been all so unclear to me till now. I'm glad to hear my information was wrong. But even if you don't let them kill each other, they still hurt each other pretty badly, right? How come you don't have pity on him?"

"When you watch two men boxing in the ring, do you feel any pity for them when they bleed or when they're tired? They're gladiators, they know they have to suffer pain when they fight, yet what motivates them to continue is not the fear of pain but the will to defeat the opponent, to put all their energy and skills into winning the fight, into being the last man standing. It's the same with these dogs. They don't have to be trained or forced to fight, they start doing so as pups. Pit bulls that come from a combat line start fighting when they're two months old and they have to be separated so they don't kill each other. It's in their genes to dominate, they have alpha dog features; that's where they get their aggressiveness from. The training you do with them is to increase their resistance and muscle strength, not to make them aggressive or stuff like that."

“I get it now. Still, I’d feel a lot of pity watching them fight, although I understand what you’re saying, especially after today, seeing how much Bronco likes to train and the strength he generates. It was a really interesting experience for me. But after the fight, doesn’t it hurt? What does he look like?”

“These dogs recover a lot faster than other breeds, even though, the first few days after the fight, they’re a bit puffy and they are a bit slow, but after a week or two, they look exactly like they did before the match. Well, plus a few scars. And the fact that he’s a little upset after the fight has never diminished a pit bull’s will to fight, the same way a boxer wouldn’t quit sports just because he has broken his arch during the match. These things are part of a fighter’s way of life, human or canine.”

Chapter 13

One evening, after a day spent in the heart of the mountain and a hot twilight in front of the fireplace with his new girlfriend, who was now asleep on the bearskin from which it was hard to convince her to move away, Radu went to the attic to watch Joker's fights for the umpteenth time. As the date of the fight grew closer, he became more and more jittery, knowing the stakes of the match. It wasn't only about the twenty thousand dollars he had bet on it, it was more about, finally, being exactly where he wanted to be, having a real chance of one of his dogs winning the title of national champion.

Even in his tender years, when he first grew fond of the pit bulls, this had been Radu's dream, to have the best dog in the country, one who never lost a fight and be absolute champion. And this moment was near; in less than two weeks, his dog could become a champion. He had trained many dogs, some of them of exceptional quality, but none of them had Bronco's caliber. He had known since the dog was only a few months old that he would grow up to be the absolute champion.

While he was watching one of Joker's matches in order to find his weaknesses, which were practically nonexistent, and to analyze, for the thousandth time, his way of fighting and moving in the ring, trying to prepare Bronco as well as possible for this title match, Sophie had woken up. Feeling the need to be cuddled, she had climbed the wooden stairs and entered the attic.

"What's up, babe? Aren't you sleepy? What are you watching? Is this the champion Bronco's going to face?"

Radu nodded and the girl from the Netherlands curled up next to him on the couch, lighting up one of the joints on the table. The ferocity with which Joker was subjugating his opponent and the strength with which he was shaking once he took hold of him, horrified Sophie, all the more so as, having spent most of her days since she came to Romania with him and Radu in the woods training, she had become really attached to Bronco

"I'm glad I won't be here when the fight takes place. I couldn't watch a thing like this. Bronco is such a lovely dog and you want to push him towards that monster's snout. Sometimes I get really upset when I see how much you like the pit bull fights..."

"You haven't seen Bronco fight. If you want, I'll show you some of his matches and you'll see him in a new light. Indeed, his father is very good but Bronco is sturdier and has a more complex fighting style. Of course, anything can happen in the ring and you can never be certain who will win, but Joker has never faced a killer like this devil, one who dashes again and again and never stops attacking. And I've trained him over these couple of months as he has never been trained before. I think he's going to defeat Joker and if you put another dog in front of him in the ring, he's going to defeat that one too. He's used to acting like this since he was a puppy, since he was four, five months. He'd fight one of his brothers and, after defeating him, I'd let another one fight him and he defeated that one, too. This is why, every time he's in a fight, he is mentally ready to fight another dog after defeating his first opponent."

"I hope he defeats his father so that you can finally have what you've always wanted, the champion of champions. Maybe after that, you can cool down and stop letting him fight...this dog is so beautiful and intelligent, it would break my heart to see him ripped by another dog..."

"Don't worry about it; he'll be the one doing the ripping. I'll let him fight till he's four or five years old and in maximum shape, regardless of this fight's result, but I won't be breeding other ring dogs. The truth is, I'm kind of tired of training them all day long. I'll always have dogs but, aside from Bronco, I'll never have another ring dog."

"I'm happy to hear it...and there's something else I don't like about this sport, besides its violence: the fact that these quadrupeds are being used to help you make money. I don't find it fair that a dog should fight to exhaustion just so that his master gets rich!"

"In the first years of fights, there was no money to be gained from the matches. There were very few pit bulls in Galati and, in fact, in the whole country. For three or four years, I didn't earn anything from the matches, I just invested in the veterinarian, nutrition and so on. But, in time, if you're really into the pit fights, you want to have better dogs so you need more money to buy and nurture them, and the only way you can do that is if you bet on the outcome of the match. The first fights for money demanded symbolic sums, a couple of hundred dollars max. I was spending more on training the dogs, anyway, even if they won all the fights. But the better your dogs are, the better the opponents are, and nobody lets a dog he invested a lot of money in fight for free. So you're forced to bet money on the match, even if you don't necessarily agree with this idea, if you want better opponents for your dog."

"Yes, but it's still cruel to let the animals fight so that you can make money off them, don't you think?"

A vein started pulsing near Radu's temple, as it did every time he got mad. He had heard these arguments the Dutch girl was using so many times before, and he loathed those who couldn't see the essence of things, and instead judged other people's actions solely according to the moral standards imposed by this society, which Radu perceived as yellow-bellied and hypocritical. Despite all this, he was trying to temper the nerves the Dutch girl had stirred and talk as calmly as he could.

"Okay, I understand that so far you know nothing about pit bull fights but despite that, you loathe them because you consider that the animals are forced to do something they don't like, and those who organize these fights do so, so that they can get rich on the poor quadrupeds' account, right? Okay. Now, please try to get your head out of your ass a little bit and see things from a different perspective, one you've never analyzed before, because the "moral leaders" of this society, rotten with fear and mendacity, are only against the things that don't bring them any profit, such as pit bull fights. For instance, zoos are okay, right? I bet you've been to the zoo many times and you haven't thought for a second about the life those animals live. You were just glad you could see them, right?

"Wild animals, whose genes dictate they run and move around constantly, looking for food, are forced to spend their entire lives in tiny pounds where they can barely move. Just so that we can see them up close. And for that we pay money so that those zoos can capture other thousands of life forms and put them in cages for the rest of their days. But that's okay 'cause it's civilized, right? Circuses are one of the biggest aberrations man has ever invented, where the poor animals have to do exactly the opposite of what their instincts tell them, otherwise they face serious punishment. They have to spend the rest of the time in cages, but that's okay, right? It's not cruelty against animals when you see beautiful lions standing on two legs, terrorized by the tamer's whip; no, that works, because that's civilized and we take our kids to the circus and the zoo to see the pretty little animals. Well, ain't that cute? Yeah, and that's all okay because taxes are being paid and the blimps who pass laws gain some bacon from it, so the way in which these wild animals live doesn't matter. But when two dogs, which were made for this, fight, all of a sudden, it's cruelty against animals, because nobody pays taxes and nobody profits from it, except for the organizers. And the fact that the Chinese and the

Koreans boil alive hundreds of dogs daily and have them for supper, that's okay also, but not the pit bull fights!

"Or, the thing I hate most about the way in which we treat animals, the bullfight! Isn't that cruelty against animals? Every time I see those beautiful bulls stabbed by a coward hiding behind a piece of cloth sticking swords in their backs, I wish that the bulls would tear the stinkin' coward apart! What chances do those poor bulls have in the ring? What chances do the innocent wild animals, held captive in a cage their whole lives, have? But the chances a pit bull has in the ring are always equal to those of his opponent. They are two athletes of the same caliber, doing what they were meant to do; fight. They are not forced to do anything else than what their genetic legacy dictates; unlike the other animals I've mentioned, which have to endure the sufferings inflicted upon them for their malignant pleasure, making them do exactly the opposite of what they were told by nature. But, of course, it's pit bull fighting that's the big issue, not abusing the other animals for profit.

"These dogs have a very good life, as you can see with my dogs. They are very well fed, they get training and outdoor exercise daily, and you saw with your own eyes how much they like training, because, I repeat, this is what they were made for. But in the public's view, a public that feeds on anything they see or hear on TV like sheep feed on grass, the tens of thousands of whales or sharks that are slaughtered every year for profit aren't the issue; nor the bulls killed in the arena, dragged with hooks outside afterwards, and thrown into trash cans so that more can be slain; nor the millions of wild animals who spend their entire lives in cages they barely have room to move in, being the subjects of experiments, one more sadistic than the other. No, all of these are okay because they happen everywhere and people take them for granted, without even thinking. The same way they do when they passionately criticize pit bull fighting, without having the slightest idea what these fights are all about and the manner in which they take place.

"At the beginning of the 20th century, every week started with pictures of the dog that won that weekend's fight in the American newspapers, and the short description of the fights. It was their national symbol, they were very proud of it. It was used by the army, the police, and it was America's favorite breed. A pit bull called Stubby was the most decorated war dog in World War I. He participated in seventeen fights, saved the lives of his platoon members from a gas attack, and caught a German spy before he could divulge their location. He was the only dog in history ever to be ranked a sergeant, and the newspapers of the time were filled with stories of his deeds. And nowadays, the same Americans have created the animal police, whose role is supposed to be to protect the animals but every time they find pit bulls that have been used in fights, they kill them. Even if the dog is retired and hasn't fought in years, the fact that he was once in the ring makes him dangerous for people, in their view, so they take him from his owner and kill him. But somehow, this is supposed to be for their own good, I mean, it's those who get paid to protect the animals that do this, right? And most of the times they kill them even if they were never used in fights, because this is what the law dictates.

"In many American states and not only in America, the breed is now forbidden. I recently saw a report of a young family with kids, who had a male and a female that had just given birth. The dogs were very friendly, they had never attacked anyone, and they didn't show any signs of violence, even when the coppers came in the yard with an aggressive attitude. But a neighbor had called them about the pit bulls in the yard, and they were forbidden in that state, so they took all the dogs, including the pups, and killed them. Both the parents and the children were crying, but they were told that this is the law and they had to obey it! I'd piss on their damn laws and on those who make them!"

Even though Radu had set himself to be calm in the discussion with Sophie, he didn't manage very well. This subject was way too touchy for him. On the one hand, there was his love for these dogs and the way in which their fights impressed him; and on the other hand, there was the deep hatred he felt towards everything civilization meant, the cowardice and deceitfulness of those around him and, implicitly, people's attitudes about his favorite subject made him lose him temper every time someone stirred him by expressing their uneducated opinions about ring fights. The vein near the temple was pulsing strongly, becoming highly visible, and the cadence of his speech, even in English, had sped up remarkably. The hatred with which he spat his words frightened all those who provoked him with their arguments, which, they now realized, had actually been unfounded.

The Dutch girl had never witnessed such a degree of violence, verbal or otherwise, before, and had never felt what she was feeling now. It was a very ambiguous yet very profound feeling. On the one hand, she was revolted by Radu and his attitude but, at the same time, extremely attracted by the strength of his convictions and the almost demonic ferocity with which he defended his arguments.

One thing was certain: this man loved and respected his dogs more than anyone she had ever met, and the way in which he used them was none of her business. The other thing that was clear to her was that she had never met, and probably never would again, a man so intense in every respect, like this man who lived in the heart of the Carpathians. Radu's features were starting to relax as he was returning to a more carefree mental state. Sophie took his face in her hands and jumped on him, kissed him heavily and sticking her tongue deeply in his mouth, while her right hand was greedily opening his zipper.

On the last evening spent in Poiana Tapului, before she returned to The Hague, Sophie went for a walk with Radu and the other two pit bulls he kept, Bronco's mother, Cindy, and old

Samson. Even though he was a bit older than twelve, this beautiful specimen hadn't lost much of his earlier elegance and agility, although he hadn't fought in more than six years. He was white with black spots. Half of his head was covered with a big black spot, perfectly symmetrical and the rest of his body was evenly proportionate between the two colors. Sophie observed that Radu was more affectionate towards him than he was towards Bronco, playing with him all the time and speaking to him in a very friendly voice, without that roughness he had during Bronco's trainings. When she asked him if her observations were correct, Radu confirmed beyond any shadow of doubt.

"You have a great sense of observation, babe! Indeed, I'm a bit more severe with Bronco because he's a ring dog. He has to follow my commands exactly because that makes the difference during a fight; plus, he's young and he needs it. This old dog, Samson, is my beloved. He doesn't have Bronco's fighting qualities but he's an extraordinary dog. He was one of my first pit bulls and the only one I've kept since then. He is a grand champ too, meaning he won more than five consecutive fights, six, to be exact. He also lost three matches. Also, he is ROM, register of merit, which means that from his many pups, some became champions. This dog saved me and my parents once when we were with him in the mountains."

"Really? How come?"

"Samson was two years old, and me, my girlfriend at the time and my folks were on a vacation in the mountains. Back then I was still living with them in Galati. We drove the car on the forest roads and when we hit a dead end, we got out and started walking in the middle of nowhere to find a beautiful glade for a barbecue. At a certain moment, me and my girlfriend had wandered away from the place my folks were having the barbecue, when I heard my mum call me in quite a nervous voice. I rushed back to see what was happening and I saw a Carpathian shepherd dog, weighing over seventy kilograms, climbing down the mountain furiously.

"These dogs live for fighting wolves and bears, they are very wild, and they live their whole lives in the mountains. They never see any people other than their shepherd, and they attack any other creatures found on the territory of the herd they are guarding. There have been many accidents in Romania when tourists unknowingly entered their territory and were devoured by these monstrous dogs. The one that was coming to attack us was a huge male and, without realizing it, we had entered his territory. He was coming to do what he'd been trained to do: kill anyone entering the world he was supposed to guard, even at the cost of his life. If we hadn't had Samson there, it would have been a massacre, I don't know what we would have done. We didn't have a gun with us. But with Samson there, it was just another opportunity to train in combat with an inferior dog. Normally, when someone came with such dogs, or other breeds besides pit bulls, the match was stopped in less than ten minutes in the ring when they saw what a little devil like this could do to a monster like that. But in this case, in the middle of the woods, there was nobody to stop them, so I let them fight till the end.

"Samson had already been revved in some matches and knew exactly what to do, even though, during the first few minutes, the Carpathian swallowed him in such a way that I couldn't even see my dog from under his fur, but then Samson, from underneath, got a good grip on one of his paws and started shaking for about five minutes, during which the shepherd dog realized he had never met such an animal. For the next fifteen minutes, he shook his front paws, his chest, and his head; the Carpathian dog was on the ground and couldn't get up. I was talking to Samson like I did during every match, telling him what to do and encouraging him. I was starting to feel bad for the shepherd dog. He was becoming so desperate, he wasn't even trying to bite mine anymore. I don't know how but he gathered his strength and started running, limping visibly. Samson ran after him a little way until the dog disappeared in the direction he had come from, and then he came back to me, victoriously wagging his tail. After I washed the blood off him, I realized he didn't have a scratch; all the blood belonged to the shepherd dog. Even if the Carpathian had bitten him, he didn't have the necessary force to pierce his skin. And when you think that this dog kills a wolf or more almost effortlessly and that he fights bears with even chances, you can imagine how impressive the pit bull is if he is able to silence him in less than twenty minutes.

"That's because the pit bull attacks again and again, without minding the pain or the initial superiority of the opponent, until he wins, and no other animal does that. Do you think he'd do all these things if he didn't enjoy fighting? This is why I'm against other breeds of dogs fighting. It is unfair; they don't stand a chance against these genuine gladiators. The only dogs that should fight are the pit bulls."

The next day he drove Sophie to the airport then he returned to Poiana for the last week of training with Bronco before the final. The day preceding the fight for the title, he just walked him through the woods, without running with him or making him hang on to the rubber circle, to help him preserve all his energy for the moment of the match. Despite all this, the lead collar remained attached around Bronco's neck; it would be taken off just minutes before the fight. The dog had never been trained this well and, the day before the match, both Radu and his quadruped knew that he could defeat any opponent they put in front of him.

Chapter 14

The day of the match, Radu left Poiana around six in the morning. The fight was scheduled to start at eight so that the two champions could fight in cool weather conditions. Irinel was sitting in the passenger's seat; he wouldn't have missed this match for all the money in the world. And he deserved to be present at the match, not only because he had trained Bronco almost as much as Radu, but he had also trained him by himself for a couple of days, the week Sophie came to visit, to give the lovebirds a chance to enjoy some time together. He had religiously followed Radu's instructions, as he did every time, and he was proud to have been a part of influencing the outcome of this match, which was about to be probably the tightest pit bull match ever held in Romania.

The fight was organized in Bucharest because that's where the champion was from, and the challengers are supposed to come to the champion's hometown, not the other way round. This wasn't necessarily a disadvantage for the challengers, much less for Bronco, who was used to training a thousand meters above sea level as opposed to less than a hundred meters above sea level where Bucharest was situated. This offered him extra resistance and ease in breathing during exertion.

For this fight's sake, no other matches were scheduled that day. The few dozen people invited to watch this match of maximum interest for the pit bull fight lovers came from every corner of the country. After the fight, Radu, Irinel, and Bronco were going to go to Lorin's house, stay there for a day or two to let the gladiator rest, and then return to Poiana. Radu couldn't afford to leave the plants in his basement without water and chemicals for more than two days, and he would never let anybody else do it for him. Stefan also flew in from Prague the night before the match. He couldn't miss this show. It would be unlike anything any of them had ever seen because never before in the Romanian fight rings had there been two dogs of the same caliber as those who were about to fight that day. Moreover, he knew how much it meant for his best friend. He knew the depth of Radu's passion for pit fights too well, and he was aware of how important it was for him that one of his dogs should become an absolute national champion. It had been Radu's dream since he was a teenager, when they used to walk the streets of Galati from dawn to dusk. He landed sometime in the evening on Otopeni airport in Bucharest, where Lorin was waiting for him.

On the road winding through the core of the Carpathians, Irinel was much more anxious and nervous about the fate of the match than Radu. He was trying to encourage his friend and mentor, although he was actually the one who needed encouraging.

"Relax, Radu mate, you'll see what Bronco's gonna do to his dad, he'll get matches out of his head for good! He's never been trained so well, and he's been kicking asses without much effort. You'll see he's gonna do the same to Joker, I can't wait to see that!"

With the exuberance specific to his tender years, he turned towards the back seat, where Bronco was sitting bolt upright like a sphinx, and kissed him on the snout while petting him on the head.

"Yes, there you go, boy, you'll mop the floor with him, my beloved doggy. Show him who the champ is, boy!"

Radu appreciated the boy's enthusiasm and his total attachment towards Bronco, even though he was a bit irritated by the fact that he wasn't letting him and Bronco focus on what was about to happen, and they really needed to reach that mental state where everything else disappeared and all that remained was the image of the opponent, who needs to be defeated at any cost.

"Joker has experience on his side; he's got more matches under the belt, while Bronco has the advantage of breathing. He's used to the mountain air here; when he descends to the plains, it gives him extra energy towards the end of the fight when they're both exhausted. And now, let's keep quiet till we get there. I wanna focus on the match, and you know that Bronco is connected to what I feel."

The boy nodded silently, a bit embarrassed, and didn't say another word until Radu parked the jeep in the yard of the disused factory where the guys from Bucharest had organized a professional fighting ring. The factory, situated in one of the industrial areas existing in Bucharest during the communist regime, was now disused and in a state of deterioration. In one of the factories, a considerable distance away from the main roads, there was one of the rings, built according to the standard dimensions of the American rings. The old hangar was big enough for ten times as many people as those invited to the match, and behind the factory, there was a parking lot that had once been used by the trucks that supplied the factory with raw stock. There was plenty of room for the few dozen cars that were there that morning in May.

All the people invited were already there, including Lorin and Stefan, and Remus, Joker's owner, and his friends. Radu left Bronco into Irinel's care, to walk him through the factory yard so he could relieve his bowels and stretch his legs. He told him to run with him for five minutes, keeping him on the leash, and then amble to warm up his muscles. Meanwhile, he went inside the factory to greet his friends and acquaintances. All eyes were on him. He shook hands with Remus, who had the champ on a leash. The dog looked to be in the best shape he'd ever been, his muscles, hard as rocks, moved like serpents under the animal's thick skin with every move he made.

Joker was, indeed, a very impressive dog, but when Radu looked at him, it wasn't the overall impression of strength generated by this dog that penetrated him but the thought and the feeling attached to it, on which he had focused since he started training Bronco for this match. That is, his quadruped would be point-blank superior to his dad and would defeat him easily, and now that the moment had come and he laid his eyes on the opponent, a strong feeling of satisfaction took hold of him, as if this thing had already happened.

Both he and Remus handed the money to the referee, who returned to each of them the five grand they had sent a couple of months before to make sure the match would happen. Then he went outside and called for Irinel to bring him Bronco, after which he took him to a distant corner from the entrance to the factory, in order to spend some quiet moments with his gladiator before the fight, like he did every time. Bronco knew exactly why he was there. The electricity in the air, the energy generated by Radu, and all the other details present every time before a match were all very familiar to him now. Although he was very jittery and he could hardly wait to get in the ring to do what he was best at and what he liked doing best, Bronco knew that this was the moment to relax before the sustained effort that would follow. He wallowed in the petting and encouragements his master, the man he would give his life for at any given moment, gave him. Radu was on his hunkers, his forehead pressed against the dog's forehead, whispering encouraging words to him.

"Don't worry, boy, we'll take this one down too. It's gonna be harder than before, but we'll do it, boy, 'cause you're the champ!"

The intensity of these moments always brought tears to Radu's eyes. The gladiator's calm before the match, even though he knew exactly what was about to happen, was, probably, the thing that impressed him most in life, except for the moments after the fight was over and his beloved dog was declared the winner.

He kissed his quadruped on the snout then he got up and they both started walking purposefully towards the ring. Any other image than that of Bronco being a winner that morning had disappeared from Radu's universe, and the feeling propagated by this image was so deep that it made him tremble. Watched from afar, Radu looked like a man who was about to commit murder. His tense figure, his determined walk, the way in which he stared blankly into space while he was walking towards the ring, wrapped everyone present in an apocalyptic energy, except for Lorin and Stefan, who knew exactly what was going through the mind and soul of their lifelong friend. They were, nevertheless, as moved by the intensity of his feelings as those who didn't know him that well.

Radu handed Bronco over to Lorin, to be washed by Remus, while he made his way towards Joker to wash him with water from one of the buckets on the side of the ring. While he was washing him, he felt as if tons of negative energy had sprung from the depth of his being and were directed towards the champion; he felt like biting him himself before letting him bite his quadruped, which he loved and respected more than himself.

Then he turned towards Bronco and took the leash from Lorin's hand. Both he and Stefan told him words of encouragement before he got in the ring.

"Don't worry, bro, he's gonna take this one down, like he did with the others, you'll see. I placed a three grand bet on his ass, 'cause that's all I have now, but I'm not worried that I might lose it."

"Yes, Radu, mate, you're exactly where you've always wanted to be, in the ring with the champion," said Stefan. "And in about half an hour, you'll have Romania's champion. I placed a three thousand dollars bet on Bronco too, and I'm gonna go home with six, I have no doubt about that."

Radu didn't know that his friends were going to bet on this match, and the faith they had in Bronco moved him deeply, a feeling that added to his emotional baggage concerning this match, giving him the certainty that his dog would be victorious.

He turned to Remus, who was petting Joker, and addressed him in an aggressive and impatient tone. “Come on; let’s let them go, shall we?”

After that, without waiting for the reaction of his opponent, he took Bronco in his arms and stepped in the ring with him. Being in his element, in the pit, just like generations before him, Bronco was focusing on the opposite corner, waiting to see his enemy, wagging his tail impatiently. His opponent arrived shortly after that and the moment the two dogs looked at each other, they started pulling in the direction of the adversary and howling out of frustration at not being able to reach him. The referee entered the ring and looked at both of the owners; each of them was glancing at the opponent. The stakes were high, not because of the money involved but because neither of the dogs had ever lost a fight before and neither of the owners could accept the possibility of losing. The dogs were of a similar size; Joker was a bit broader in the back than Bronco, who had a more supple stature than his opponent. The referee counted to three, at which point the wrestlers were released. They flew at each other’s throats at the speed of light.

The first impact between the two champions was very powerful, each of them grabbing the opponent’s face and starting to shake frantically. Less than two minutes after that, Joker started doing what he knew best. He let go of Bronco’s head and started searching for his paws, bending and trying to go underneath his chest. Radu was waiting for this moment and was anxious to see Bronco’s reaction. He immediately told him to “guard.” Bronco, keeping hold of his adversary’s head, pulled his paws underneath him, thus leaving all of his front weight on his “grab and hold,” almost touching the rug that covered the ring with his chest. Joker kept pushing himself under Bronco’s chest, trying to grab one of his front paws, but couldn’t advance enough because Bronco had a hold on his head. Radu heard Remus telling Joker “get out of there, boy, come on, get out,” at which point he stopped trying to grab the paws and turned his head, clutching Bronco's throat. This showed Radu not only the fighting qualities of the champion but also his tight connection with his owner. This only hardened him more and made him yell at his dog with an almost inhuman voice, sounding more like a demon choir than his normal voice: "Come on, Bronco, shake it there, shake!" That moment, Bronco started shaking insatiably, without stopping wagging his tail for even a second.

After the first ten minutes of the fight, Joker managed to grab one of Bronco's front paws, stirring cheerful roars among those who had placed their bets on Joker: "Well done, Joker, you go, boy, rip off his paws, boy!"

Radu spoke to Bronco in a calm voice, trying to engender the same sensation in his dog. "Come on, boy, get out of there, guard, you get out of there!" But Bronco didn't seem like he was going to be able to get out of that clutch. Joker had already been shaking his right paw for more than two minutes. He had a hold on the champion's ear but couldn't create in him enough discomfort from that position because he couldn't shake strongly enough without having both of his front paws on the ground. Bronco let go of the ear and grabbed his father's snout, the latter gave a short whimper, proving that this clutch hurt because of the extraordinary strength in Bronco's mandibular muscles. He started shaking the opponent's snout and Joker finally let go of his paw. He turned towards him, trying to grab his face, hoping that Bronco would stop biting his snout. This is exactly what happened. The dogs returned to their initial positions, each of them biting the adversary's head.

Less than a minute later, Bronco made a move that stirred a noise of admiration among the crowd gathered at the match, a move that he had never tried before and took even Radu by surprise. Bronco suddenly let go of his clutch on Joker's head and went from one side straight under his father's chest, grabbed his throat from that position and, turning his head to the right after that, with all his might, propped on his front paws and started pulling backwards, thus lifting Joker from the ground. Joker made a complete circle in the air and collapsed on the same side Bronco had made his clutch. The crowd started applauding and cheering, even some of those who had placed their bets against Bronco. This move had never been seen before, not by any of those present anyway. Bronco had that judo fighting style but, until that moment, he had just placed himself parallel to the adversary, grabbing his throat and pulling him towards himself while pushing him with his shoulder in order to make him lose his balance. Never before had he gone under the dog to take hold of him and make him go down that way. Radu's heart filled with pride when he saw Bronco's move, and he started yelling as if out of his wits: "Well done, boooooy! Bravo, Bronco, my boy! Shake him, take him down, you go, boy!"

The crowd became much noisier and the factory hangar was now echoing the interjections of the public. Unfortunately, Joker didn't stay on the ground for long and, before Bronco had the chance to inflict on him wounds that could prevent him from continuing the fight, he managed to get on his feet and seized the same paw he had taken hold of just minutes before. It was time for Joker's supporters to scream with joy. The speed with which the champion had managed to get out of that difficult situation was impressive.

The next twenty minutes were equally dominated by each of the dogs at a time, who took turns being on top and shaking frantically until the opponent was able to take a better hold and take the lead. All the people present there knew that they had never seen such an even, well-balanced battle in the ring. Thus, after more than half an hour, both dogs were similarly exhausted; it was still unclear who was about to win.

After they had reached the fortieth minute of the match, both breeders realized that neither of the dogs had ever fought for so long. They were both used to winning the fight by this stage. Despite that and the fact that Joker wouldn't let go of his clutches, his teeth had started to dither while biting; barely, but it was a clear sign that his mandibular muscles were starting to wear out. Radu looked closely at Bronco's bite to see if the same thing was happening to him. He jumped out of his skin with joy when he saw that his dog's clutch was still perfect, showing no signs of exhaustion. For the first time since the beginning of the match, he was certain that he would win. He had seen this in many dogs before, and when their teeth started to dither upon biting, that dog didn't have enough strength to grab the opponent properly within the next fifteen minutes. Seeing this made him yell frantically at Bronco in an already hoarse voice from all the advice he had given him in the last forty-five minutes. When he smiled at Lorin and Stefan, the two of them, who couldn't see that tiny detail in Joker's bite from the edge of the ring, realized that Bronco was soon to be the new Romanian champion. They knew Radu well enough to be sure that he wouldn't have relaxed during the game unless he was confident of victory.

Remus had probably noticed the fatigue in his dog's jaw himself because he became more desperate in his gestures, standing with his face close to the rug and slapping his palm strongly against the ground, yelling encouraging words in the hope that Joker would be able to make the decisive move before his bite loosened completely.

Bronco felt that the strength with which he was bitten had grown weaker and that his opponent wasn't going for his paws with the same energy, and this discovery, along with the energy generated by Radu, full of confidence, made him shake more insatiably and use his best skills to defeat this remarkable opponent. He managed to bring him to the ground once again with his classic judo technique then he grabbed his father's chest, pulling backwards as he was shaking. Clutching the chest is one of the most dangerous things in a dog fight. Because the chest has a big surface from which it can be bitten, as a rule, the clutch is stronger in such a soft spot as the chest, where the fangs go deeper into the flesh. The dog that gets bitten on the chest can't take good hold of his adversary, the distance between his snout and the opponent being too great, plus, from that position, his moves are very limited, no matter if the dog is grabbed while on the ground or standing up.

When Joker managed to finally get off the floor, after more than three minutes in which Bronco had continuously shaken his chest, he couldn't stay up too long, because, with his chest muscles weakened now, the strength in his front paws was greatly diminished. When he fell back on the ground, Bronco seized the opportunity to grab one of his front paws and started shaking powerfully, encouraged by Radu, who was about to lose his voice.

Less than five minutes after that, the referee decided to stop the fight. It was obvious that Joker wasn't up for it anymore while Bronco, even though he sometimes stopped to catch his breath, was shaking powerfully every time he took hold of his opponent. In order to see how game Joker was, the pieces of hard wood were introduced in the mouths of the fighters to break them up and they were taken to opposing corners of the ring. Then, while Radu was preventing Bronco, who was trying to break free with all his might, whimpering in frustration because they wouldn't let him fight anymore, from attacking, Remus set Joker free. After taking a step towards his opponent, Joker tripped and fell, the bites on his chest preventing him from keeping his balance. However, though unable to hold his head up from all the effort of the last hour and moving forward mostly by dragging his chest on the floor rather than walking on it, Joker managed to reach the opposite side of the ring and grab Bronco, to everyone's applause. The moment Radu set Bronco free, he brought his opponent to the floor and started shaking his neck. Radu introduced the piece of wood in his mouth once again and released Bronco from his clutch. After that, with everyone's screams and applause amplified in the factory hangar, he lifted Bronco above his head, kissing his snout and getting his face smeared with blood.

The image of Radu, twisted with emotion, bloodstains all over his face, raising his champ in the air over his head as he was screaming in ecstasy, would have been on the front page of the newspapers of the age a century ago, as photos of the champions were published weekly back then. But in the current situation, only those present were able to enjoy the intensity of that match and the strong feelings of those involved. And in the minds of everybody present, no matter which of the dogs they had placed their bets on, there was now the same thought: Romania had a new champion.

Chapter 15

After the match, the four guys went to Lorin's place. On the way, they stopped at a vet's, one of the few in Bucharest who granted medical care to pit bulls after their fights. Bronco was given a dose of antibiotics and some stitches where his skin had been torn, without any anesthetic because, during the first half an hour after the match, the animals' bodies are still flooded with adrenaline and they feel no pain so it's better not to use any anesthetic, unless the dog gives signs of discomfort while he's being stitched. The boys went on towards Lorin's home afterwards, which was situated close to the old center of Bucharest, the only part of town that still preserves the former beauty of this East European capital.

Cristina and their dog, Paco, had gone to a friend of hers so the guys and Bronco could have some peace and quiet. Radu made his dog a bed on the floor out of some blankets he had especially brought from Poiana Tapului. He didn't want to have to make him climb up on the couch, given the fact that his paws had been bitten during the match. Bronco had already started to swell a little and to move slower, and in the following days, the situation would get worse. Only after five or six days would the swelling start to go down and Bronco would again move with ease. But, just like any other ring dog, Bronco was used to this and endured it stoically, spending most of the time during the days after the match sleeping or drowsing in the bed Radu had made for him.

After arranging his champion on the temporary bed, Radu took a seat next to his friends around Lorin's living room table. He then yelled: "Fuckers, we have the new champion of Romania!" and he banged his fist against the table, making the entire apartment vibrate.

Radu was radiating happiness. A big smile and an expression they hadn't seen on his face for a long time, probably since they were kids, were now ingrained on his Mephistophelian-featured face. Lorin and Stefan embraced him while Irinel sat, a bit embarrassed, in his chair, watching them with tears in his eyes, deeply moved by the atmosphere his idols had created and by the love they shared. He wanted to be a part of it. The fact that Bronco, whom he loved with all his mountain man heart, was the best dog in the country moved him also. He felt he was living a dream.

Radu beckoned to him, hugged him, and kissed him on the head. "My brothers, had it not been for this little devil here, I'm not sure we'd have had the same match. He has trained my Bronco from dawn to dusk during the days I couldn't go out with him and he has come to help me every day of training."

Then he turned to the kid, who was now smiling uneasily and looking down, while his heart was pounding wildly in his chest.

"Irinel, I swear to you, the best pup Bronco's gonna have I'll give to you, brother! I have seen how much you love these dogs, and now that you know how to train them by the book, I'll give you a pup to show all these bunchy bastards in Bucharest and their poor excuses for a dog how it's really done."

He kissed the kid on the head one more time and then turned towards the host of the evening. "Lorin, put something on the table, bro, will you? Let's celebrate!"

"Yeah, Radu, mate, I have made special preparations 'cause I knew we would come home winners. Bro, let me congratulate you! You have a dog like I've never seen before and I don't think I'll ever see again. Are you mad, bro? Did you see how he was jolting the champion of my dick? Had they cloned Joker and brought the two of them in the ring, he would have eaten both of them alive! There's no match for him, bro; maybe only in Serbia or Russia could there be a decent challenge for him. The dog is way too good. I was expecting him to beat his dad, but not by dominating him like he did. Apart from grabbing him by the paws, that one didn't manage to do him any harm, and before that he used to beat his challengers as if they'd been made of wax. Way to go, Radu boy, you've managed to get what you've wanted all your life. You have the best dog that ever was, bro! Now, let's celebrate!"

He opened one of the drawers of the living room cabinet and drew out a bag with a big white hunk inside, coke of a better quality than the one he had brought to the New Year's Eve party. It came from a new source. He had gone into business with some Albanians who had come to Bucharest to open a new market for their product, which was pretty good. Lorin had been one of the first people the Albanians had contacted, upon hearing that he was one of the biggest dealers in the capital and that he had connections in the entire country. They saw Romania as a far better market than the neighboring countries due to its larger population, and, implicitly, the number of customers. Romanians also had a partying spirit compared to their colder neighbors, Romania being the only Latin country in Eastern Europe.

Lorin took out the hunk and put it on the table ostentatiously, smiling widely. "I'll bring a mirror right away. But I've got no booze. Irinel, will you go downstairs and buy some bottles of rum?"

Irinel agreed and left the table to run the errand he had been assigned. "Should I get anything else, do you have any juice?"

"No, bro, you can buy a few bottles of soda too. Get four bottles of rum and four big bottles of juice. Take this money and use it to buy the things."

By the time Irinel returned with the bottles of liquor, Lorin had cut a line for each one of them on the mirror he had placed in the middle of the table.

"Radu boy, you and your dog made me three grand today, bro!" Stefan told him while putting his arms around his shoulders. "Thanks a lot. It would be awesome if all money could be gained so effortlessly!"

"I'm glad I could help, Stefan, my boy! Don't thank me, thank Bronco! And, speaking of money, I've done some research these past few months and I think it's best if you go to Peru, not Bolivia. Peruvian coke is a little bit better, it's considered the second best next to the Columbian one, plus there are a lot of tourists going to Peru. Machu Picchu's there, the ruins of an Inca settlement from around the 15th century, and loads of people go to see it, so you won't stand out in the crowd. It also has the advantage of a large opening towards the ocean, which means a lot of ports, which means a lot of cargo boats leaving there. I think it's the best option we have."

"Okay, bro, that's how we're gonna play it then. Anyway, it's all the same to us, it's not like we had someone waiting for us in Bolivia. We'll manage on the scene."

"I've also looked for plane tickets. The best deal is if we buy them now, about a month in advance, it's much cheaper this way. You'll be flying from Madrid, that's where most flights to South America are. You'll buy a round trip ticket, and after you get the little devil on board the ship, you return by plane. You then wait for him in a car where the ship docks in Europe, after you make sure that nobody followed him, and take him to Prague. From then on, Stefan, it's on you to cut it and get rid of it."

"Yeah, man, I've already spoken to the chemist. He's very happy to cut it, he doesn't even want money 'cause he's fuckin rich. He just wants us to give him a few pure grams 'cause he really is a joy rider. And the investors are waiting for us. I've got a market where I can sell all of it at once. When we push it, I think it's better if you come with me, in case they try something. I don't think they will, the Czechs are peaceful people plus they'll keep needing merchandise, but you never know. They could go apeshit when they see all that good shit."

"Yeah, bro, when it's time for us to push it, we'll come with you to Prague and oversee the transaction. We all put in the money for the deal, anyway. Oh, and talking of the money for the business, I've made a rough calculation, and ten grand should be enough. You might even return with some money. You won't be spending more than one grand on the snort, and the rest is for further expenses, for Irinel's boat ticket, for hotel expenses, for renting a car, and so on. I'll chip in five grand out of ten, since I've won today. You can each contribute two thousand five hundred, meaning the money you've won today, minus five hundred that stays in your pocket. We'll split the money like we said, thirty percent to the two of you and Irinel, and ten percent to me since I'm not coming with you guys."

"So you contribute the most and profit the least, bro?"

"Don't worry about it, Lorin. I'm just glad we have the money to invest. If it all goes as planned, that ten percent is gonna be a lotta money, anyway. Man, this Albanian shit is good, way better than the stuff at New Year's Eve."

"Yeah, I told you, these Albanians are semi-interesting, at least now, at the beginning, as they're making their way into the market. I bet it won't be long before someone fucks them up when they grow, but for now, you can do good business with them."

"These Albanians are evil and dangerous motherfuckers, but they only jump and sting as a group. If they're alone, you can beat three of them at once. Plus, in Romania, they have no muscles they can flex. They can bring in their whole mob and still get eaten alive here, just like the Russians, but if you meet them in the Italian and Greek joints, where there are plenty of them, you're in serious shit. They control all the drugs on the inside, and there's a motherfuckin' load of them. You remember how they clipped Columbianu and two of his crew from Brasov few years ago in Milan, don't you?"

Meanwhile, Irinel returned with the bottles of rum and the party really started. They told the boy about their new plans for the trip; each of the three friends giving him advice on the way he would have to behave once alone aboard the ship until he joined them in one of the European harbors. The boy displayed a calm and detached attitude, but they weren't sure how much of this attitude was line shooting and how much was authentic. They were all sure of one thing, though: if, worst-case scenario, the lad got caught and was arrested, he would spend his detention years with the same willpower they had spent theirs, without saying a word about their involvement to the cops. The story he was supposed to give if he got caught was that he had just been on a trip to Peru and, being naive because of his age, he had accepted to transport to Europe a package of homeopathic medicine that could be found only in South America; the package being handed to him by the same people who told him it would be more interesting to travel by water than by air. That way he would be able to get a taste of what only true adventurers experience. They were Brits, he was to say, who had paid him well enough to carry the package, and had told him they couldn't leave South America yet because they had business there but that the medicine had to reach a sick person. Someone would contact him upon his arrival on European soil. Even if the story was transparent, they couldn't prove it wasn't true, and the boy's age and innocent looks would surely help him in this undesirable scenario.

The boy was aware of the possibility of serving time in South American jails, but he didn't let this thought scare him. On the contrary, he regarded it as an opportunity to become more experienced and pernicious. Moreover, this would make him more like the guys he admired so much, Stefan being the only one of them who hadn't served time. Lorin had spent four years in prison in Germany, and Radu had been imprisoned in Romania for three years for kidnapping and torture. This had happened years before, when someone who owed him money decided there was nothing Radu could do to him to recover the money because he was the godson of one of the leaders of the local gypsy mafia. Wrong decision. Radu waited for him at night in front of his house, hit him a couple of times with an iron crowbar, put him in the trunk of his car and took him to his place. After a few hours of torture, he agreed to pay him back the money and called a member of his clan to bring the money to Radu's house. The guy he called was aware of the situation and realized that his friend had been kidnapped, that's when he tipped the police off about a person being held at the relevant address. Radu had learnt a lot from that mistake and from the time spent in jail, getting out a tougher, more determined, and perceptive man than before.

After the first few liters of rum had been consumed, the discussion returned to the subject of the fight that had taken place that day, and about the new champion that had taken everyone by surprise with his never-seen-before wrestling technique and with the giddiness with which he had defeated his father, even though everyone present had hoped it would happen. The only one who had been absolutely sure of Bronco's success was Radu, and this had been pretty obvious even before the match, judging by his extreme confidence. Irinel, who had started to read Radu's mind and predict his reactions, albeit not understanding exactly where his mentor's inner strength or blind belief in his convictions came from, had also noticed. Normally, he would have been ashamed to ask Radu very direct or personal questions but now the consumption of alcohol and coke had opened the gates of his soul wider. And he felt now he could dare to do so, that he had earned Radu's trust and respect. The boy asked him a question none of the guys had expected or asked, even if they had grown up together, being used to analyzing people by their deeds, not by their words, and very seldom confessing their feelings and thoughts.

"Radu, let me ask you something 'cause I'm very curious to know how you do it."

"Go ahead, my little brother!"

"How do you manage to keep your faith intact all the time? You always give the impression that you are one hundred percent sure of what you do and what you say. Don't you ever have your doubts, don't you ever lose faith in what you feel and what you think?"

Radu smiled widely and felt the love he had towards this boy was growing more intense. Not only did he like the fact that he was curious about this issue and that he had found the perfect moment to ask this question, but he also felt flattered by it. And when he snorted, he became more talkative and tended to share his creeds and experiences, but he only did this with the few persons close to him.

He would have never given an explanation or opened his soul to strangers.

"Irinel, in my opinion, the most important thing is that you don't wait for validation from the people around you, dear brother! You shouldn't let yourself be influenced by the feedback you receive, otherwise your universe becomes what you perceive as the image of yourself in the eyes of others, and you should never let this happen. Neither positive nor negative feedback should influence you. You should analyze it but without any emotional involvement; this way, your inner self remains unaltered, no matter how the people around you perceive you. Don't let the praise lift you up and don't let the disappointments get you down. Keep yourself at your own level and in continuous connection to yourself. This way you never diverge from your own path and from who you are; this is the only thing we truly have in life, not the things we possess or the people we love. The only thing we truly own is ourselves. This attitude is regarded by this diluted society as self-sufficiency, when it only means, in fact, being who you truly are."

Chapter 16

The next day, Radu nestled Bronco on the back seat and, along with Irinel, set off for Poiana Tapultui. But that did not happen before his friends had made a new decision regarding their trip to Latin America. Stefan was the one who had come up with the idea; in his adventurous way of being, he was always at the ready for visiting new places and experiencing various sensations.

"Listen, Lorin, how 'bout we go to Barcelona for a few days since we're going to Madrid anyway? We can go sunbathing, make a li'l racket in the clubs, maybe meet up with the acrobats. We haven't seen them for ages; after that, we can go about our business."

Lorin had no objections to this plan, especially as, unlike Stefan, he had never been to the Catalan capital before and it was a city he had wanted to visit for a long time.

"Okay, Stefan, we can go there for a couple of days, why not? Do you have the acrobats'contacts?"

The acrobats were a gang of guys, most of them from Galati, all of them sportsmen, who had gained this name because of their occupation. They scaled people's balconies, being able to climb even to the top of the apartment buildings, from the outside. After they had been in Greece for a while, because the Greeks were in the habit of keeping their valuables, usually jewelry and money, inside their houses, the acrobats migrated to Spain. Their reasons for doing so had been diverse. On the one hand, the language was quite similar to Romanian and any Romanian could speak Spanish in just a few months after arriving in Picasso's country. This is why Spain had been flooded with hordes of Romanians, who were coming for either work or to steal. On the other hand, the architecture of the buildings in this country was very convenient for their occupation: the apartment buildings were close to each other to keep the shade and channel the wind on the narrow streets, which facilitated their acrobatic movements. The guys were able to jump from one balcony to another situated in the building opposite without any difficulty. There was no lock or alarm system they couldn't disable in less than half a minute.

Radu had no objections to this change of plan, as long as the boys met Irinel at the Madrid airport on the day of the flight. "You may go, boys. Just be careful to get to Madrid on time, particularly since the little devil here has never been out of the country before and I don't want him to get lost. Meet him on the day of the flight, in front of the airport, let's say at the departure gate to a non-Schengen destination 'cause that's where you'll be boarding the plane. It leaves there at 10 p.m., you should be there at seven and find Irinel. You should also have his phone number. I'll switch on his roaming, but for now it's settled that you meet at seven in front of the airport, okay?"

"Yes, Radu man, it's settled! Don't worry, we won't lose him, we'll meet him there. Buy him a ticket from Bucharest to Madrid, we'll buy the ones from there to Lima. And you, Irinel, when you get to Madrid, get out of the airport and hang around, but make sure you don't go too far 'cause at seven, we'll come to pick you up. We'll keep in touch on the phone until then, anyway."

The boy agreed then they said goodbye, got in the car, and drove back to the heart of the Carpathians. Radu would not see his friends again until their return from South America.

Three weeks later, Stefan and Lorin landed in Barcelona's airport, El Prat. They had made reservations for a room at a hotel situated in in the Gothic neighborhood in the center. Stefan knew the center of Barcelona very well, he had been to this superb city a few times before for both business and pleasure.

They spent their first afternoon peacefully, going out to the sea front to eat the renowned paella Lorin set his heart on from the first taste. After that they bought a piece of hashish from one of the dealers who could be found at every street corner and relaxed on the beach, admiring the impressive view of the sun descending behind the sea curtain, while the waves were gently lapping the fine sand. The sounds of the waves, along with the *mélange* of languages spoken around them in very relaxed and detached tones, gave the guys a feeling they had rarely had in their native country, much less while surrounded by strangers. It was a primordial sensation that people are positive entities, in communion with all living forms, and that all of us belong to the same larger entity, being united by the energies that, without us knowing it, define us.

In the evening, they strolled along La Rambla, Barcelona's main street, which was teeming with tourists, gift shops, and various artists, most of them painters and caricaturists ready to sketch the portraits of the passers-by for a symbolic fee. The last hours of that day were spent on the hotel room balcony, which had a superb view of Rambla, smoking hash and planning the details of the trip to Peru.

Next day, after a few hours of lying in the sun that bathes Barceloneta beach, the closest beach to the center of the city, a shower in the hotel room and a another portion of paella about which Lorin was so crazy, the two guys took the subway to the building that had impressed Stefan the most of all the places he had visited before.

"Bro, I know you're not very enthusiastic about seeing a cathedral," he told Lorin, "but when you see what I'm talking about, you'll change your mind. It's called Sagrada Familia."

"Okay, Stefan, let's see what you want to show me! Then we'll go meet the acrobats; they said we should call them when we get to the city center."

When they got out of the subway station that was named after the cathedral, Lorin was stunned. Stefan examined his reactions very closely; he had anticipated such a response on his part.

"Bro, are you mental? Fuck, this is beautiful! Let's see it at close quarters!"

"Do you think I would insist that we come here for no reason? In my opinion, this is the most impressive edifice ever built. And just wait a minute, this side we're looking at now was not designed by Gaudi, but by modern architects. Wait until you see what he designed!"

"Wait a sec, dude, let me look closer! Oh, such beautiful details it has and it's so tall! Superb! I love it! I had heard about this Gaudi fellow, but I didn't know his worth."

"Yes, well, Barcelona is full of buildings designed by him. There's also a park to die for, Parc Guell, which is on top of a hill and gives you a panoramic view of the whole city and the sea. It used to be the dwelling place of a very wealthy man, a huge fan of Gaudi's work, who told him to design a park in his psychedelic style. The man reinvented architecture. It's been a century and they haven't been able to finish this cathedral he started, and what they've managed to do is, in my opinion, not as good as the part projected by him by a long shot."

They went round the cathedral to get to its front, designed by the rock star of architecture himself, at which point Lorin, already ecstatic about what he had seen up to that point, was gobsmacked.

"God, it's so beautiful! I've never seen a more amazing thing, bro, I swear! "

Stefan was smiling, satisfied with the effect his favorite building had on his friend. "See how many details it has, bro? Even if you stare at it for a whole hour, you can't see all the details. Every time I came to Barca, I came here. I used to sit on this big rock right across the street from the entrance with a joint in my hand and stare at it like a fool for hours, trying to assimilate this brilliant creation. True, what these new architects have done on the other side is also beautiful, but it can't be compared to what Gaudi did. It's much more organic, visceral and full of details. I don't think he would like it if he saw the way his cathedral looks now."

"You're right. When I saw the front, I didn't quite get what you meant, that it's not that cool, but after seeing this one, you're absolutely right. Dude, this man was on psychedelic drugs, I'm sure of it, otherwise I don't think he could have had these visions."

"Man, I think you're right. I've heard that when he died, he was hit by a tram, nobody recognized him. He had no ID or cash on him and he was dressed like a tramp. In his pocket, he had nothing but some magic mushrooms and everybody thought he was just a junkie so they didn't give him much care and attention after the accident or at the hospital. By the time they realized who he really was, it was already too late. I'm not sure whether the part about the mushrooms is true or not, but I think it is, his works are way too psychedelic. You get the impression that you've just taken LSD and stepped into another dimension when you see what this man created."

After another hour spent in the vicinity of this sublime piece of architecture, the Romanians took a subway train to the center of the town to meet their childhood neighbors. Only two of them came, the rest of them were at work; they would all meet up in the evening at their place. They hugged each other, delighted by the encounter that came after more than ten years, then they sat at one of the many mini gardens strewn around Barcelona's center.

"How's it hanging, brothers? We haven't seen you in ages! Is everything okay?"

"Yeah, man, we're here for a flying visit. Stefan's showing me around 'cause he's been here before; after this we're going to Madrid, we've got some business to take care of. What's up with you guys, how's everything going?"

"It's going great, bro. We've got accustomed to this place, we have a good team, we make good money, the laws are mild. We can't complain."

"Are you still acrobats?"

"Yeah, bro, well, it's a living...but there are more of us now. Some little devils from Suceava and Bacau have joined us, they're good pickpockets and sometimes we go mugging together. We usually do the tourist areas by day, and at night we break into balconies. In the end we split everything evenly. The cops here hold you for a little while and then they let you go; Spain sure is a sweet country. Next week we're going to Ibiza 'cause the season has started. It's full of tourists, drunk as fuck and high as kites, it's like they're asking you to rob them. We'll stay there for a month and then we'll go to Pamplona for the bull festival. It's general madness then, bro, everybody shouts and jostles and it's very crowded, you can accidentally end up with someone's wallet, even if you're not a thief. Dude, how's Radu, still with his pit bulls?"

"Yes, bro, he's the owner of the current Romanian champion, who defeated his father, the former champ, last month. Apart from that, he's still the same. He was in prison a few years ago for kidnapping and cutting Relu, the Zabareans' godson. I don't know if you've heard the story. He owed him some money and had spread some shit about him in town."

"Yes, yes, I've heard about it. It served him right, those gypsy crows in Galati are way too full of themselves. So Radu's still that batshit crazy guy we all know? He's really hardcore, bro. We went with him on a couple of actions and he scared the shit out of us."

"He's exactly the way you remember him, maybe a bit more mellow 'cause we've all grown older, but he's got the same style. He may be hardcore but he's the most soulful person I've ever met."

As they kept talking to their old friends, the sun set imperceptibly and the life on La Rambla started changing, the gift shops and the caricaturists being replaced by prostitutes, most of whom came from Africa and Latin America, although East Europeans were also present. Despite the fact that the people were different, their purpose was similar: to clean the tourists out of their vacation money. Besides the female prostitutes, there were also transvestites, Barcelona being considered a Mecca of prostitutes and transsexuals, which is pretty obvious at nighttime, particularly in the old city center where the boys were.

"Man, look how many strumpets have sprung on the streets while we were making small talk!" Stefan exclaimed as they got back on Rambla Street.

"Yeah, it's full of them during the night, bro. But you know what the really cool thing is? All the bitches sit and wait on Rambla, no matter where they're from, but a block from here, there's a street where only Romanian hookers wait and there's more of them there than all of these combined."

"You're not kidding! Romanian tramps have their own street?"

"Yes, dude, come with me and I'll show you!"

The acrobats made a turn on one of the narrow streets perpendicular to Rambla and, only a few meters farther, they entered a street that resembled the biblical image of Sodom. The whole street was flanked by prostitutes, all of them from Romania, and some of their pimps, who didn't let anyone else show their merchandise on their street.

"All of these are Romanians, man? Well, there's more of them here than on Rambla!"

"I told you that's how it is. The Romanians have terrorized everybody here since they showed up; before them, the Moroccans were in power but some crews of driven Romanians came and broke their bones. Two Moroccans were killed by some folks from Barlad, and ever since then, nobody has had the guts to mess with them. We let them sell their drugs in the street but they pay us a fee. Sometimes we even take everything they have on them if we haven't made money that day, but the suckers don't dare say a word 'cause we have a big army here, bro, and they've seen what happens if they try to show us that their dicks are bigger."

As they were talking, they passed by one of the guys who took care of the girls, staying in the street with them all the time. He greeted them. They weren't the real pimps, just their soldiers, gaining a percentage of the profits for making sure that everything went smoothly without incident in the street. The acrobat addressed him cordially: "What's up, Gheorghita, are you working?"

"I'm taking some air, what else can I do? How 'bout you guys?"

"Same here, we've got some old friends visiting, so we thought we'd show them around. Have you found out anything concerning our business?"

"Not yet, man, but I'll let you know as soon as anything drops in."

"You do that! Take care!"

"You too, bro."

"Are you in business with the pimps?" Lorin asked his friend, smiling.

"Yes, bro, it's good to have them close, they're up-to-date at all times. They tip us off from time to time and we give them a share of what we make."

Half an hour later, Lorin and Stefan said goodbye to their friends from Galati, apologized for not going upstairs to their place because they wanted to hit the clubs, and sent their greetings to the other guys they hadn't met that evening. The acrobats were regarded by the two friends as being good fellows, reliable in case of need but, after a while, they became a bit irritating. All their talk revolved around thievery and robbery, things the boys didn't really have any particular respect for.

Stefan and Lorin entered several downtown clubs and snorted some lines of coke they had bought from one of the Moroccans who hung around the corner of every street in Barcelona's center during nighttime, but they weren't very impressed with the city's nightlife. The atmosphere was somehow too cheerful, too fiesta-like. A great number of gay people who, feeling at home, were getting quite ostentatious with their lascivious gestures so the boys got out of the club after they had imbibed a few glasses of rum, and walked towards the beach to see the sunrise.

"Come on, bro, let's go chill a little bit on the beach with a cute little joint. I'm tired of everybody bouncing around me!" Lorin told his friend.

Stefan agreed and they went towards the very same beach where they had sunbathed that day, Barceloneta. There was approximately half an hour left before the first rays of sunshine would turn the horizon red. The boys sat down on the cold sand and shared a joint, chatting, and exchanging impressions about this gorgeous Catalan city.

While they were talking, they noticed the graceful silhouettes of two girls who were walking on the seashore, letting the water touch their bare feet. The girls had noticed them too and seemed to be talking about them, laughing, and turning their heads in their direction. When they approached the Romanians, one of them asked, very rakishly: "Hello, guys. There's a very nice smell coming from your direction; may we join you and have a few puffs?"

"Of course, it will be our pleasure. Come sit next to us. I'm Stefan and he's Lorin and we're Greeks."

"Oh, we could have sworn you were Spanish, you look just like the local people do. We're Hanna and Maia and we're from Sweden."

Lorin, puzzled by his friend's assertion, asked for an explanation. "Why'd you tell them we were Greek, you fucker?"

"I didn't wanna scare them, bro. Foreigners don't usually have the best impression about Romanians, and I thought of a country where the people look similar to us but whose language the girls were probably not familiar with. If I said we're from Italy or Portugal, they might have spoken the language, but I don't think they speak Greek."

The girls were talking to each other and the one that had opened the conversation, being the bolder one, while her friend sat behind her, a bit embarrassed, addressed them again. "Hey, we know you're Spanish, we just heard you speak! Why won't you admit you're from here?"

Stefan laughed heartily and answered her with a smile on his face. "Okay, you're right, but only half-right. We're not Greeks, that's true, but we're not Spanish either. We're from Romania."

"Woow, the country of Dracula! But why didn't you say so in the first place?"

"People are usually afraid of Romanians and we didn't wanna start by scaring you. We wanted to tell you we're Romanians after we had gotten better acquainted and you had seen that we're good guys."

"The truth is I've only met one Romanian guy, in a club in Stockholm. He was very nice at first, he came to me and gave me a flower, which surprised me, especially since we were in a club. We talked a bit and then he disappeared. I only found out later that he had stolen my wallet and my phone from my bag."

"Well, now you know why I prefer not to admit we're Romanians from the start!"

As they were chatting with the girls, they noticed three men approaching them with reeling but firm steps. They came straight towards them and one of them spoke in a drunken, or supposedly drunken, voice. "Hey, guys, may we join you and have a smoke? We haven't smoked in who knows how long."

Lorin's first reaction was to send them away but Stefan, who was more used to foreigners, passed them the joint. "There you go, have a puff if you're so desperate!"

The boys looked carefully at the new arrivals and, from the beginning, they had no doubt that these people hadn't accosted them for the purpose of smoking hash. Two of them had backpacks and had tied their shirts around their waist; and the third drew out a thick iron chain from his pocket and started wrapping it around his fist. The second foreigner, they seemed to be from somewhere in South America, with typical American-Indian features, drew a knife from his pocket and started playing with it, spinning it around his fingers and drawing lines in the sand with it.

When he noticed that Lorin was getting ready to jump over the one with the knife, Stefan addressed him in a calm voice, mostly because he didn't want to scare the two Swedish girls, who were already petrified with fear, even more. "Wait a sec, bro, let's see what they do. If they make a move, we break their bones on the spot!"

As he was saying this, he observed that the third man was sitting down next to his sneakers, which were lying in the sand. The shirt around his waist covered them, and he put his hand under the shirt, grabbed the shoes, and tried to hide them with one hand behind his back in order to get them in his backpack, all the while looking at the Romanians. Stefan couldn't believe their guts and, at the same time, their stupidity. Their method could be fruitful only in the case of tourists terrorized at the sight of the weapons, who might have preferred handing them their belongings to fighting them. He leapt from his spot like a spring, grabbed the sneakers from the thief's grip, and kicked him in the chin as he was sitting on his hunkers. When he turned around to hit the other thief who was standing next to him, he, along with his friend with the chain, jumped to their feet, their faces completely changed as if they had been woken up from their sleep. They put their palms in front of their faces and screamed at Stefan and Lorin, who was now also on his toes, "Wait, guys, wait a minute! Where are you from?"

"We're from Romania, fuck your puked Indian slut of a mother! You think you picked the right people to rob, you fucking dickheads?"

The expression on the attackers' faces, upon hearing the origin of those they had seen as prey, changed from astonishment to horror. The only thing they managed to say being: "Romania! Oh my God! We're sorry, guys, forgive us! We thought you were tourists!"

"Well, that's what we are, tourists, you motherfucker! Get lost, quickly, before I make you swallow your knife, you slimy bastard!"

They seized the one who had received a knee in his mouth and who still hadn't recovered and hurried away, looking back from time to time.

The guys burst out laughing. They had seen the same expression on the faces of other so-called predators. The ones who had tried to attack them were nothing more than petty thieves who were counting on intimidating the tourists and who'd had prior encounters with Romanians on Barcelona territory. They had nothing in common with the Latin gangs from South and North America, whose strength and ferocity were renowned worldwide.

Even though the boys were having great fun, the Swedish girls' morale was pretty low. They had overcome their initial fear provoked by the three thieves, only to get even more scared by the reaction of the two Romanians they had just met. They got up from the sandy beach, said goodbye, and left hastily.

Still laughing, the boys said goodbye too then lay back down on Barceloneta beach and watched with their hearts full of vitality how the first rays of sunshine appeared. They felt ready and anxious to set off on their new adventure.

Chapter 17

After they picked Irinel up from Madrid airport, there was a boring flight that lasted almost twelve hours, then the guys finally landed in the Peruvian capital in the evening. They took a cab from the airport to Lima's central area. It left them in Plaza de Armas, the place where the famous Spanish conquistador who conquered the Inca Empire, Francisco Pizarro, had founded Lima in 1535. It was also known as Ciudad de los Reyes, the City of Kings. Pizarro was even buried in the Roman Catholic church in the eastern section of the plaza.

The boys rented a hotel room with three beds for two nights. Being tired, they weren't in the mood for a night in town; instead, they went for a short walk around Plaza de Armas, which was humming with tourists and locals, who were assiduously trying to sell them various souvenirs, articles of clothing, or traditional appetizers. The three Romanians weren't very interested in the landscape or architecture, they had come here for business, and they didn't allow themselves to get absorbed by the checkered crowd swirling around them, even though the atmosphere was completely different from anything they had experienced. None of the boys had ever been outside Europe before.

They bought some edibles from a nearby mercadillo and some weed from one of the dozens of dealers that populated the more crowded areas of Lima then they went upstairs to rest in their hotel room. The following day was going to be very important. They were going to find out which part of the country it was best to travel to in order to buy the best cocaine at the lowest price. Buying it from Lima, even if it could be found at every corner, would have been stupid. The merchandise here was a lot more expensive and less pure than in the mountains where the coca plantations were.

After they took a shower, they went out on the balcony to eat and smoke, admiring the central square and its hustle and bustle. It was the first time that Irinel had been alone with Radu's two friends, but he felt as light as rain with the guys, especially as they were treating him with respect and he could sense that they were fond of him.

"How's it going, Irinel? What do you think about this place? You've never left the country before, but when you did, you came all the way to the other side of the world!" Stefan said, smiling at the boy.

"I like it, bro, what can I say? It's completely different from our neck of the woods...but such a throng. I haven't seen so many people in one place since I went to the football stadium in Bucharest with Radu, to see Steaua's match with Galatasaray Istanbul."

The boys were very amused by Irinel's comparison, and Lorin, upon handing him the joint, inquired about his morale concerning what was about to happen: "So tell me, little devil, are you ready for the adventure? So far you've had Radu around, you've had us, but there, on the ship, you're going to be on your own, and all the responsibility is on you. You've gotta handle everything with maximum care, not only on board of the ship but, especially, when you get off. The most important thing is to not be afraid, or let the dark thoughts and worries overwhelm you during crucial times. You have to act naturally, as if you have nothing to hide, or else someone might target you. Always be observant of everything that happens but don't lose your temper, not even for a second, little brother, 'cause those are the moments that make the difference between freedom and the black hole, and that's when you can tell a man from a pussy. But I'm sure you'll do great, from the little I know about you so far and from the confidence Radu has in you."

"Yeah, bro, chill, I won't lose my head, no matter what. And I'm not afraid either. I understood a long time ago that you only stand to lose when you let fear dwell in your soul. What will be, will be, I'm ready for anything. Don't worry, everything's gonna be okay."

"Very well, boy, I can tell you've been taught at Radu's school. After we see which direction we have to go, we'll rent a car. There's no point in carrying the load with us on trains and buses."

"And how do you plan on finding out where it's best to go?"

"We'll go to town tomorrow and mingle with the people. It's full of foreigners here, some of them are just visiting, others have settled here in Lima; and a lot of them come here to buy coke. We'll find out where to head somehow, either from them or from the locals. No worries, boy!"

"Lorin, don't you think we should take some guns with us on this adventure? We don't really know how things go down around here. These guys might pull one over on us and put a revolver to our heads as if we were some shmucks. I think it would be better to get ourselves a couple of pistols to be on the safe side, how about that?" Stefan voiced an idea that had already crossed Lorin's mind a couple of times.

"Dude, you know, that's not such a bad idea, particularly if we're to go through the jungle where these guys grow the coke. It's better to make sure we don't go like fools and put our heads in the lion's mouth. When we go out tomorrow, we'll also ask about a couple of guns."

The following day, they woke up with an overflowing lust for life, having precise objectives that had to be carried out that day. They went out for a walk on the very colorful streets of the City of Kings and became one with the crowd that bustled around them, stopping at a garden placed strategically on one of the narrow central streets. After ordering an English breakfast each, they noticed that none of the people there were Peruvian; they heard German, French and English. Stefan looked at the two Englishmen who were talking in a relaxed and jovial way at the table right next to theirs, and learned that the two of them were planning to go to Machu Picchu. He believed that they might have some useful information, so he waded into their conversation.

"Hello, guys, may I ask you something?"

"Sure, mate, what's this about?"

Stefan got up from their table and pulled a chair over to the one with the English party. "May I?"

"Please, have a seat!" answered one of them. He seemed delighted with the idea of meeting new people on this adventure.

Both Lorin and Irinel were very impressed with the lightness and tact with which Stefan had addressed the foreigners; it became obvious to them that he possessed a few qualities they lacked. And that apart from the qualities that made him so attractive in the eyes of the gentle sex.

Stefan continued talking to the Englishmen in a very polite and amicable manner but in a low voice, bending a little towards them over the table so he could be heard and understood by the British but not by those at the neighboring tables, in case someone had nothing better to do that morning than eavesdrop on their conversation.

"Here's the deal, guys. My friends and I have come to Peru to buy coke and take it back with us to Europe. We'd like to buy the best merchandise possible, since we've come all the way here, and I don't think we can find the best quality in Lima. The merchandise here is for tourists. What I wanted to ask you is if you have any idea where we could find quality stuff, I mean, something as close to the source as one can get?"

The Englishmen gave him a friendly smile and exchanged a quick look, which gave Stefan the impression that they were also users and that, maybe, they hadn't come to Peru just for the sightseeing. One of them answered him in the same low voice Stefan had used, slightly bending over the table to be closer to his interlocutor.

"We also want to buy some good stuff, not a lot, but high quality. Indeed, there's no point in buying it from here, especially if you want a larger amount. You have to go to the mountains where it's being grown. I would advise you to go to Cuzco, it's the capital of the former

Inca Empire, and it is located at an altitude of over three thousand kilometers. See what you can find there. Maybe you'll come across someone who knows some growers or has some at a fair price; anyway, you've got more chances there than you have here. We're heading there ourselves. We want to go to Machu Picchu and Cuzco's on our way too, so if you find something good, give us a call."

"Thanks a lot for the information. We might head in that direction, but today we're staying in Lima. We want to leave tomorrow. Have fun at Machu Picchu and thanks again for your advice! Have a nice day, boys!"

"Thanks, we wish you the same, and good luck finding what you're looking for!"

Stefan returned to his table, they finished their breakfast and, after saying goodbye to the two kind Englishmen, they rejoined the waves of people coiling noisily through the lanes of the Peruvian capital.

"What do you think, dude? Should we go where these guys said or should we keep inquiring here?"

"Bro, since we came all the way here, let's do it right. Let's buy the best stuff possible, right? I believe those English folks knew what they were talking about but we should keep asking other people and see what they tell us. I propose we buy something to snort from around here and see what the dealers have to say, maybe we find out something useful. Plus, we need to get some guns."

In the central plaza, even though there weren't as many dealers as in the evening, the guys spotted some locals whose obvious purpose was to sell drugs to the tourists. Stefan approached the one who seemed better off than the others, as he was dressed more stylishly and displayed a breezier attitude than the rest.

"Hi, we wanna buy some coke. Do you have anything good for us?"

The Peruvian analyzed the Romanian from head to toe. His East European accent and his body language eased the dealer's initial fear he felt every time a new client approached him; namely that he might be an undercover cop. He could never be sure but this muscular, tattoo-covered Romanian, who moved and talked with the attitude of a European gigolo, looked nothing like a cop.

"Yes, I've got some premium stuff for you guys. Where are you from?"

"Romania."

"Ah, Romania, we don't have many Romanians coming here, but I've met a few before. How much do you want to buy?"

"Not a lot, about two grams are enough. We just want it to do the trick this afternoon."

"Sure, no problem. Follow me, please!"

While the Peruvian was leading him through one of the lanes winding towards the plaza to the more secluded place where he usually took his clients, Stefan tackled the subject that was, in fact, the real reason he had approached this dealer.

"Listen, I want to ask you for a piece of advice. If we wanted to buy a slightly larger quantity but as pure and cheap as possible, where in Peru should we go?"

"Well, you don't have to go anywhere. I can obtain as much as you want, right here in Lima."

"No, we want to go where it's grown, get it straight from the source, uncut. We need it as pure as it gets."

"Well, the one we have here is very pure. Try it and you'll come back for more, trust me!"

"Here's what we're gonna do: if it's as good as you say it is, I'll look for you again and we'll talk some more. But should we decide to go somewhere else after all, where do you think it's best we go? I heard Cuzco is a viable option, what do you think?"

"People are real savages there, I don't think you're gonna like it, but, hey, if you really wanna go, you can find the stuff there too. It's grown in the jungle. But it's quite far; you've got to travel for a whole day to get there. Why don't you buy it from here where it's just as good?"

"Okay, we'll see what we decide to do." He took the two grams, gave the dealer the money and then he tackled the other subject he wanted to discuss with him. "I have another question for you. We want to buy some pistols for protection. Can you recommend something?"

The Peruvian scanned him from head to toe again as if to reassure himself the Romanian wasn't an undercover cop, after which he got closer to him and told him, mostly whispering: "I don't sell guns but I know someone who does. Still, if you want me to get you in touch with the man, you should buy some more grams from me 'cause I have to go about to find the guy."

"Look, let me tell you what we'll do. When you bring me the guy, I'll give you fifty bucks for your effort."

"Okay. Wait for me in an hour at the place you first approached me."

An hour later, the boys spotted the Peruvian, followed at a certain distance by a compatriot with rough features who was analyzing his surroundings with suspicion. The dealer gestured towards them. They followed him and, together with the newcomer, walked the crowded streets then turned into a winding lane. After walking for another five minutes, they entered the yard of an old colonial-style house.

Once they entered and felt the cool of the house, the second Peruvian, who owned the house they were now in, addressed them in impeccable English. "What do you need, guys?"

"Nothing too complicated. We just want three pistols to have for protection around here. If you want, when we leave, we can sell them back to you at a lower price 'cause we don't plan on going back to Europe with them."

The Peruvian nodded, went out of the room for a moment then came back with three pistols, all of them nine millimeters and in excellent condition.

After they agreed on a much lower price than what the boys had been ready to pay, they bought the guns, gave fifty bucks to the guy who had introduced them to the gun seller, and concluded that they would look for them as soon as they returned to Lima, to sell back the pistols at a lower cost.

Once back on the street, the boys were in a much better mood than the previous day, not only because they knew where to go to procure the best quality merchandise but they had also obtained the guns they would probably need during this trip. At least for their psychological comfort.

"My dear brothers, I say we shouldn't waste any more time around here. Let's rent a car and hurry up to Cuzco. You heard how long the trip is. If we leave this afternoon, I think we'll be there by tomorrow morning."

The boys agreed and went to a car rental company, where they got a Chevrolet for a week for only two hundred bucks. They stopped at the hotel to pick up their belongings and set out, full of energy, for the capital of the Inca Empire.

As they had predicted, they reached Cuzco the next morning, but, even though they had taken turns driving the car and they had had the cocaine to keep them in shape, the guys were exhausted and nauseated because of the altitude, approximately three thousand, four hundred meters above sea level.

Cuzco was a totally different city from Lima, so much so that they were finding it hard to believe they were in the same country. Not only was the architecture completely distinct, the influence of the Spanish architects being practically nonexistent here, but the people also looked different. They were smaller in stature, had darker skin, and the European features evident in Lima had disappeared completely from the faces of the locals. These people weren't dissimilar to those in the capital only from a physical point of view; they also dressed very differently. Their clothes were a lot more colorful and seemed closer to what they had imagined they'd find in Peru before taking this trip. Several of the colorfully-dressed people had lamas they kept on leashes, as if they were dogs. Another aspect that surprised the Romanians was the fact that coca leaves were being sold everywhere, for chewing. At the first garden they stopped to eat at, they were brought a tea made from coca leaves, called mate de coca, which, although it didn't have a very pleasant taste, had the role of diminishing the effects of the high altitude and altitude sickness.

They decided that, since they were at a stage of doing things for the first time, they should eat something they'd never tried, so they each bought a dish of guinea pig, one of the local culinary specialties. Even though the food looked a bit awkward, it proved to be extremely tasty, and the boys declared themselves perfectly satisfied with what Peru had had to offer them up to that point. They were about to find out if it would also offer them what they were looking for.

Upon arriving at the center of the city, they were stupefied to discover that the central square, where they rented a hotel room, had the same name as the one in Lima, Plaza de Armas. In the evening, after they rested, they went out on the streets to look for information. Just as in Lima, the town center was studded with dealers, making their work easier. After they waded into conversation with several of them, Stefan stopped at one who had interesting information. He told them he was from the heart of the mountains, from one of the jungles where coca leaves are grown, and that he could take them there to talk to some growers, but only if they intended to buy more than a kilogram. He also warned them that they would have to drive for a good couple of hours through the Peruvian jungle, but the roads were in pretty good condition.

Without taking too much time to decide, the guys got in the car and, together with their new acquaintance, started their nocturnal journey to the core of the mountains, covered by the luxuriant jungle. On their way to the native place of the Peruvian, they found out that he despised the inhabitants of the capital city. He regarded them as a different race, corrupted by the rotten values of the Spanish conquistadores, who had subjugated them and tried to destroy their national identity. The very name of the capital founded by Pizzaro, the City of Kings, reminiscent of Winnetou's stories, made this man of the mountains feel sick at heart.

By morning, exasperated by the huge distances they had to cross through this weird country, they finally reached the destination.

Ricardo, for this was the name of their guide, introduced them to his relatives, and there were plenty of them, who welcomed them with a large smile on their faces and a friendly attitude. This the Romanians weren't accustomed to, especially coming from strangers. After they had discussed the reason for their visit with the head of the family, an older man in his sixties, but still fit, he said a few words in Spanish to one of his grandsons. Stefan made out "Go and get me a kilogram." The old man explained to them that in their country, it was legal to grow coca leaves, but it wasn't legal to process them into coke. The benefit plans from the government weren't enough to cover the expenses necessary for any other kind of crops so they always grew coca, which they sent to Colombia for processing, but they always kept a few kilograms for themselves. He also told them, before his grandson's return, that they made a paste of maximum purity out of the coca leaves, to which they added different chemicals to transform it into a powder, and that the product he had was the purest one in Peru.

Up to this point, the boys had been very pleased with the meeting, but that didn't mean they trusted the growers. They still wore the pistols at their belts, handy in case these highlanders tried something funny.

To their utter surprise, the young boy came back with a bag full of a white-yellowish paste, similar to the Romanian salty cheese preserved in sheep stomachs. Their satisfaction tripled after they tested the quality of the merchandise. None of them had ever tasted anything like it before; the cocaine had several times the purity of any other product they had tried. A very strong feeling of well-being took over, a sparkling energy replacing the exhaustion that had intensified on their way through the jungle. It was, without a shadow of doubt, what they were looking for. They agreed on a lower price than what they had initially expected for this transaction, took the whole kilo, thanked their hosts and, before leaving, told them they would send the youngest of them again, alone, for further supplies. They shook hands with these very hospitable people of the jungle, and went on their way to Cuzco with their valuable package.

That afternoon, back in the Inca capital, after they had given Ricardo their three 9-millimeter guns as a present, they made inquiries about the cargo ships that sailed to Europe. Several people told them that most of the ships departed from the port of Callao, built by the Spanish in 1537 and now the main commercial harbor in the Pacific.

The next evening they were in Callao harbor. Stefan approached the captain of a ship bound for Europe the following week, explaining to him that he had a friend who wanted to return to Europe by sea, and asking if it would be possible to take him, of course, for a fair amount of money. Stefan noticed that this captain had had similar experiences. From his casual attitude and his way of talking, it was pretty obvious not only that he had understood the reason why the boy wanted to return by ship rather than by airplane but also that he had done this before. After keen negotiations, Stefan had to agree to pay the sailor three thousand bucks, a higher price than what they had initially estimated but they needed the captain and his ship, and he knew it very well. They set the date for when they would bring the boy, payment would be made after he had embarked, and the captain promised them a good room for the boy and no problems upon his debarkation.

The trip was going to last more than three weeks, and the boy would debark in the Belgian port of Antwerp.

A few days later, Irinel boarded the Peruvian ship, his heart pounding wildly in his chest but he was delighted by this trip. And the guys, after giving him some last pieces of advice and paying the money they had agreed with the captain, headed towards the Jorge Savez airport in Lima for another twelve-hour flight back to Europe.

Chapter 18

Meanwhile, Radu was looking forward to another visit from his Dutch lover. Since the year started, his rather dark inner universe had become brighter because of the feelings he had begun to nurture for this woman. Impatience at the thought of seeing and touching her, the frustration caused by the distance between them, reading the messages she had sent again and again, and a general state of restlessness, both psychic and sexual, were all new sensations for Radu. His love life had never been terribly rich. Radu lacked the natural way with which Stefan, for instance, approached a woman he fancied and that animal magnetism his friend sparked, about which the boys cracked jokes, likening him to a bull turning on all the cows in his proximity.

He also lacked that loyalty to one woman that Lorin had to Cristina. He soon got tired of the presence of the same woman in his life if it lasted too long. Being attracted only to the sexual side of the relationship, he found the attitudes of women and the discussions he had with them rather boring and he loathed the wishy-washy, weak ways of his partners and their lack of conviction. However, now, for the first time, things had changed dramatically. What he felt for Sophie belonged to an altogether different category than the feelings other women had stirred in him before. Aside from the exceptionally strong sexual attraction, which made him want to possess her in a more visceral way than he had ever done before, and that it was enough for him to become hyper-excited and restless, he also had other feelings for her. Feelings that were completely new for Radu and completely turned his inner compass upside down. He felt a kind of admiration and respect for her, putting her on a pedestal he had built without even realizing it. How much this was due to the fact that the woman was a foreigner, and her attitude was very different from the Romanian women he had come across, and to what extent it was because he had grown up, he couldn't say. Age had toned down the flame that always set his belligerent being on fire, making room for some feelings, which, though as intense, were of a different kind.

Never before had Radu allowed happiness to overwhelm him in the rare moments when he had come across it because he wanted to keep his inner balance. Now happiness had flooded him in waves bigger than before, and those waves were knocking at the gates of his soul, seeping under the sternness with which he controlled his inner universe just like ocean waves ceaselessly lapping a tough cliff, slowly wearing its edges away. Although this sensation was pleasant, it made Radu anxious because he felt he was slowly losing the complete control he had on his inner realms, these being increasingly lit by something outside of him. Well, Radu had never allowed anything outside of him to impact his world, and the sense of this change was bitter-sweet, like scratching a wound you wouldn't let heal, giving you a morbid pleasure.

His sense of restlessness was also rendered more intense by the fact that not only had his feelings for Sophie brought happiness into his soul, but also that the dream he had had for more than a decade had come true; and that was being the master of Romania's champion.

This mix of positive feelings meant Radu was, for the first time in a long while, overwhelmed and confused. A sense of restlessness had taken hold of him just as a snake, creeping into the thickets, sneaks into the complexity of local flora. As a consequence of his approach to judging and looking into things, too many positive feelings could only mean that something serious was about to happen because there was balance, in his experience. When you reached the top too quickly and unexpectedly, the price was a dramatic plummet into the abyss of disappointment and dejection. For this reason, he was trying to harness his feelings for Sophie, because they were running wild through his being like the herd of wild horses he had seen years before in the Danube Delta, the only population of its kind left in Europe. In spite of all this, he could not help wishing to hold his lover in his arms again and to soak himself in the odor of her hair and the flavor of her pheromones, which assaulted his nostrils when he kissed her on the neck.

The day the Dutch woman arrived at Poiana came at last. The impact between the two was stronger than ever as they kissed feverishly and clutched each other's faces in their hands in order to quench their desire to possess each other, before the clothes fell off their quivering bodies and they gave themselves away, completely consumed by the flame of passion.

After several hours of animal instincts alternating with moments of tenderness and delicacy, of which Radu had had no idea, the two of them rolled over the familiar bearskin in front of the fireplace, completely knackered but charged with another kind of energy. Sophie took his face in her hands again, imprinted it with a kiss, and then she looked deep into Radu's pitch-dark eyes, which she perceived as gates to a deep abyss where she liked to take shelter and which were now lit by the blaze in the fire place, highlighting the flame of his ceaselessly-scrutinizing glance. She told him as straightforwardly and firmly as possible: "Radu, I want to have a word with you. These last few months I couldn't think of anything else but you, and the distance between us is killing me. I was thinking I could move here, at least for a while. I'm in love with this place, that's why I bought myself a house here. They said I could work from home with less pay, as long as I submit my work in time. I'd be able to spend more time with you. I would live in my house lest I should invade the privacy I know you care for so much, but we'd be at a stone's throw from each other. However, I'll do it only if you want it. If you think it's pushing things too far, please let me know, and I won't mind. Nothing will change between us. What do you think?"

Radu was hearing exactly what he had wanted to hear, and while the girl was speaking, joy took hold of him; maybe that's why he felt the cold snake of fatality coiling lasciviously within him. He drove the unpleasant feeling away, trying to ignore it, but Sophie felt in his voice that something was wrong. However, she put it down to the butterflies she imagined men felt in such a moment.

"Sophie, I would love it. I wanted to suggest it myself but I thought you had your own commitments in The Hague and you could not move here. Having you with me at all times would make me very happy. You know, maybe this sounds like a cliché, but I think you know me enough by now to realize that I say what I mean, and I've never felt for a woman what I feel for you. This desire to wake up beside you and the way I miss you when you're away in the Netherlands has been gnawing at me since I met you. Yes, move here, it'll be fantastic!"

Sophie caressed the Romanian's face, her heart pounding wildly in her chest. That's what made the difference between them. The happiness Sophie felt in these moments did not give her a sense of restlessness; on the contrary. This was what she had always wanted – to fall head over heels in love with an authentic male who could take her breath away by his way of being and who loved her with every fiber of his being. That this was happening at last meant, for the Dutch woman, the fulfillment of her destiny.

She went on. "Well, Radu, if I move here with you in the mountains and far from any kind of civilization, I have to know and understand you first. You're still an enigma for me. I cannot understand exactly what motivates you to be the way you are. The only thing that's clear to me is that you're very self-confident and you strongly believe in your convictions. For instance, I cannot understand your contempt for humankind; I've noticed that, except for your friends, you treat people in a way that makes them tremble with fear, and I'm not very comfortable with that. Why do you dislike people?"

"Yes, you're right. I love and respect animals more than I do people. That's because we are too self-sufficient, we deem ourselves superior to the other living organisms on the planet and we destroy everything in our way in order to possess more of the things we don't need. Tell me, why is the well-being of each of us more precious than, for instance, a spider's? Well, it's not in the least more precious. What makes the difference is the fact that we are more intelligent and we use our power in the most selfish and wicked manner one can imagine. The truth is we don't deserve to live; we are a pest on the planet that gave us life. We influence other forms of life in the most negative way possible, we take everything without giving anything back and we defile everything we touch, taking it for granted that it's our right to do it only because we can.

"But this is not going to last forever. There will come a time when the Earth will have had enough of the poison we inoculate it with daily and it'll destroy us. Then humankind will disappear from the face of the Earth, and all the other creatures will enjoy a better and more peaceful existence, living in perfect harmony; even the predators that kill just as much as they need to survive. The day when the human race is exterminated will be a celebration for the rest of the animal and vegetable world. I hate civilization and everything it stands for. Why do you think I've come to live here in the mountains? I prefer the dogs' company a lot more to that of humans. The dogs are perfectly loyal, they have no notion of perversity, hypocrisy, or wickedness and, especially the pit bulls, don't know what fear and cowardice is. You cannot lie to dogs, they can feel your fear, and they feel what kind of person you are, no matter how you act. To be more specific, I prefer the company of dogs to that of most people, but luckily not all people are like that. Those I love, I love with all my heart and I'd do anything for them any time."

"Yeah, I've noticed that about you, and I perfectly take your point and your disdain for humanity, even if I don't completely share your opinion. I think that we still deserve a chance to change and that right now we are like spoilt kids who have forgotten to respect nature but we will respect it when we realize our mistakes. I am a bit more tolerant towards people, maybe because I am a woman...Oh, and there's something else that baffles me about you, which I need to make sense of, given that I haven't been able to think of anything else in the last months – where does this appetite of yours for violence come from? And how come you're not afraid to face such risks? In each fight, you run the risk of being seriously wounded or even killed, especially here in Romania, where people are so vain and trained and ready to fight."

"When you do something that implies an immediate risk and especially an act of violence, you have no idea how you'll react until you're forced to plunge into action, and all of a sudden, instincts you didn't know you had take control and guide your actions, showing you that you're a superior being to the one you thought you were. Basic instincts, seemingly forgotten, buried deep in our souls by centuries of cowardice and comfort, emerge and take control in moments that make the difference between life and death. And being aware of these instincts and the feelings activated by these moments are probably the loftiest ones a man can have. This, and the feeling you have when you manage to defeat your enemy in a battle in which you forgot about self-preservation and gave the best of yourself to save what you love. And if you have to die, leaving this world fighting in the name of what you love is the most honorable way a man can do it."

"You were born in the wrong century. You belong in the battlefield, sword in hand, leading an army!"

"I know. You have no idea how much I'd love that! I've always had this feeling that I was born in the wrong century. If I could make a wish, it would be this; to turn back time several centuries and live then, defending my land and my people as an army leader. All through history, Romanians did not attack other peoples but they were constantly under the attack of neighboring empires because of their strategic position at the Black Sea and their rich natural resources. And they could opt between submitting or fighting against all odds. That's why my idol is Stefan cel Mare, or Stephen the Great;

for me he's the most outstanding person who has ever tread these lands. I've loved him since childhood and I'll always love him. Few foreigners know that if it hadn't been for him, the first wall of Christendom in the way of the Muslim Ottoman Empire would have fallen, and most of Europe would now be speaking Turkish."

"Hold on a sec, I thought your greatest ruler was Vlad Dracula?"

"Vlad Dracula is most familiar to foreigners, and that's mostly due to Bram Stoker's novel, which turned him into a vampire. Vlad never had anything to do with the vampire business, but he was a ruler who impressed the whole of Europe with his brutal fighting methods. What the foreigners don't understand, though, is the fact that this was the only way the leader of a small country could face the huge Ottoman Empire; through terror. For instance, when the vast army dispatched by the sultan to conquer Vlad never returned, he himself went to war in order to punish the Romanian ruler. But, as they were coming closer, they could smell something they had never smelled before, and soon the sight that met their eyes terrified them and sent them fleeing back to Istanbul.

"After defeating the Turks, Vlad had had a forest cut down, and the trees carved into sharp stakes, and then all the twenty-three thousand Turks, who had come to set them on fire and who had survived the battle, were impaled. Can you imagine that apocalyptic sight? An endless forest of sharp stakes, and tens of thousands of Turks screaming in agony. That's why the greatest ruler of the time trembled with fear and returned home defeated."

"My God, I knew this Vlad Dracula of yours was sadistic! But what does impaling mean exactly?"

"In the first place you must understand that this was the only possible way one could fight an army which was several times bigger. If he hadn't done this, the sultan, who had brought with him many more soldiers this time, would have killed all the Romanians in order to make his way to Christian Europe. This scared him, even if he was one of the cruelest leaders ever, and he returned home, bearing the shame of defeat. Vlad was forced to do it, his sadism was not ungrounded.

"As far as impaling is concerned, he invented a method more sadistic than the classic one. The tips of the stakes were normally sharpened and pierced the victims' chests, and they died relatively soon. However, Vlad invented another impaling technique; he didn't sharpen their tips, he left them deliberately blunt, and he didn't pierce the victims' chests, but their asses. Thus, the stake touched no vital organs, and it took them several days to die. They were laid on the ground, face down and arms tied, their legs were spread and the stake was thrust into their asses. Then the victims were lifted, slowly sliding into the stake due to their own weight and gravity. Indeed, that was a terrible way to die, and now figure a forest of tens of thousands of such stakes. That's quite shocking, isn't it?

"However, in a straight confrontation, Vlad's army would have been decimated, as they were several times less numerous than the Ottoman army. When the sultan returned, Vlad continuously staged commando attacks. He would place small army cohorts in the forests, or he would pursue the Turks and attack them where they could not engage their whole army, then the Romanians would withdraw into the woods. He also charged during the night after dressing the Romanians in Turkish garments in order to confuse the Turks, who are said to have continued killing one another long after Vlad and his army had left the scene.

"Indeed, he was a brutal prince, but being brutal in those times was the only way one could cope with the huge Ottoman Empire, the greatest of its time. Vlad had hated the Turks since his childhood. He and his brother were given to the sultan as a warrant of submission by their father, and while his brother grew up to become the sultan's lover, Vlad grew up hating their guts and observing their battle techniques in order to be able to vanquish them afterwards. Years later, his brother was dispatched with a Turkish army to defeat him, but he failed.

"One wrong idea foreigners have about him is that he was the ruler of Transylvania, whereas actually he ruled over Wallachia. Another wrong idea is about his castle. The Romanians advertise Bran Castle as Dracula's castle because it's located in a tourist area, while actually Vlad never lived there; his castle was in Poienari, on the border between Wallachia and Transylvania, and it was built on the peak of a mountain for strategic reasons. The irony of it is that this castle was built by the noble class, who worked their asses off to achieve it. He couldn't stand the boyars, which were the noble class, these being the equivalent of today's politicians; they changed rulers like socks, pursuing only their mean interests and getting rich on the backs of average people. Vlad summoned them all to a feast and, after a discussion that confirmed the wickedness of these people, he ordered that all of them be impaled, except for some whose lives he saved in order to have them build his castle in the mountains. Legend has it that they worked until their garments got so tattered that they fell from their bodies, and then they continued to work with no clothes on until they all perished.

"Vlad formed a new noble class out of lower social classes, who were loyal only to him. He was a true warrior, but he was betrayed and murdered. Stephen the Great was never betrayed, but was respected and loved by everybody during his rule of almost half a century."

"I find this very interesting to learn, all the more so as I'm planning to move to this country and I barely know its history. Tell me, why do you say that Stephen the Great was a greater ruler than Vlad Dracula?"

"In the first place, Vlad ruled only eight years, in three separate periods, while Stefan ruled for forty-seven years in a row. The two of them were cousins. Vlad helped him at some point with some troops against the Turks, and Stefan crowned Vlad after defeating his brother. However, this doesn't mean the two of them got along well. They actually hated each other, both of them being very powerful and proud rulers. In fact, Stephen the Great died from a wound he got during the siege of one of Vlad's fortresses. Stefan waged forty-eight battles, of which he won forty-six! I am no historian, but I don't think there's ever been an emperor who has fought and, especially, won so many battles. And he always led his army and fought without spilling a drop of blood although the inimical armies were always more numerous.

"Besides his exceptional courage, he had an exceptional sense of strategy. For instance, he used nature to win in the battle of Podu Inalt against a huge Turkish army. He chose a narrow mire between two high hills for the battle, which prevented the Turks from engaging all their troops in battle. Then he used the mist, sending his drummers to beat their drums across the mire, and the Turks got themselves deep into the thick mud following the sound. Then he attacked them, and the Ottomans had no escape from that spot; they were trapped and decimated by Stefan's tiny army. This battle is considered the greatest victory of Christendom after the fall of Constantinople, and the Pope named Stefan "Athleta Christi," Christ's athlete.

"He also defeated Mehmed II, who, when he was twenty-one, conquered the Byzantine Empire and Constantinople, today's Istanbul, though he could not defeat this Romanian ruler who defended his territory with his tiny army in a bout of unmatched courage and tenacity. Stefan lived each day of his life as if it was the last, with death snapping at his heels. The first monastery he built was his grave, the Putna monastery, and that is why he achieved so many things and ruled for so long. He did not fear death and was always ready for the supreme sacrifice.

"Back then, the only method of healing wounds received in battle was burning them with hot iron, a pain we can only imagine. Think of the pain you feel when you touch hot iron and the pain you feel if you have a deep wound, and now figure out the pain caused by that hot iron on the wound. Normally, a man had to be held to the ground for this procedure, but Stefan never allowed anybody to hold him during this painful treatment, saying that the day he was not able to master his pain would be the day he was unfit to be a leader. It's amazing that, although his entire body was covered with scars from various battles, all healed, except for one made by an arrow in his heel while he was charging one of his cousin Vlad Dracula's fortresses, while he was fighting the Turks. That wound never healed and troubled him for many years. The last time he was burnt with the hot iron was two days before he died. My own explanation is that, despite his belligerent nature, which readily shed blood, he felt guilty for having charged an attack against his cousin, whom I'm sure he highly esteemed. The physical manifestation of that sense of guilt was that unhealed wound."

"Wow, thank you very much for this superb history lesson. Now I can better understand your people and, implicitly, your own way of being. You love your ancestors dearly, don't you?"

"With all my heart. In those times, the world was ruled by mighty people, who understood what leadership meant and who motivated their subjects by their own example. There's no trace of that now. We are led by bookworms, a bunch of cowardly and corrupt politicians whose only concern is to line their pockets, even if their fortunes are much more than what they and one hundred generations of their offspring need. I'm afraid this civilization was designed to be a screen behind which the weak and the cowardly hide. Just like religion.

"Phrases like "the more clever will give up" and "turn the other cheek when slapped" tell you everything about it. And both have been indoctrinated by the same method: fear. Fear is man's worst enemy and has always been used against him by his peers. A long time ago, they used to control people using fear of the devil and an eternity of burning in hell, with the possibility of booking a seat in heaven if they gave money to the church. How many thousands of people did the Inquisition torture and burn at stake in the name of God, and how many hundreds of thousands died in his name for the idea that "my God is the true one, not yours, and if you don't have faith in him, I'll kill you"?

"In the first centuries, the Romans drastically persecuted the Christians, and then because Christianity gained popularity and the collapsing empire needed to keep its subjects loyal, they suddenly became the most pious people and built the Vatican as a holy symbol of Christianity. And no, that was not a political move, maybe some angels showed themselves to the politicians and told them which was the right path, right? In the meantime, the people became aware of certain things, and now they've changed the devil. Now they're keeping us under their thumbs through fear of terrorists, whom they use as scarecrows to ensure our collaboration while they control and monitor our every move. Even if the tools have changed, the manipulation method is the same, fear; just as their purpose has always been the same, control. The desire to control others can rise only in persons who lack self-confidence and who are wicked, the very people who are at the top of this corrupt machine called civilization."

"I gather you've never voted?"

"Haven't you been listening?" he asked with the suggestion of a smile in order to tone down the tough tone he realized he used whenever he talked about it because of the waves of hatred flooding him. "Anybody who makes political commitments does so only for mean purposes, in order to have power and control over others and to line their pockets, not because they want the best for the country. Just like cops, who don't choose this job to help their peers but to be in a position of power. They are those who were bullied as children, and they decided to become cops in order to have the power they think that badge gives them, which actually means nothing. If I need you, I will look for you and wait for you, cop or no cop. Maybe all the more so if you are a cop.

"A long time ago, leaders were chosen because they were brave and they had a leading spirit. Back then, the standards according to which leaders were chosen were the opposite of what they are today, when those in power are people who have always hidden behind petty red tape, some accountants holding diplomas in political sciences. And people debating and arguing who the best leader is, are like sheep having to choose between a lion and a wolf as leader of their herd. Lions and wolves will always look at the sheep only as a source of food, and so it is with politicians, who were not born predators but prey. However, they wear the predator's skin and get power as a reward for the time they spent studying, this weak society giving them the opportunity to overcome the humble condition nature equipped them with.

"However, in this civilization, the strong are considered pariah, and the warriors are imprisoned more often than not together with rapists, pedophiles, and other social scum, while the weak lead the world from behind a desk. However, a warrior will always fight, no matter where you might put him and how much you might attempt to destroy him, because the flame in his heart can't be put out by the measures against him, but only stirred. And that flame will perish only when he does."

Chapter 19

Lorin and Stefan were waiting for Irinel's return from Peru in Prague. Lorin had decided that he would stay there until they had sold all the merchandise, so that he did not have to come back in just a few weeks. Cristina had never been happy with this arrangement, but she respected his decision as usual. She put up with it at the thought that her man would return with a handsome amount of money from this adventure, part of this amount being already planned for a holiday abroad since they hadn't taken a trip for a long time. She longed for an escapade; the two of them as a couple, without the company of his friends. They intimidated her, especially Radu. If Radu filled her with fear through the brutality of his actions and his way of being, Stefan intimidated her through that detachment from worldly things, which she considered unnatural. The ease with which Stefan treated any kind of problem and the endless party he always inspired inhibited her whenever her man was in the company of his childhood friends. Yet she would have never dared say this to Lorin. She knew that those two were closer than brothers to him and that he would do anything for them, and she had realized that if she tried to interfere with their relationship, the result would have been a chill on her relationship with him. Besides, even if the boys made her anxious, she respected them too, not only for their way of being but especially for the love she knew they nurtured for her man.

In the long years they had spent together, she had had many occasions to observe how strong the bond between the three boys was. She knew that any of them would have given his life for the other without flinching. And this impressed her deeply. She had never had such a close friendship with any of the girls, neither did she notice it in the case of her intellectual parents, who, although they had many friends, cultivated an artificial kind of friendship, adorned with many compliments, flattery, and fake politeness. She knew that the kind of friendship the boys had was something rare in our times, when everybody is preoccupied with their image in the eyes of the others and whose relationships are based firstly on interest, and not welded by the intensity of extreme experiences of the kind these boys had gone through together.

While waiting for Irinel, who was due to return in about two weeks, Stefan took his friend to see the wonders of Prague. That morning, in glorious weather, he planned to take Lorin on a paddle boat on the Vltava River, which runs through the Czech capital. They rented a tiny boat for an hour and started paddling in the clear water under the arched bridges built centuries before, the oldest being the Charles Bridge, an impressive Gothic structure erected in 1357. The bridge was defended by three towers, one from the old center and two from the opposite side, and it is framed by statues of saints and historic characters, initially lit by oil lamps, then gas lamps, which were electrically adapted in the early 20th century, and are still in use today. Even if the statues flanking this historic bridge are blackened with the passage of time, two of them preserve their original golden color, at least partially. Tourists hope their desires will come true if they touch images representing a vicar being pushed into the water from this bridge in the spring of 1393 because he wouldn't reveal to the king the secrets confessed by his queen.

Passing a joint, the boys admired the beauty of the Golden City, with its parallel bridges teeming with tourists and its buildings, which harmoniously combine all the architectural styles, the Gothic one prevailing and defining this aspect of the capital. They paddled past the national theatre, an impressive neo-Renaissance structure built from the donations of the Czech citizens. Its golden roof reflected the sunlight in a grand manner, and the statues of the ancient chariots pulled by foaming horses adorning the roof of this architectural wonder enhance the majestic impression. Several minutes after they passed by the theater, another building on the bank of the Vltava River caught Lorin's attention; this time a very modern structure. The dancing house, known by the name of Fred and Ginger, in tribute to the famous dancers Fred Astair and Ginger Rogers. Surrounded by buildings in the neo-Gothic, neo-Baroque and Art Nouveau styles, it was initially one of the most controversial constructions in Prague only to become, later, a benchmark of the capital. It is considered one of the most avant-garde, modern buildings in the entire world because of its innovative architecture and the sense of movement it suggests.

It was not just the majestic architecture of Prague that impressed Lorin in a most pleasant way, but also the beauty and relaxed manner of its inhabitants. While they were paddling, other paddle boats were sliding by them, steered mainly by young people, all of them smiling and radiant with happiness; they even saw some boats where beautiful topless girls were basking in the sun. They waved to the two boys in a very relaxed, uninhibited, and friendly manner.

"You know Stefan, you've chosen a great city to live in, bro! Now I see why you like it here so much. I've never felt such relaxation and harmony as I feel here. I'd love to live here myself, I bet I'd be the happiest man ever!"

"Yeah, man, you know I've been to all the nice places in Europe and lived in some for a while, but this is the coolest city in the world if you ask me. The liberty and beauty you find here are unique. This place holds you in its grip once you've visited. I've met lots of people who came just to visit and never left, they found a way to earn a living and made a life here. Prague is special, it keeps you hooked. The atmosphere of this city has an unrivaled glamour.

"Well, bro, come and live here if you like it so much. Just think how cool it would be if we lived here together! That's the only thing I miss, a colleague from home, you know, a buddy to mess around with. I'm not complaining, I've got plenty of friends, but none are my folk. They're colleagues, they party and stuff, but they've got another style, they're more reserved. If you came here, we'd take this city by storm."

"I'd love to move here but I can't. In the first place, Radu needs me to transport his merchandise to Bucharest. What else can he do with the grass? You know he wouldn't trust anybody else to do it. Plus, I don't know what Cristina would think of it, she might like living here, but her job's in Bucharest, and besides, what could she do here?"

"You're right about Radu, but we could find a solution, and Cristina would immediately find a job here. Prague is the paradise of international companies because this is a polyglot city. You find all the nations of the world here, and these firms need as many native speakers as they can get for their businesses. And, because prices here are comparatively lower than those in other European capitals, the companies pay lower taxes, they hire cheaper offices, and pay less than in other big cities. I'm sure she'd find a job with one of these firms without a hitch. I've noticed she's an excellent speaker of English, she has a higher education diploma, and the extra training she might need would be paid by the firm."

"I'll talk to her and see what she thinks about it...and we'll also talk to Radu, but I don't think he'll be very pleased with the idea. But you never know what to expect, he always thinks of a solution. It'd be awesome if he moved here but he wouldn't think of leaving his mountains for all the riches in the world, the nutty bloke!"

"No, I don't think he'd change it for the world. He belongs to the place, the Carpathians perfectly agree with him and he wouldn't move to a city crawling with people. Anyway, when he comes here in about two weeks to ship the merchandise, let's talk to him and see what he thinks. You never know what ideas he might spit up."

The relationship between Lorin and Stefan was more open than the one with Radu, but, at the same time, each felt closer to Radu than to each other and both thought of him as their best friend, even if they had a brotherly love for each other too. Radu had a different approach though. He loved the two boys equally with all his heart, considering each his best friend in his own way. Stefan was the party-man, the soul of the party, always surrounded by beautiful women and invariably relaxed and jovial, as if nothing bothered him. Radu liked Stefan's adventurous spirit, always in search of new experiences. His sole purpose was to have as much fun as possible. And life had always given him chances to keep the endless fiesta going. His style got him occasional nicknames from his friends like "The Prodigal Son" or "The Traveler."

On the other hand, Lorin was the most loyal man Stefan had ever met. Hard as a rock, he had always been there for him when needed, and he knew he would do anything for him and for those he loved. Even though he lacked Stefan's versatility or Radu's depth, Lorin was the top number one reliable friend and confidant.

Likewise, the families of the three boys were very different, even though the three of them had spent their childhood in the same neighborhood. Radu came from a family of intellectuals with a very old pedigree; his genealogical tree could be traced as far back as the 1600s. Lorin's family was modest, his folks were factory workers - the first generation who had migrated from the country to the city. Stefan and his sister had been brought up by their mother, their father having deserted them when the boy was very little in order start a new family with a younger woman. Stefan hated his guts and had forbidden him to ever get even near his mother, his sister, or himself.

"Hey, Lorin, guess who's coming by next week.The thugs from London, Razvan, Bogdan, and some other guys in their gang. Bogdan called me yesterday to tell me they're coming."

"That's so cool, I haven't seen them for ages. I guess they're coming to do some card cloning. What the fuck else could they do in Prague?"

"Well, he didn't say when we spoke on the phone, he just said they'd come by. Of course that's why they're coming – to clone cards and dick around here and elsewhere. They've eaten away at England."

These boys' way of earning a living was rather complicated, both because they used illegal, top quality equipment in their activities and because they ran a high risk of being spotted by the authorities, their businesses always leaving virtual traces behind. Their method of making money was to put card information-reading devices onto ATMs; this device was called "the pussy," and when the pussy was taken back from the ATM, it was connected to another device called "the tomcat" in order to clone the respective credit cards used by the bank's clients. Thus, the card owners had no idea that somebody else has had access to his bank account until it was too late. The boys shared the credit cards amongst themselves before they had been read and before knowing the amount of money in each account so they all had an equal chance. If, at the beginning, the execution methods were rather rudimentary, they improved in time, as they had to be one step ahead of the police who used their own hackers to spot the criminals. The main difference between this kind of crime and others is that here they needed IT people, without whom these devices could not be made. Even if most of the risk is assumed by soldiers who place them and then take them back from the ATMs, this could not be done without those who calculate and invent new programs and new devices for this kind of activity.

This kind of crime is committed mainly by Romanians, who make up more than 95 % of this category of criminals. This is so not only due to the Romanians' resourcefulness and their endless search for shortcuts to getting rich, but also to the fact that Romania has the most, and widest range of, hackers. The cases of Romanians breaking the accounts of the most important governmental or private institutions in order to withdraw information are considerable. In Romania, the line between being a criminal and a taxpayer is very ambiguous, every person being a potential criminal when given the opportunity. The high level of knowledge the IT graduates have and the large number of calculus specialists in this country combined with the low salaries and the low standard of living make almost any IT graduate a candidate for the profitable business of credit card cloning.

When their friends from London arrived at Prague, Stefan and Lorin were waiting for them in one of the coffee shops in the center, giving them the address of the bar for their GPS. Five of the boys had come, which was almost their whole team of eight; the other three being away in Russia at that time for the same purpose, that of withdrawing the money from the cards cloned in London.

"It took you some time to get here, folks!" Stefan greeted their friends when he saw them at the bar entrance. They had had to ring the doorbell and were granted access after a sign made by Stefan to the barman, whom he knew very well.

"Hi there, good to see you, guys. I hadn't heard from you for ages but Gigi told me you're in Prague and he gave me your number."

"You mean Gigi Japca? Oh, yeah, I talked to him a month ago. He said he'd come by for some card cloning. How are you doing, you wackos? You're here on business, right?"

"Yeah, man, you never know where to do business these days; they've set limits on cards everywhere. Last month we went to Costa Rica to take money out, now we have some guys in Russia, and I've heard Slovakia's a good place too. There's almost no place left. England's kaput, and so are France, Germany, the Netherlands, Italy. How are you doing, you're dicking around here, eh? Well, you keep it bouncing, bro, the city's gorgeous. I've been here before. Are you nuts, rolling your cigarettes here on the table? Don't they start barking?" asked Bogdan, noticing Lorin had just finished crafting a joint.

Stefan answered with a smile: "Hey, cool it, man, this ain't London. In Prague you smoke where you want, and this bar's a coffee shop. You buy your grass from the bar and you smoke it here, if that's what you prefer. Can't you see everybody's got a joint?"

"Yeah, man, you're right, I see it now. That's a fucking free country, bro. I thought only Amsterdam was so fucking cool!"

"No, there's more freedom here. In Amsterdam they're closing down the boutiques, the place is full of pricks fucking it up. They say they're planning a bill providing the right to buy grass from coffee shops only for local people, they'll be given a card from the city hall and only they'll be able to buy it. On top of that, I've heard they're planning to close down the Red Light District; they've had enough of its racket. So, this'll be the capital of fucking entertainment, bro. I picked the right time to moor here. How are you, men, how are things in London?"

"It's okay, basically, as you know, it's crazy like hell and hectic as ever, but the hub of everything. We've recently had problems with a crew there but we sorted it out. We paid the Russians for protection."

"Are you nuts, man? What crew, bro, Romanians?"

"Yeah, man, there's a gang of Romanians, most of them from Moldova, two of them from Galati, Ucu and Faur, and they scare the shit out of those who clone cards, bro. They wait till they see you've taken out big dough, and they know everything 'cause they're involved in all the monkey businesses the Romanians run in London, and when they hear you've hit it big, they break down your door and torture you till you give them the money. Most of the people send the money home once they've taken it out, and that's why they work them over for a whole day till the victims call home to ask for the money to be sent back so that they can pay them. They burn them, cut them, torture them, and nobody can turn them in 'cause they bully only Romanians cloning cards.

"They're a big crew, about fifteen assholes, and nobody dares fuck with them in London. They're the most famous infamous Romanians there. They worked us over a few months ago, and took from us all the money we'd made, the fucking bastards, but now we give a share to the Russian mafia and they leave us alone. They can't fuck with the Russians, no matter how fucking hard they are."

"Well, Ucu and Faur are friends with Radu, they were in the same room in prison; they're still in touch on the phone. I've known Faur since he was a child, we were schoolmates. I've never had anything to do with Ucu, he's too fucking insane, but Radu gets along well with both."

"Yeah, I know they're buddies. Radu is wackier than them, bro, I bet they get along well. By the way, how is he? I haven't seen him for many years."

"He's fine, man, happy to be the owner of Romania's champion. He trained him into an invincible gladiator. He's got himself a Dutch lover, and when the pussy pays her visits, he's in cloud number nine. I haven't seen him so happy for a long time. What else can I say? He's the same guy living in the mountains with his dogs and a joint in his muzzle to calm his demons down. The dog he has now, Bronco, is one of a kind, bro. When he fought his dad in the final, he used a new technique, raised him from the ground, and then played his game through. There's no other dog to compete with him."

"I'm glad to hear that. I know he's always been keen on pit bull fights. It's good to hear he achieved his goal, and I know the three of you have always been like brothers. That's what truly matters, man. Money slips through your fingers, women come and go, but true friends are there forever."

After one more hour of chatting at the bar, followed by a copious Czech dinner and a few hours spent snorting lines of coke and drinking rum in a club downtown, Stefan decided he should show them the true face of Prague. He took them to one of the most successful after-hours in the capital, whose owner was an acquaintance of his. The friends from London appreciated the atmosphere in the club: an intimate orange light filtered through beautifully colored fabrics hanging from the ceiling and enveloping the leather couches in the cubicles. Relaxing music rendered the club atmosphere even warmer, just the kind one needs at that late hour, unlike the tough beats they had listened to in the other club. There was also a lower level, much darker, lit only by dark light neons behind the bar, and from the main room, if you wanted to get to the toilets, you had to walk along a long and very dark corridor, flanked, on one side, by sofas where people were engaged in touching and kissing, and on the other side by tiny dark rooms, lit only by black neons, where the most interesting activities were carried out. Although this lower level, where the atmosphere was more underground than above, was more to the taste of Lorin and Stefan, their friends from London preferred to be above where they could see and hear each other better. They were quite surprised when, going to the gents, they saw that it was packed with women who were waiting in line. The toilets being taken, the boys had to use the urinals, and they did so rather reluctantly, given the fact that many feminine pairs of eyes were staring at them, looking like wild creatures with smiling faces.

Bogdan, hesitating to take his dick out yet amused by the situation, asked the girls: "Why are you queuing up here? The ladies' toilet is over there."

A smashing blonde, with typically Czech features and an intensity in her glance given by the nocturnal cocaine consumption, told him in a most sexy tone: "Well, the ladies' toilet is full of gents. Everybody goes there for a fuck and a snort 'cause it's cleaner than the gents' so we come here. The queue's shorter. But don't be shy, go ahead, do it as if we weren't here!"

"I'm not shy, I'm just worried I might scare you with my dragon, 'cause I'm not sure you've seen anything like it before!"

"Well, well, let's have a look. I've seen some dragons before but I always love surprises. Maybe when the toilet's free, we can go in and I can have a closer look."

While they were talking, one of the toilet doors opened and a couple went out laughing, and the Romanian guy, wasting no time, took the blonde by the hand and dragged her in. Her friend hurried in, saying she had to pee too.

When they left the club around lunch, together with some of the girls they had taken with them after deciding to continue the party together, the boys felt extremely high. They made for a bungalow near a lake, recommended by Stefan, who had rented bungalows on other similar occasions, and the party continued until next morning when, knackered and smoking a last joint before falling asleep, one of the guys from London told them: “Now I can understand why you love living in Prague so much, bro. I’ve been living in London for ten years and I’ve never had the fun I’ve had here!”

Chapter 20

When Stefan entered the house, Jana was waiting for him, obviously out of sorts. She burst out the very moment the Romanian closed the door. "Stefan, are you out of your mind? You've been missing for two days. You text me and then you switch off your mobile? Where have you been? You're not getting enough pussy at work and you need to fill in your spare time with more of it? Since your friend came here, you seem to have gone completely nuts. I don't see much of you, in fact, too little! Here I am, worrying like crazy about you, twisting the worst scenarios around in my skull, and you're fucking around with your buddies, is that it? I have no idea if the Romanian chicks you've been with agreed to it, but I sure don't! So, you'd better make up your mind if you want to be with me or not, and change this attitude. You're not eighteen anymore when life's a continuous fiesta! And now, tell me, where have you been?"

Although Stefan had expected this kind of reaction on the part of the Czech girl, and in the cab on his way home he had tried to be prepared and refrain from letting himself get pissed off by it, the verbal fierceness with which Jana had 'welcomed' him and her attitude drove him insane. This was because he very often got this kind of reproach from women, whom he dumped without exception. He hated it when somebody was trying to force their point of view on him and limit his actions. He also had a hangover, which made his head pulsate with pain and a sense of fatigue that called for peace and a soft bed where he could sink and sleep for the next ten hours. The happiness he had felt was soon replaced by its opposite.

Dark clouds of anger were gathering on the sky of his soul, warning of an imminent storm. Stefan hated this sense of disappointment when he moved from a mood which uplifted him and became his supreme *raison d'être* to negative feelings, which he felt took him down to the abyss of frustration. It was the same kind of feeling he had after each successful party, when he knew the show was over and he had to put up with the thought of returning home, which was ten times more intense because of the drugs leaving his body.

It made him feel like a child being taken to bed by his parents when he wanted to stay up and play with the other kids. He loathed with every fiber of his being this sense of frustration and everybody causing it; these persons being, more often than not, girlfriends waiting for him at home, full of reproaches. This is why he had had no long-term commitment. He could not understand why the beautiful thing he had with each of them had to be debased by these feelings of possession and reproach. He had always felt better on his own, enjoying what women had to offer, but turning the tables when he felt things had become too serious and the respective woman started to claim him and his way of being.

He replied to Jana in a very sharp tone and a coarse voice from all the booze and cocaine over the last two days. "Listen, Jana, I can do without all this big fuss! I thought that you were different and that you liked me for what I am, but I see you're like the rest of them; you only want to change me and turn me into your pet. I really wanted to be with you, I've never felt so good with a woman before, but it seems that's not possible. I see no point in continuing the argument. I'll rent a flat one of these days and I'll pop by and take my belongings. Nice to meet you!"

Jana was wrong-footed by her boyfriend's attitude. She had expected he would apologize and promise he would not repeat it, as most Czech men do. The fact that women are the dominant partners in the Czech couple is well known. Before she could say anything, Stefan had turned around and left. He called for a cab and gave the driver the address of Lorin's hotel. His friend was half asleep when Stefan knocked at his door.

"Hi, bro, what's the matter, has your woman kicked you out?"

"The fucking bitch. She started fucking my ass as soon as I got in. I thought we'd be together, but no way, man, I'm just fine on my own. I don't know how you could live with the same woman for all these bloody years, bro."

"Well, Cristina ain't the woman to do that, bro. She lets me mind my own business as long as she knows she's my one and only love and I'll always come back to her. Plus she has more confidence in me. I'm not a gigolo like you, so she doesn't expect women to jump at me. I hardly ever cheat on her. Well, cool it, bro, let's smoke a last one and then let's go to bed, I'm knackered. I haven't partied like this in ages. You'll see what you'll do when we wake up."

"Yeah, bro, you're right. I'll rent a condo somewhere and that's that. Why I was planning to stay with that mad woman I can't say. You should have heard the loudspeaker, bro, I thought she'd hit me. Well, this is the custom here, the bitches bully the goofs and they grow up thinking this is normal. That's why most of the chicks here turn into sluts, nobody dares argue with them. Do you know what Napoleon said about the Czechs when he conquered them? That the women are whores and the men cowards. If you read any novel written here centuries ago, you'll see how the counts and nobles all over the world would come here for the beauty of the women, and that's become the legend: that they are the best fucks and they can do whatever they fucking please.

"Most of the Czech women I talked to told me they don't like Czech guys because they are neglectful and careless. And they're right. Look at the discrepancy in their appearance. Men are usually big-bellied from the beer, which is cheaper here than water, and they wear the same clothes for a whole month, while the women are chic and sexy. And they know it and accept women's infidelity as something normal. There were several times when a woman with the boyfriend or husband in tow, and even holding his hand, came to me and gave me her card or asked for my number. That could not happen in Romania; there'd be a hell of a show if somebody did that. But it's okay with them.

"A few weeks ago, I was with a Czech guy in a bar and I knew his partner was a slut. She'd fucked other colleagues of mine and she cock-teased me once when he was at the gents. Anyway, the guy was furious with her, they had just had a row, but on other grounds. And I thought that was the right moment to ask him, and I interrogated him whether he thought his woman fucked around or not. He said he wouldn't know, maybe she did, but that was not the problem. What really mattered was their domestic dispute. In Romania, if a woman does that, she is considered the greatest slut and no man hooks up with her again, but here, most of them are like that. That's why Prague is the perfect city to be a bachelor, but if you commit yourself to them, you're done for; they have you under their thumb."

Meanwhile, Lorin had finished rolling the joint and let his friend cool his nerves. He had always admired him for the way in which he would always find an explanation in any situation and the way in which he always turned the tables in his favor. This gave him far more freedom than if he had known feelings like guilt or remorse.

"You'll manage, bro, you know you always find a way out. I think you'll be with her. I've never seen you so head over heels, but pay her a bit more attention. She's a woman, you know, not merely a slut from Galati who falls for you just 'cause she's well fucked. Anyway, you'll see what'll come of it. Now take a whiff and let's have some sleep, I'm dead tired. Tonight we're meeting the Londoners again, they're leaving and it will be a goodbye get together."

In the evening, they met up with their friends again, who thanked them for the good time they had together in Prague and then left for Bratislava. They hoped that the capital of Slovakia would offer them a more significant capture than that in Prague where, even if they had had the time of their lives, they hadn't withdrawn so much money with the cloned cards.

When he switched on his phone, Stefan had more than twenty missed calls from Jana, which confirmed to him what he wanted to believe; that she loved him too much to lose him just because he wouldn't make any concessions for her. That she had actually fallen in love with him, knowing exactly what kind of person he is, and she would not try and change him. Even if he would not admit it to Lorin, he also wanted to be with her. He already missed her touch, though only a few hours had passed since he had seen her. At the same time, he knew that they could not be together unless she stopped reproaching him and wishing to be in control, because he liked his life style too much to pay heed to changes or adjustments for anybody's sake, even the woman he was in love with as he had never been before.

Two weeks later, they picked Irinel up from Antwerp harbor. The lad was beaming with joy and he was delighted that he had accomplished his mission without a hitch. Even though he didn't know exactly the amount of his share, he knew for sure he will never have seen so much money before, and he had already mentally spent a few thousand euros on stuff he had dreamed of for a long time.

Back in Prague, Stefan contacted the chemist who was to turn the paste into powder; the fellow owned a lab and was not going to charge anything. He wanted, in exchange, a share of this pure cocaine since he was an avid consumer and was always in search for a pure product. The fact that now he had the paste in his hands – and that it was the purest product possible – was a dream of his. As a Czech, he was used to the flexibility of the law, and he knew he had nothing to fear since he was not involved in selling the product. The risk he was taking was fairly small, and the reward a lot more significant than the risk.

Stefan, Lorin, and Irinel witnessed the whole process of turning the paste into powder because they couldn't put their entire confidence in the drug-addicted chemist. One kilo of paste gave one kilo and a quarter of powder after the drying process. They gave the quarter to the chemist, and they cut their kilo twice, getting two kilos of fantastic purity, which they cut again in two, thus getting four kilos. Even though cut twice, their product was approximately sixty percent pure, compared to the twenty to thirty percent in the merchandise sold in Prague and in Europe in general. They split the four kilos into one-kilo bags then they called Radu to let him know that the process was over and that he should join them for sell-off.

"Hi, Radu, are you coming over on the trip you were planning?"

"Yeah, bro, sure thing, everything's fine with you?"

"Yeah, yeah, fine. So when are you popping over?"

"Well, I'm leaving tomorrow so I'll be there the day after. I'm driving over 'cause I'm bringing puppies back with me. I've already made arrangements with two dog kennels and booked my Staffie pups. I'll take two bitches and a male. They have such cute faces, I can't wait to see them!"

"Okay, Radu, you let us know when you're in the neighborhood, bro!"

"Okay, Stefan, see you soon."

Radu's decision to buy Staffordshire bull terrier pups from the Czech Republic had not been made because Stefan lived there or he had planned a trip to the area but primarily because the Czech Republic has one of the best dog kennels in Europe. He had made arrangements for a bitch and a male from the biggest hatchery for the breed, which had more than twenty dogs, all of them champions and champion lines. Right then, there were three bitches with young pups, the pups being from different lines, and from the second hatchery he had booked one more bitch. He had arranged to take them after they had finished the transaction with Stefan's clients.

Radu embraced his mates when he reached Prague and afterwards they went to Stefan's new flat. Modern and furnished, it was situated in a very old building in the historic center of the capital. Although he was very pleased with his new place, he was aware that he had only rented it to show Jana that if she wanted to be with him, she had to be more flexible. Irinel was the first person Radu addressed after they were seated around the table in the living room.

"Well, Irinel, how was your trip, bro? Any problems?"

"No, Radu, everything worked as planned. I had my own room on the ship, I hid the skeleton in a closet in a little hideaway. I used a screwdriver to make room for it and hid it safely, but I didn't have to worry, nobody checked my bag. When I got there, I got off with the sailors, as the captain told me. They looked at my passport and then off I went. I can hardly wait to do it again. Now I know my way, I don't need any company."

"Are you that sure you want to keep doing it? You know that this success may be a failure next time, don't you?"

"Yeah, Radu, I do, I want to do it. If I get caught, at least I'll have my own savings."

"OK, we'll see whether you need to do it again. Let's finish with this one first. Stefan, when are we seeing our people?"

"Well, we made an appointment with one of the guys tomorrow, and after we sort it out with him, I've got someone else to do business with. We'll place at least three kilos right away, maybe we can get rid of the whole amount, let's see what they say. Anyway, they've never seen such good quality stuff, and if we sell it at a reasonable price, we'll start a competition."

"Listen," said Radu, "a gram is worth eighty euros here, right? This means people need to buy it for forty to make their own stuff. I suggest we sell it for thirty to make sure we set up a good market. We'll get a lot of profit out of it anyway, let's not be greedy. What matters more is that people come and buy from us again. If we sell it for thirty, they'll probably cut it again, so they buy it for fifteen, and if they sell it to dealers for sixty, the dealers get a profit of twenty per gram out of the eighty they sell it for on the streets, they still get a profit of almost fifty per gram. Bro! I don't think they ever got so much money before. We sell it for this price once or twice, and if it works, we go for a higher price when they are hooked."

Lorin and Stefan agreed, even if they initially had in mind a slightly higher price. However, Radu was right. Being a new business, it was very important that they target faithful clients who would, in turn, target their faithful clients; that is, the dealers, and, most important, their clients, those who consumed the product.

Radu continued the dialogue with his friends: “Stefan, what other businesses do you think we might do here? It’s fairly cheap, the laws are good, it’s full of tourists, I’m sure there’s more potential. What other businesses would you recommend?”

“Bro, chicks would smash the business records. I know a Russian who’s got a few chicks, and he won’t have them work in a club, he makes arrangements over the phone. He’s rented a few condos downtown and brought a few chicks from the former Soviet Union. He put an advert in the newspaper and now his mobile won’t stop ringing, bro. There are inconveniences, though, you know, when you’ve got chicks on the market, there’s trouble. I wouldn’t bother getting into that!”

“Yeah, you’re right, let’s stay away from the pimping business. We could bring somebody over to deal with it, though, and we’d take our share. We’ll see about that. Anything else? Does “agriculture” stand a chance?”

“Yeah, man, it’s okay. If you rent a house outside the city, not very far, and you don’t raise any suspicions, you can do your business for an eternity and you’ll never get any visits. This business is done mostly by the Vietnamese but the best quality stuff is grown by the locals. You only have to rent a house with a cellar and hire a person to do it.”

“Well, that’s the business, bro. If we rent one of those old houses with a huge cellar, we can get fifteen to twenty kilos in one go. But we need somebody reliable to grow it and an outlet to sell it to. There’s no point in selling it here, it’s too cheap in this country.”

“No, there’s no point selling it in Czech, we need to find some other place. I know where we can find the best place. In the countries with a lot of Arabians and blacks ‘cause they bring hashish and you can hardly find grass there, countries like France or Spain, but I think the best is Italy. All you can find there is hash. I had a terrible time getting grass when I went there and it was very expensive and not very good. You have to be cautious in Italy, though, it's full of pigs and snitches."

"Yeah, man, you're right! We can easily get a few kilos per month to Italy, only if we have a contact. Do we know anybody reliable there? We need a good fellow to either do it or to know mother fuckers interested in buying wholesale."

Lorin broke in: "I have a friend in Turin, bro, he was my mate in jail in Germany. The fucker is from Suceava, he's been living in Italy for several years and distributes hash there but not in the street. I don't know where he takes it or who he sells it to, but I went to his place once and he had a few kilos of it. I could talk to him and see what he says."

"You do that. After we conclude this business, you take a trip to Italy and talk to the guy, but make sure he's serious. We could give him a few kilos from my cellar first and see how it goes. There's no point in growing it and not being able to sell it. There're no customs between the Czech Republic and Italy, we can load it in the car or on the train and off it goes. I'd like to close down my cellar. I've had enough of watering the plants and taking care of them, plus if I get a visit from the cops, I won't be able to find a way out of it, I'm sitting right on top of it. Sophie is planning to move to Poiana and I'd like to ease it, be less stressed. It would be good if we sorted it out that way, plus there'll be more money."

"Are you crazy? You want to stop growing the plants? First you say the only pit bull fights you'll ever do again are those where Bronco fights, now you're saying you no longer want to grow grass...you're getting old, bro! If you no longer grow it, you no longer need me to take it to Bucharest. I was saying to Stefan the other day that I'd like to move to Prague but I can't because you need me."

"Are you serious, you want to move here? Well, go ahead, mate, the city's great. Besides...there's one more pair of eyes on this merchandise from Peru. If it works, we'll get a lot of money, more than ever before, and we'll need to be vigilant about our moves."

"Hey, Radu, wouldn't you like to move here too? Do you realize how cool it'd be if we all lived in the same city again? It'd be like in the old days, only in a much nicer city. Plus we'd take Prague by storm; this is an excellent place for many businesses."

"No, bro, I'm not leaving Poiana. You know I don't like the hustle and bustle of the city. I like the mountains, especially now if Sophie moves there, it'll be cool."

Although a worthwhile attempt had been made, the lads knew that Radu wouldn't move from his beloved Carpathian Mountains for all the money in the world. The wilderness of the place echoed the depths of his dark and independent being. He felt a metaphysical bond with those Transylvanian mountains; they gave him shelter and protection, as they had done with his ancestors for thousands of years. He wouldn't leave that place for the world. The Carpathians were his home in a more visceral sense than owning a house means in the modern sense of the word.

The next day they met up with Stefan's Czech friend, to whom they sold a kilo, and the following day they got rid of two more kilos. One was sold to a wholesale dealer who worked with Karla, the former German pop singer who now ran one of the most successful clubs in Europe, Jana's good friend; and the other kilo to an acquaintance of hers, the owner of the biggest gay club in Prague. Not only was he a great consumer but most of the homosexuals in Prague got their supplies from him, thus he turned the clients of his club into faithful clients.

They decided that Lorin should take the remaining kilo with him to Bucharest to get it sold there for a higher price than the price they asked in Prague. Before he went with Irinel to buy the Staffie pups and return to Romania, Radu gave Lorin his last piece of advice.

"Take care not to have it with you at the customs, bro. Take a train and hide it in a compartment somewhere. There's a panel in every toilet, open one with the pliers and hide it there behind the pipes. Take care and wipe your fingerprints off the pack before putting it there, and don't place it in the toilet of your car; find a place a few cars from yours. And take a whole kit with you, not just the pliers. That'd be the only evidence against you in case they find the merchandise; take the most expensive kit and, if asked, you tell them you bought it because in Romania you can't find quality stuff, and so they have no evidence against you."

After they shared the money for the three kilos of coke, which was ninety thousand euros, the boys each went his own way. Stefan stayed in Prague, he was about to start shooting a new porn production in a few days; Lorin took the train to Bucharest with his luggage of over thirty thousand euros, and Radu and Irinel got into the car and set off to the Staffie hatcheries, where the pups were waiting for their new owner.

The male was two months old, very stout, with a big head and broad back, obviously more of a bull than a terrier, exactly as Radu had wanted it to be. He called him Bullyson, even though his pedigree name was different. The bitch was one week younger than him, a bit slimmer and with a more slender waist, but very swift and clever: he named her Atris. A few hours later, they got out of the jeep in the yard of the other hatchery, in the east of the Czech Republic, closer to Romania, where he bought the other bitch; she had a wonderful temperament, and he named her Drucilla, or Dru for short.

This was a decisive step in Radu's life. For the first time since he had his first pit bull, he was able to opt for another breed. And he was very happy with his choice. These lovely pups were exceptional quality and had a fantastic temperament, playing all the time as if they hadn't just been taken away from their mother and siblings.

On their one-day long trip home, the two boys chatted, and Radu thought it was time he had yet another discussion with Irinel that wasn't about dogs, especially if the lad was so determined to be part of his world and this kind of business.

"Well, Irinel, in this kind of business, you need to be exceptionally cautious at all times and to choose only the people you trust without any shadow of doubt and you're sure won't turn you in if caught. If it weren't for snitches, the authorities would be able to prosecute only five percent of the people they catch. They will always try the same method. They'll tell you the other people you got arrested with have turned you in and your only way out is to turn them or others in. Mind my words, don't you ever do that in your entire life, you young thug! That's how the fools get caught in the net and they turn one another in; very often, they have no evidence against you to keep you there, but you turn yourself in if you start talking. No matter what, you never talk to the police.

"That's why it's very important for you to completely trust the people you do business with, and that they trust you, and you know you won't turn each other in. Those who squeal are the most despicable scum of the world, and they only deserve to be razor blade fucked. But the fuckin' system has made separate compartments for them and other pedophiles or raping scums to protect them from the rest of the inmates, fuck the son of a bitches. Prisons are full of people who have to share their cells while the cocksuckers who snitch and the pedophiles enjoy all the privileges. There's minimum security for them. I got my hands on one of those while in jail, I won't tell you what I did to him, or you'll throw up. Lorin too has worked for a week on the fucker who snitched on him. That's what all these assholes deserve, fuck their bastard families. If you're turned in, you do your penance and you never speak to the cops, little bro!"

Chapter 21

A few weeks later, Radu received a new match offer for Bronco. This came from an old friend of his, Leon, or Varan, which means Komodo Dragon in Romanian. An addict of pit bull fights, he was now only a spokesman for those who wanted to organize this match. Leon was from Iasi, one of the largest and most picturesque cities in Romania, situated in the north east of the country, close to the border with the Republic of Moldova. The guys who requested the fight were from Bessarabia, and they owned the champion of the city of Chishinau, the capital of the Republic of Moldova. The inhabitants of the Romanian city always had business with their neighbors across the Prut River, and although the Moldovans used to belong to the former Soviet Union, the Iasians had more to do with them than with their Romanian co-nationals. Moldova was annexed to Russia only in 1812 and named Bessarabia as a consequence of their victory in the war between Russia and the Ottoman Empire; up to that point, the people on both sides of the Prut belonged to the same nation. The language of the Republic of Moldova is, in fact, Romanian, spoken with a heavy Russian accent, even if the people from Moldova often use phrases that sound funny to Romanian ears.

The inhabitants of this small republic are brave people, toughened by the hardships they've had to face along the centuries, and the members of the local mafia, also known as rackets, are among the most famous and feared criminals in Europe. The Romanians, being familiar with the fierceness and efficiency of these mercenaries, use their services for paid killings, attempts on people's lives or reclaimings. They are also popular because of the relatively low prices for which they carry out these contracts.

This fierceness is typical of the inhabitants of both sides of the Prut River, the Romanian Moldavians being considered the most feared inhabitants of this country. Since time immemorial, the chroniclers used to say that one hundred Moldavians were more efficient in battle than hundreds of other soldiers, the Moldavians being famous both for their bravery and for their extreme drinking and partying. These characteristics have remained unchanged to this very day. Iasi and the neighboring cities are plagued by the conflicts between meddling clans, which cause havoc whenever they meet, whether at a crowded crossroads, gyms, or, especially, clubs. Most of the DJs in Bucharest and other places in the country avoid the clubs in Iasi because of the extreme violence they witnessed when they had to do with this easily-irritated area.

However, Iasi is not famous only for the rather violent outbursts of its inhabitants; it is also one of the most important cultural centers of the country. This city on seven hills is the source of some of the greatest Romanian artists, and the first modern university in the country was founded here. Being much closer to the capital of the Republic of Moldova, Chishinau, than to its own capital, Bucharest, and speaking a Moldavian idiom fairly different from the rest of the country, the Iasi inhabitants are a bit ostracized when they travel across their own country, which increases the disdain most of them feel for the rest of the Romanians whom they consider deficient in stamina and spoilt.

Leon, an inhabitant of Iasi, with solid roots there, belonged in this category; he had a particular contempt for the people in Bucharest and, in general, for all the Romanians who were not from his area. This he displayed ostentatiously whenever he had the chance. Towards Radu, on the other hand, he had nothing but respect and admiration, seeing in him all the qualities of a warrior, which he admired so much in his ancestors. The two boys idolized the same historical figure, namely Stephen the Great, Moldavia’s ruler five centuries before. Leon was one of the leaders of the world of interlopers in Iasi, being in charge of a fairly numerous and very tough group, and he had approached Radu proposing this match at the request of the Bessarabians because he had many business dealings with them, from weapons through drugs to prostitutes. Everything that came from the Republic of Moldova through Romania, and then further to Western Europe, would go through IaSi first, and Leon had both hands and arms up to the elbows in these dealings.

Radu gathered information on the nature of his relationship with those he was going to organize the match with. "Well, tell me, Varan, do you know these guys? What kind of dog do they have, and have you seen it fighting?"

"Yeah, Radu, I've had some dealings with them. What can I say? You know what the Bessarabians are like. They have a very good dog called Caligula. He's a tough one and he hasn't spared any opponent so far. They called me today to ask me to talk to you, as they've heard you've got the champion of Romania, and they wanted to know whether you would let him face the champion of Moldova. They said you should set the stake if you approve of the event. And if you do, Iasi is the best place, being halfway between their place and yours. So...what do think? May Bronco go ahead?"

"Yeah, bro, why not? I was looking for a match for Bronco and I see nobody in Romania dares let their dogs compete with him after he battered his dad. Tell them that if they want to do it, we can arrange for it to happen in two months for about fifteen grand. Talk to them, and if it's okay with them, it's a deal."

"Okay, Radu, I'll let them know. And how are you, everything's okay?"

"Yeah, yeah, I'm not complaining. Well, maybe we can have a chat when I come over, like in the old days. We barely saw each other at the match with Joker."

"Yeah, bro, I cannot wait to see you again. I'll make arrangements for a party when you come. You'll stay at my place that night or as many nights as you wish to spend in my city. Anyway, we'll have another of Bronco's victories to celebrate, I'll bet on it!"

"Okay, Leon, I'll start training Bronco, and I'll see you in Iasi in two months."

Radu knew he had to take advantage of Bronco's physical condition and his youth, because this condition started to decline once the animal reached the age of four or five years old. Besides, a few months had already passed since the fight with Joker, and Bronco had completely recovered. He had already begun the light training sessions for a few weeks now. Another two months of intensive training were going to get him in prime condition and ready for this Caligula. He had heard of the dog, though he had never seen it fight.

Irinel helped him with the training only in the first month; in the second, he went to Peru again, this time on his own. Lorin had sold the kilo transported in the hull of the train to a cocaine dealer who, after buying half a kilo, had returned a few days later for the other half, with nothing but praise for the Peruvian product.

"Lorin, this sells like bread fresh from the oven, people won't stop asking for it. This Saturday I placed two hundred grams in just one club. The word has spread and there's an endless flow of demand, bro. You'd better get some more of it, there's never been this top quality stuff in Bucharest. This'll get both of us rich so when's the new load coming?"

"I can't tell you if there'll be more of it, but be sure if there is, you'll be the dealer!" Lorin answered, pleased with the response to their product, both in Prague and in Bucharest. Anyway, his new dream was to move to the Czech capital, so he could not promise he'd bring cocaine again to Bucharest, especially since it was much more risky to transport and sell it there than in Prague.

The following month, Lorin went to Turin, at Radu's suggestion, in order to talk with his friend about the possibility of setting up a network of grass traffic, since in Italy they smoked mainly the hashish brought from Morocco. Lorin's friend from Suceava, with whom he had spent two years in the German prison, received this proposal with open arms, as he was always in search of new products and he knew that quality grass would sell there much better than hash, which was not as strong and with which people were very familiar. He told Lorin that he sold around two kilos a month, and if he had grass, he would probably sell around three or four kilos a month.

The joy Lorin felt on account of the increase in turnover in the last few months was somehow spoiled by a thought that had started to plague him lately: he felt that his two friends were taking unfair advantage of him. An inner voice kept telling him: "Of course they sent you over again – you place the merchandise in Bucharest, you go to Italy and talk people into new combinations, while we're resting our dicks in bed and waiting for our share in the profit." He always silenced this voice, feeling guilty for the thought, and he invoked reasons to silence the voice talking against his friends: "Stop talking this nonsense, they're busy. Radu's got a fight with Bronco, Stefan's got shoots, you're the only one who has the time to travel. Plus this is your business, you've always been the one who gave business a jolt, even if Radu has been the architect. Money's better than ever, you're free and healthy, stop whining like a pussy."

It so happened that, on the day of the fight, none of Radu's friends was in the country. Lorin hadn't returned from Italy, Stefan had shoots in Paris, and Irinel was on board the ship on his way back to Europe. Radu had never been without his friends around for any of the fights he had organized, but he wouldn't let himself be disturbed by this. He left in the morning of that day for Iasi with the same winning spirit he always had before a fight. Nevertheless, that feeling of doom that had found a nest in his soul a few months before kept gnawing him, and he couldn't get rid of it despite his best efforts. All he could do was to drive away those feelings for the time being, but his inability to completely root out that cold snake salaciously coiling through the thickets of his emotions intensified his anxiety and that strange premonition that something bad was about to happen. He was aware of the fact that, under those circumstances, he'd be better not going through with the fight since he transmitted all his feelings to his dog, but at the same time he would have never allowed a feeling springing from any weakness change his plans or way of being. However, it was the first time that he had doubts about the result of the fight, even though he had complete trust in Bronco and his unmatched gladiator qualities.

When he arrived at Iasi, Leon was waiting for him at the place they had arranged, and he beckoned to him to follow him. They drove to the exit from the city, and soon they reached the Bucium Forest, where Leon turned at some point down a forest road that ran to the heart of wilderness. Radu knew this place. He had been there a few years before, for some fights in which he had taken part. The pit was in the middle of the forest, not far from the log cabin of a friend of Leon's, who also had some fighting pit bulls.

He soon set eyes upon Caligula; a very stately dog, yellow with a white chest, whose ears had been cut off, which he thought was rather strange. However, he knew that for certain dogs it was an advantage if they had a compatible fighting style. If they were bitten on the ear, they would not attempt to set themselves free from the grip but, instead, they would bite their opponent's nose or chest. Caligula was a bit taller than Bronco and a bit broader in the shoulders, around two kilos heavier but well-conditioned. This pleased Radu. He knew that Bronco was used to fighting slightly heavier dogs, and it even gave him an upper hand in this situation due to his fighting style, which was to get under his opponent and use his weight to upset his opponent's balance.

Radu met Caligula's owner, a Bessarabian with the looks of a pirate, a skinhead dressed in a waterproof tracksuit, just like the three compatriots with whom he was in tow. He left Bronco in Leon's care while he was washing Caligula, after which he returned to his beloved dog, which was now in a serious state of agitation, feeling the static electricity before the fight. He kissed him on the muzzle and whispered in his ear: "Get this one down too, boy, knock him out, boy!"

At first impact, Caligula knocked Bronco down, being obviously more stout and stronger than Romania's champion. Bronco jumped to his feet and, grabbing Caligula's chest, he started to shake him frantically, while his opponent thrust his fangs deep into his neck and started to pull with all his might.

Ten minutes after the fight had started, Bronco bit his opponent's ear, and Caligula, as Radu had expected, did not attempt to extricate himself from that position, which would have made Bronco's fangs thrust deeper into the soft tissue, but instead he grabbed Bronco's paw in a very strong grip. Bronco gave out a short whimper when the bones of his paw cracked under the strength of Caligula's bite. He let go of his ear and grabbed his muzzle, which forced the other dog to let go of Bronco's paw and grab his muzzle as well. For a few seconds, the grinding sound produced by the two fighters' fangs, which were now grating against one another, produced awe in the spectators. It was clear to Radu that this was the strongest opponent Bronco had ever met; even if he missed that elegance which characterized Joker, this and other slight drawbacks were compensated by an extraordinary rough force, tenacity, and a very aggressive fighting style.

Half an hour after the beginning of the fight, Bronco already had some rather deep wounds, and the Bessarabian dog was repeatedly knocking him down, which he achieved with relative ease when Bronco managed to stand for a few moments.

Caligula's force was impressive but Radu would not let himself disappointed by this. Deep in his heart, he was sure Bronco would be the winner again even if, in that moment, he did not know exactly how this might occur.

Fifteen minutes later, Bronco was still on the floor, gripping onto the opponent's neck. Caligula, though he was still shaking Bronco, had started to let go for a few seconds in order to be able to breathe. The effort he had put in it, his slightly heavier structure and his fighting style, which meant that he gave his best from the beginning without saving energy for the crucial moments that closed the fight, meant Caligula was breathing more and more heavily. He was failing to exert the impressive strength he had displayed thus far, which Radu took as an evidence of the fact that Bronco would be the winner again. Even if he had been tossed as never before, Bronco had enough energy left to allow him to fight for at least another half an hour, while his opponent could not continue to fight for more than ten or fifteen more minutes. The fact that he had been fighting on the floor gave Bronco extra energy compared to if he had fought standing throughout the fight, even if the wounds suffered were more numerous and deeper than ever.

Feeling that Caligula's batteries were fading, Radu was yelling his heart out, and Bronco obeyed. He managed to stand up without letting go Caligula's neck and, pulling with all his strength towards him, he knocked his opponent down. It was only the third time Caligula had been knocked down during this fight, but it seemed he would remain there this time; he had given up the intention of biting Bronco in that position for almost one minute, despite the Bessarabians' encouragements.

Ten minutes later, the referee separated them, sent them to their corner positions, and let Caligula attack first; the Bessarabian dog tripped twice. He had no stamina left until he got near Bronco, who knocked him down immediately. A few minutes later, the fight was stopped and Bronco declared a winner again.

Radu kissed Bronco on the muzzle and raised him above his head to the crowd's acclamations; except for the four Bessarabians, each person present had hoped Bronco would be the winner. After which, before taking the money from the referee, Radu left the pit to wash away the blood from his dog. Confused feelings were running through his soul at light speed, but the prevailing one was relief at the thought that Bronco had won that fight, despite the negative feelings he had had in the last few months.

While he was leaning over his dog, wiping his body with a damp cloth, he felt suddenly that he couldn't breathe and that somebody was pulling him backwards. He felt a sharp pain in his neck as if he was going to swallow his tongue. He had to straighten his back and, letting go of Bronco, he reached for his neck, without realizing what had happened. Only when he heard the Bessarabians' yawps and saw one of them putting a noose hanging from a long rod around Bronco's neck, like those used by dog catchers, and saw two more Bessarabians with an Uzi machine gun in each hand, did he realize what was going on. He tried to fling himself forward with all his might in order to rid himself of the grip cutting his neck. He was pulling the thick nylon with which the third Bessarabian was holding him from behind, but it was in vain. This one was holding him with the force of a demon, yelling in his ear: "Stop fidgeting, blea, or I'll strangle you! Stand still and you'll live!"

While he felt he was passing out, Radu saw how the one who had taken Bronco away was putting him in the trunk of the second SUV with which they had come, Caligula occupying the first one. His master, who was obviously also the leader of the group, was pointing both Uzis at those present, yelping: "Nobody moves, pizdet! If any of you tries anything, I'll shoot all of you dead! This dog is ours now!"

Then he stepped towards the referee, who stood completely baffled, and took away the money gambled at the fight. After that he turned towards Radu, who was struggling with his last scraps of conscience to get out of the suffocating grip with which the Bessarabian was holding him, and told him: "And you, blea, don't you dare follow us to get him back, or I'll thrust a bullet in that skull of yours! The dog's ours now. After we do a few fights with him, we'll give him back to you, when he gets older."

After that he hit him with the weapon in the under-jaw, making him pass out completely and fall. The one holding him let him drop and took a gun out of his back pocket, which he pointed towards the Romanians. The last words uttered by Caligula's master were: "Don't you try to follow us or we'll shoot the dog and throw him out of the car while driving. You chill and wait for him to be returned to you in a few years, if he lives through it."

When Radu came back to his senses, he saw the two SUVs driving away, leaving behind a cloud of dust. Leon was leaning over him, slapping him to his senses, and telling him in a worried voice:
"They took Bronco away, bro, they stole Bronco!"

Chapter 22

When Stefan found out about Bronco being kidnapped, he was in Paris, shooting a French porno production. Radu briefed him on what had happened and told him he needed him because the next day they were going to Chishinau in order to get Bronco back. He also told him Lorin was due to arrive in Iasi that evening. As soon as he found out about the terrible event, Stefan logged on using one of the laptops in the studio and bought a plane ticket to Iasi, with a stopover in Bucharest for that evening. When he told the director that he had to leave the studios before the film was shot through, the Frenchman was very annoyed, reproaching him by saying he could not just leave whenever he felt like it, that he had a contract-based duty and that he could at least put his business off for two more days or as long as that shoot lasted. All this was uttered in a raised and disrespectful tone. Stefan had no particular sympathy for the Frenchman, and that lack of sympathy had now turned into hatred; he took the contract which the Frenchman had flung in his face, crumpled it, grabbed the director by the collar and forced the crumpled paper into his mouth, his predatory look piercing the scared and baffled look of the Frenchman like a blade reddened in the fire pierces a lump of butter – without a hitch, as things are meant to be.

With a Mephistophelean smile on his symmetrical face, he told him: "Fuck your money. Keep it, and take yesterday's and today's shoots as a gift from me. But if you ever raise your voice again when you speak to me, I'll cut your tendons, you French cocksucker!"

When he let go of him, the director lost his balance, took a few hurried steps back, and went behind his desk, seized with panic, without uttering a single word. While Stefan was leaving, he managed to tell him in a trembling voice: "I'll sue you, you Romanian asshole!"

Stefan took his leather jacket and turned towards the Frenchman, grinning. "Go ahead, but are you sure that this is your best move? I've been to your studio and I can come for you any time."

He left the studios, went to the hotel to pick up his belongings, and then took a cab to Charles de Gaulle airport. During the flight, thinking of the event that morning, he was a bit sorry about his own jumpiness but he could not stand that plump arrogant Frenchman, and even though this incident could cause professional problems in the future, he also knew that the people in the porn business did not appreciate or hire him for his moral qualities, common sense, or way of being.

A few hours later, he landed on the airport in Iasi, where Radu was waiting for him. Lorin joined them later that night; he had flown from Turin, with a stopover in Bucharest.

All this time, Radu was waiting for them in Iasi, feeling worse than ever. Even the toughest and most unpleasant experiences he had had before could hardly compare to the feelings of helplessness, worry, and frustration that he felt now. He felt his heart break whenever he imagined his most beloved Bronco, his body swelling with the bites suffered during the fight, transported in an unfamiliar car full of strangers and kept in improper conditions. Bronco had been born in Radu's house and, apart from the Carpathian woods where he was trained and the pits where he fought, he had not seen any other places and he had never been anywhere without his owner. The fact that he could not help Bronco was a very strong overwhelming feeling for Radu; he had never felt anything like it.

He had always been in control and the attacker, but this time he was the prey and, besides helplessness and frustration, he felt this was utter disrespect directed against him, a very personal insult on the Bessarabians' part. Even if they did not know him, and he was aware that the affront was not personal but strictly about the money, the hatred he felt for those who did such a thing was a feeling of a far greater intensity and magnitude than everything else he had felt before. He felt sick because of this tsunami of hatred which hit and overwhelmed him, and the violence of the images occurring to him whenever he thought of those who had stolen Bronco from him was beyond any horror film script.

Oddly enough, when he managed to cool his nerves, he also had a feeling which took him by surprise at first but for which he eventually accounted: a feeling of relief, as if a burden had been taken off his shoulders. This was due to the sense of doom that had been with him in the last few months, that cold snake which had now manifested physically.

That the misfortune had happened made the uncertainty and apprehension in the face of fate disappear, and the relief when that burden was lifted, combined with the hatred for his attackers, was translated in his inner dictionary where he deciphered his feelings as a natural and normal result of what he had felt before; he kept saying to himself that he had to go through this experience in order to toughen himself, since he had grown too soft and unprincipled of late. This realization gave him wings to fly and took him out of that feeling of lethargy and depression that had plagued him in the last few hours, arming him with motivation and meaning, the weapons he needed in order to regain the balance of his warrior spirit.

Leon felt not only guilty about what had happened but, like Radu, somehow violated and offended, which he had not felt since he was a child. That these Bessarabians had the guts to do what they did on his grounds, especially when they knew him, his strength, and his power, both financial and the number of soldiers he commanded, plus his connections in the world of interlopers, caused a sense of emptiness in Leon's stomach, which gave him a knot in the throat. He had never been so disrespected, and that this had happened at home and, to make it worse, that he had been tricked and then caught in this trap without having the slightest idea of what was going to happen, gave him a sense of frustration and hatred comparable to Radu's. However, Radu had not only had his pride wounded but the most precious thing he owned had been stolen from him. The sense of guilt added to the collection of negative feelings, and he felt he had to share this with Radu.

"Radu, I'm terribly sorry about what happened. I invited you here, bro, but it did not occur to me, even for a second, that this could happen. Never mind, I promise you, we'll break into their den and we'll get Bronco back as soon as your friends arrive. Fuck the bloody Russian bastards and their guts to do such a thing on my territory! The mother fuckers will get slaughtered, you can bet on it!"

"Do you know where they live?" Radu asked in a voice that seemed to come from the world beyond.

"I've seen these Russians only twice before. They supplied me with weapons when I needed them, but they are Goarja's folks. I don't know if you've heard of him, he's their papa in Chishinau. He's a former KGB member, who had serious businesses during the communist regime and, after the Iron Curtain fell, he created the most powerful network in Moldova. He commands more than fifty men and everybody in the area pays their tribute to him if they want to do business in Chishinau, legal or illegal. He sent a lot of people over, including these motherfuckers, but I bet he didn't know what they were planning. The man has serious businesses in Romania and in Europe, and everything goes through this filter; he wouldn't risk losing hundreds of thousands of euros for a dog, I'm sure of that. Plus he's not interested in pit bull fights. Tomorrow we'll pay him a visit and ask him for their address, and then we'll break into their den."

Late in the afternoon, Leon received a phone call from Goarja. He beckoned Radu to come closer, and then he used the speaker mode: "Hi, Varan, I've just heard what happened this morning there, pizdet. In the first place, I want you to know I'm not involved in this, you know me well enough to be sure I wouldn't start a war on account of a dog. These guys were trouble in the past too, but this time they did a nasty one and they deserve to be punished for it. I'm waiting for you to come over; we'll talk and sort it out, okay, blea?"

Next morning, four cars left Iasi for Chishinau on a vendetta mission based on blood-shedding scenarios. In Radu's car, there were Lorin and Stefan, in another the twins, whom Radu had summoned and who came from Galati to help him in this mission. In the third car, there was Leon with two of his men, and the fourth car was full of four other guys from Iasi, Varan's top people.

The trunks were full of weapons of all sizes, though the stars were some recoil buffer mini Uzis, which Leon had recently purchased from the same people he was about to punish. Varan had equipped all weapons with recoil buffers since he didn't want the operation to be noisy in Chishinau, a city in which the twelve Romanians could be easily lynched by the Moldavian gangs if they had gathered in a large number.

In less than two hours, they were in the capital of the Republic of Moldova, parking their cars in front of the villa of the interlopers' boss. Only Leon and Radu entered, the rest waited in the cars. Goarja was waiting for them in his office on the second floor, guarded by more than ten armed bodyguards, all of them former military soldiers.

He shook the Romanians' hands and he met Radu, whom he addressed in a friendly tone: "I'm sorry about what happened. These guys have put me to shame. I have my dealings with Varan, and they are worth hundreds of thousands a month, and these mother fuckers chose to spoil my reputation for a dog. I understand this is no ordinary dog, that it is worth many tens of thousands, but that don't change the situation. Look, there are two things I'll ask of you – one is, please don't kill them. Beat them or torture them, but spare their lives, and the other is to leave the driver unharmed. Those who kidnapped your dog are three brothers, more evil than the devil, and they deserve to be punished, but the fourth is just a kid they used as a driver, and this kid is under my care. I'll punish him myself for what he did. If you abide by these conditions, I'll tell you where you can find these brothers or, better yet, I can send one of my men to show you where the house is, and I guarantee there won't be any consequences. If these guys ever set foot on Romanian soil again or try to get vengeance, they'll be executed on the spot. Do we have a deal?"

Both guys agreed and arranged to come by at 3 a.m. and pick up the man that was going to point them in the direction of the house belonging to the people they were looking for.

At the established time, the four cars entered the country roads that were going to take them to where the three brothers lived. Their village, situated approximately thirty kilometers away from the capital, was very poor, as most Bessarabian villages were. Romanians had a joke that the local people there hunted cats with a slingshot in order to get something to eat. At a certain point, they turned the corner of the main street that crossed the village and entered a back road, full of bumps; a few minutes later, they reached a hillier area where there were some scattered houses at a considerable distance from each other. Goarja's man motioned them to stop and pointed at the house belonging to the three brothers. The Romanians turned off their headlights and continued their journey on foot so as to avoid alerting the enemy with the engine noises. The thirteen boys, twelve Romanians and a Bessarabian, advanced quietly but quickly through the Moldavian slum, every one of them armed with a mini Uzi and a pistol. Both types of guns were buffered, and aside from the firearms, they also carried blunt weapons, such as short baseball bats, telescopic tonfas, and brass knuckles.

The house was fenced in by a concrete wall that was first surmounted by one of the guys from Iasi, who, immediately after climbing it, got out his semi-automatic gun and a few shots were burst fired. The other guys were taken aback by this gesture and jumped over the fence hastily to see what the man from IaSi had shot at. When Radu set eyes upon the victims, a wave of fury came over him quickly but he clenched his jaws and kept quiet, jumping in the yard with the others. In the middle of the garden, lying lifeless, were the bodies of two pit bulls, a male and a female, which the Bessarabians had left unchained to guard the yard.

They approached the entrance; some of the guys went around the house at Leon's signal, to make sure there were no other exits, although that old tumbledown house didn't seem to have ever been refurbished, being in a more lamentable state than a century before when it had been built. Behind the house, in the meadow, there were many dog cages, in one of which Radu hoped to find Bronco. But it wasn't the moment to check yet; first, he had to take care of his attackers.

One of the boys from Iasi opened the lock using a wire in just a few seconds. The door squeaked a bit, giving the Romanians an extra reason to storm inside the house with the guns in their hands, in case the Bessarabians had heard any noise. They hurried down the hall then entered the living room where one of the brothers was asleep with the TV on. A bowl of water and a plastic bottle cut down the middle were right next to his bed, together making up the famous Russian bong. The guys banged the doors of the other two rooms against the wall, waking the Bessarabians from their sleep. Hardly had they lifted their hands to defend themselves than they were hit in their faces and heads, after which their mouths were duct-taped and they were taken out of the house.

The Romanian boys had noticed upon entering the yard that there was some sort of a garage or deposit in the back; they broke the bolt and took the prisoners in, tying them to the garage balk with the ropes they had brought from home. After tying up their hands and legs without uttering a single word, the Romanians started kicking the bejesus out of the three brothers, using the contusive objects they had brought with them.

In less than two minutes, the Bessarabians had been reduced to nothing more than an open wound. The floor was now filled with blood, and the heavy smell of fear mixed with the stench of sweat and urine floated like a poisonous cloud over the small space.

Radu took a bag and put it over one of the Bessarabian's head, namely the one who had immobilized him with nylon fiber when his back was turned, and, strangling him with the same weapon, he whispered in his ear the words that the Moldavian had murmured the day before: "Stay still, bitch. Stop squirming or I'll strangle you to death!" Bags were placed over the heads of the other two thieves, and the plastic was immediately reddened by their blood, getting tighter and tighter as they gasped for every breath of air.

Noticing, out of the corner of his eye, a blowtorch in a corner of the garage, cheered the cockles of Radu's heart. He stopped the boys and told them: "From here on, let me take care of them. I wanna work on them by myself a little!"

Varan was against it at first but when he felt the devil in Radu's look and the latter repeated his request, this time looking straight into his eyes and gesturing in his direction with the blowtorch in his hand, reminding him that everything that had happened was his fault, the guy from Iasi motioned his men to get out. Radu asked Lorin and Stefan to guard the door and let nobody in until he got out. Then, with a smile that made one of the Basserabians empty his bladder instantly, he addressed them.

"Guys, it's between us now. In a few moments, you're gonna wish more than anything that I had killed you, but before you go meet the devil, you've got some more time to spend with me!"

After that he started the blowtorch and started blistering the one closest to him. The smell of burnt skin and the shrieks muffled by the duct tape on their mouths gave Radu a more diabolical satisfaction than anything he had ever felt before. The combination of the sweet taste of revenge and having life and death power over his attackers proved to be the strongest aphrodisiac so far. He knew he could go on for hours without this feeling being diminished in any way.

After a few moments in which he had focused entirely on the agony of one of the Bessarabians, he went on to the next; that one's skin and flesh sizzling frantically under the bluish flame. Meanwhile, he talked to them, his smile never leaving his face, even for a second:

"It was ME you picked to rob, you scum? MY dog you decided to steal, you fuckin' cocksuckers?! In the name of that dog and everything I hold dear, I'll bury a hundred shits like you, you cunts! But why are you fidgeting like this, are you ticklish? Oh, look, I missed a spot, let me help you get homogeneously baked!"

Eventually, alarmed by the smell coming from the garage, Lorin and Stefan entered the room and immediately covered their noses: "Come on, bro, I don't want the dawn to find us here. We've got Bronco, he's in your car, we took the money, let's go!"

When Radu turned towards them, though they had known him for as long as they could remember and they had seen their friend furious many times, both guys were creeped out when they saw his twisted features that, lit by the flame from the blowtorch, had transformed him into a demonic entity. He answered them in a calm voice, without losing his smile: "Yes, my dear brothers, just wait a second while I paint this one too. I don't want him to feel left out."

After that he used the blowtorch on the third victim, making unbreathable the already overbearing stench in the room. A few moments later, he turned off the machine, pulled out a knife from behind his back and put it at the throat of the gang leader, the one who had organized the kidnapping and in whose eyes there was only a kind of horror and fear he had never felt or seen before.

Radu whispered to him as the blade penetrated the burnt skin, moving down from the neck to the chest: "You're terribly lucky Goarja asked me not to kill you. If it weren't for him, I would have played with you for another couple of hours until you gave your last breath. But if you ever set foot in Romania, or if I ever see you at another match or elsewhere, I swear on my nearest and dearest that I'm gonna leave you there in a puddle of blood, without any further warnings or explanations, and your boss has agreed on this one. Consider yourselves mighty lucky, damn you and your retarded kind!"

He hit him hard in the chin with his fist, at which point the Bessarabian's whole body remained suspended by the arms tied to the balk as he lost consciousness. Radu cut his ropes and walked away. The one he had untied could set his brothers free when he regained consciousness.

Bronco was waiting for him in the front of the car, held by Lorin in a leash. Seeing him warmed the cockles of Radu's heart and he felt the diabolical state of mind that had seized him for the past couple of hours leave him, replaced by gratitude that Bronco was all right and the love he felt for the dog. He kissed him a few times; the dog licked his face, wagging his tail joyfully, even though he was pretty swollen from the wounds Caligula had inflicted on him. After that, Radu threw a blanket on the back seat of his car, he laid Bronco there and sat right next to him, beckoning Lorin to drive.

The four cars went off at a rare pace and started their journey back home towards the Romanian border. Although he was overwhelmed with happiness again, Radu didn't have that bad feeling anymore, the one foreshadowing doom. On the contrary, he felt that everything was exactly the way it should be and that everything happens for a reason, even if we're usually unaware of it. On the way home, he confessed something that took his friends by surprise.

"You know what? Before leaving Iasi, I promised myself something. Should I find Bronco alive and in one piece, I would give up the pit fights, and I intend to keep that promise. Yesterday's fight was the last match I'll ever take part in, my little brothers!"

Chapter 23

Back in Iasi, the guys stopped at one of Varanu's strip clubs, to split the money taken from the Bessarabians. They had dropped off Goarja's man in front of his house, thanking him for his help. He was the only one involved in the action who wasn't going to get any of the money recovered from the three racketeers.

The twelve boys entered Leon's office, situated at the top floor of his strip joint, and started counting the money. Radu said to those present: "Guys, thank you very much for coming with me! I only want the money from my match, which is my fifteen grand, plus the fifteen I've won. I don't need any profit. I got my Bronco back safe and sound and that's all I wanted. You can split the rest of the money amongst yourselves."

The almost one hundred and twenty thousand euro they had found under the mattresses of the three brothers was divided equally among the eleven Romanians, after Radu had received his thirty thousand. Then the guys said goodbye, but not before Radu seized the opportunity to buy the two semi-automatic mini Uzis they had had with them, silencers included, in case the Bessarabians came for him, although this was unlikely.

The five men from Galati got in their cars and left Iasi, heading for Poiana Țapului, where they were going to celebrate not only Bronco's retrieval but also his victory in the latest fight. The twins excused themselves, explaining that they had to be back in Galați by the same evening. They congratulated Radu for his and Bronco's victory and thanked him for giving them the occasion to earn a pretty large amount of money in just a couple of hours.

In the afternoon, they parked in front of Radu's mansion, where Sophie was waiting breathlessly. Radu had only told her over the phone that something unexpected had happened and that he was going to be back later than predicted. Meanwhile, the Dutch girl's imagination had been flying in every direction, one more obscure than the other. She had even started having certain regrets concerning her choice, telling herself that this wasn't the kind of life she wanted, and that the Romanian she had fallen in love with wasn't the best choice for her, with all the violence and unpredictability that followed him everywhere.

But the moment she heard his jeep and saw him get out of the car with a smile on his face, a magic sponge washed away all the dark thoughts that had crowded her universe for the last couple of hours and she dashed out of the house, rushing to fold her arms around the hefty neck of the man she loved. The fact that his two friends were also present decreased her enthusiasm a bit but she tried to hide it.

Radu hugged and kissed her while saying: "Hi, babe, did you miss me? How are the little ones, did they do any damage inside? I've got news for you, I'm sure you'll be glad to hear. This match was the last one. It's over, I quit the pit bull fights!"

"Did Bronco lose the fight? How come you made such a decision?"

"No, he won, but I don't want to get involved in any more fights. I've had enough. From now on, I'll just breed dogs as a hobby, not for fighting."

Although Sophie didn't expect the Romanian to be able to surprise her even more, Radu's statement made her knees shake. She wanted to eat this man she never knew what to expect from alive.

Radu put Bronco in his kennel and, after kissing him on the snout once more and filling his bowls with food and water, they all entered the house. Lorin and Stefan hadn't had the chance to see the three Staffordshire bull terrier cubs that Radu had bought from the Czech Republic, and their behavior, playful and friendly, endeared them immediately to this breed they hadn't heard much about. They were most impressed with the male, Bullyson, who was almost two times larger than the two females and had already started dominating them, making them behave with his thick paws or slightly biting their ears whenever they were starting to get on his nerves with their endless liveliness and playfulness.

A few thick buds from Radu's personal production were taken out for smoking, after that a bag full of the white powder brought from Peru and processed in Prague made an appearance on the living room table. The rum was poured in the glasses, the mirror with sculpted frame got covered in white lines, and thick blunts filled the whole villa with a smoke that smelled like happiness. An hour later, the atmosphere was animated, the discussion spirited, and the laughter unrelenting. Sophie drew away to one of the rooms along with the Staffie cubs, leaving the boys to party undisturbed in their barbaric style. Anyway, she couldn't understand a thing they were discussing and she felt a tad guilty every time Radu had to interrupt the talk in order to translate for her.

Stefan, while passing the joint to Lorin, addressed him with a grin:
"Bro, this guy's the reincarnation of Vlad the Impaler, only he used punishments that were a hundred times harsher than the crimes committed."

"Well, the Dutch girls don't call him Count Dracula for no reason!" Lorin chuckled.

"Do you know what the Impaler did when some of the sultan's envoys refused to take off their turbans, indicating that their religion forbids them to do so? He had their turbans bolted to their heads permanently and sent them back to the sultan like that. Radu boy's the same. Those fuckers steal his dog, and he bakes them from head to foot."

Radu, who was amused by his friends' discussion, chipped in:
"What was I supposed to do, bro, pull them by the ears? Fuck them, they're lucky I didn't have more time to deal with them properly! The truth is, I went a bit crazy in that cellar; the more they screamed, the

more I wanted to hurt them. Can you believe the guts they had, thinking they could steal my beloved Bronco? Damn them all to hell, with their filthy breed and cursed creed! Did you see the way they were pissing their pants when I started torching them?" Radu added, laughing heartily.

The truth was that there were moments when he managed to frighten even his two friends. That insatiable appetite for violence and the pleasure that lit his face every time he inflicted pain upon those he hated could bring shivers down the spines of everyone present, including his childhood friends who had had the occasion to observe this kind of behavior countless times but could never fully get used to it.

Radu added: "Can you imagine what those men must have felt hundreds of years ago, before going to battle? Did you see what wave of adrenaline came over us before bursting in those fuckers' house? And we outnumbered them, there was no real danger, but still I had my heart in my mouth when we entered the house. Imagine how those men must have felt on the battlefield, before the actual battle, face to face with their enemy, all of them armed, their sole purpose being to kill the adversary, realizing that there was every chance they'd get killed. And back then, people fought hand-to-hand, unlike nowadays when we shoot at each other while hiding behind walls, using snipers from a kilometer away like cowards! How can you compare the sensation when your blade enters the enemy's flesh, as the air leaves his body and you look into his dying eyes, with the sensation you have when you shoot someone you can barely see because of the distance between the two of you? The invention of firearms has turned us all into cowards. Like the rest of technology, for that matter, efficient but altering the spirit. We've got comfort, but we've lost our balls!"

Radu felt that he was letting his hatred flood his being once again in a way that was too extreme for those present, all the more so as they were celebrating. He decided to change the subject and get back to business. “Tell me, Lorin, mate, how were things in Turin, what did that pal of yours say?”

“Bro, it’s good news. He said he pushes about two kilos of hash a month, but he’d sell some three or four kilos of weed. I knew the jackass was going to be glad, there’s a severe weed drought down there.”

“Great, then let’s get down to business. Who do you think we could use to grow it?"Stefan stepped in. “I think we might use my cousin. The devil’s loyal, he got three years in jail but he didn’t rat the other guys out, and he’s down on his uppers just now. I know ‘cause he asks me to send him a hundred once in a while. The only problem is that he’s clueless when it comes to growing weed, you’ll have to teach him what’s what.”

“No problem, Stefan, buddy, it’s important that he shouldn’t be stupid, but as I recall, the bastard’s not slow on the uptake, right? Why don’t you call him and tell him to come by and we’ll have a little chat with him. If everything goes okay, when you get to Prague, look for a house outside the city, as secluded as possible and with a big cellar with plenty of room for as many plants as possible, and let’s get this business going! If we get at least ten kilos per cycle, that’s three months a cycle, we can get pretty good profits. I’ll come to buy everything that’s needed and set the plantation up; you just find us a house and a few seedling plants from around there and then I’ll show the guy how to grow them.”

“Perfect. I’ll give him a buzz right away. It’s even better if he comes here ‘cause when he leaves, he can take me with him to the airport in Bucharest and we can also drop Lorin home, This way we avoid riding the train.”

“Lorin, what’s the word about Irinel? When is he supposed to be back?”

“He should be in Europe in about two weeks, he’ll let us know when he’s close and we’ll go and wait for him. Meanwhile I’ll take the necessary actions to move to Prague. I talked to Cristina and she’s happy about this idea. She’s just a bit stressed that she may not find a job there but I told her to calm down. There's enough money now, there's no reason to panic, but apart from that, she's anxious for a change of scenery. Stefan said he'd browse the Czech real estate websites for a two- or three-room apartment for us to rent. I want us to move there in a couple of weeks. I won't insist that you come too 'cause I know you won't move from here. I only hope you'll at least come visit us!"

"I will, Lorin, mate, don't worry! Especially now when that is where we'll make most of our money, of course I'll come by. Think about it. I won't even be growing weed here anymore. After this batch of plants, I'm going to disband the jungle in my cellar and I'm thinking about putting a swimming pool there. I also won't get involved in any more pit fights. All my money's going to come from the Prague deals, so of course I'll come to see how things are going, especially now that you're both going to be there...I'll miss you fuckers. I hope you'll come home from time to time! Let me kiss you, fuckin' jackasses!"

Radu hugged each of his friends at a time, kissed them and, with tears in his eyes, he confessed to them: "I don't know what I'd do without you, guys, you're all I have, my dear brothers! And nothing's ever going to change this, no matter what this bitchy life hits us with!"

The party went on for another good couple of hours until they all fell asleep wherever they could lay their heads. Stefan and Lorin each slept in one of the mansion's rooms, Radu with Sophie in the bedroom. The next day, Stefan's cousin showed up at the mansion and was delighted with the boys' proposal and with the fact that he was going to move to Prague. He swore he was going to do his best to grow the plants to the best of his abilities and that, if he got arrested, he was going to tell the cops that the plantation was his own, without dragging the boys in.

A month later, Radu along with Costin, for this was the name of Stefan's cousin, were heading for Prague. Stefan had found a nice little flat for Lorin and Cristina, newly furnished and close to Jana's apartment, where the porn actor spent most of his time even though he had rented one for himself in the old town center. He was so fond of it that he just couldn't bear to let it go, all the more so as it increased his feeling of independence, which he needed like air. He had also found a house that was very suitable for their plans, situated almost twenty kilometers outside the town. It was an old house, built more than a century before, at the edge of a village but pretty secluded. The owners, who had inherited the house from their grandparents, lived in America, leaving it in the care of a real estate agency for maintenance and renting. The house hadn't been inhabited for years because its location wasn't very convenient for someone working in the city, but it was perfect for the boys' plans. The real estate agency proved to be very pleased with the prospect of renting it, and couldn't care less about who was going to live there and what they were going to do in it as long as the rent was getting paid. The most important aspect for the guys, the cellar, was exactly the way they needed it, roomy and cool, with enough space for around a thousand pots.

Upon leaving Bucharest, Lorin asked Radu to help him with the transport, his car already packed with their belongings, and Paco, his and Cristina's dog, occupying the backseat. Radu filled the trunk of his jeep with his friends' luggage, the backseat also crammed with bags. Most of those things belonged to Cristina, who refused to leave anything behind, taking the bed linen, towels, and cutlery with her. Lorin had teased her about it but he let her have it her own way nonetheless.

The next day, Costin moved into the house outside Prague, leaving all the windows open to get rid of the smell of mold and closed space that filled the whole place, while Lorin and Cristina were making themselves comfortable in their new flat, with which they were very pleased. Radu bought everything he needed to set up a plantation of weed from a grow shop in the town center then spent two days assembling the components, placing the special earth brought in plastic bags in the flower pots, explaining to Costin in detail exactly what his work was going to consist of.

He felt that an era had ended, as he would stop doing what he had been doing for the last many years, growing weed and training pit bulls for matches. Instead, he had moved all of his business to Prague and he was making more money now than before while his effort was decreasing. He joked with his friends about them outsourcing their business, just like international corporations do in India or Singapore. He also felt that he was making headway, constantly moving up a ladder he was building for himself as he went along, although it wasn't very clear to him exactly what was waiting for him on top of the ladder, or how much longer he would have to go to get there. He just knew he needed to keep climbing and that nothing could stop him.

Chapter 24

When Stefan received an offer from Berlin to participate in the shooting of a German porn production, he invited Lorin to tag along. He knew that Berlin was one of his friend's favorite cities, and that he had lived in the German capital for a long time years before, soon after the December revolution.

Lorin gladly accepted the invitation, not only because he had many memories from Berlin, a place he hadn't visited in over ten years, but also because he knew that, with Stefan, he was going to party scrumptiously in Berlin's clubs, which were so dear to him. He was leaving Cristina alone for a couple of days for the first time since they had moved to Prague, but his girlfriend had immediately plugged into Prague's energy and was very excited about her residence, being very impressed with the medieval architecture of the town and the friendly and detached manner displayed by the locals, very much unlike that of the people in Bucharest. When she wasn't going out for a walk with Lorin on the paved alleys of the old town center, or visiting Stefan and Jana, Cristina spent most of her time online, looking for a job. At first, she had searched for jobs for Romanian citizens but when she couldn't find any, she started applying for positions in customer service that required the fluent use of English, experience in the field being an advantage but not a requisite.

After a few weeks of intense job-hunting, she finally received a call from one of the companies she had contacted, setting an interview appointment for that week. While Lorin and Stefan were on their way to Berlin, she was getting ready, both physically and mentally, for her first job interview outside Romania. She would have preferred that her man took her to the interview and waited for her outside until it was over, but she knew how much he missed the German capital, and even though her memories of those times weren't the most pleasant possible given the fact that she had to wait for Lorin all those years he spent in jail, she would have never opposed his getaway with his friend for a couple of days.

She was more concerned about what they were going to do there, especially knowing Stefan's easygoing ways; he was magnetically attracted to beautiful women and vice versa. She was a bit put out by the fact that her man was going away for pure entertainment with a man who not only looked like the statue of a god, with every muscle in his body visible under his tanned skin, but who, in his clever, relaxed and direct way of approaching women, was irresistible to them. But she had forced herself a long time ago to come to terms with the fact that her beloved's best friends were people who intimidated her, no matter how much time she spent with them or how nice they treated her. On the other hand, she couldn't help feeling grateful to Stefan for helping them move to this splendid city and for finding them the flat with which she was so delighted.

At the time Cristina's interview was taking place, Lorin was flying with Stefan over the thick layer of clouds that gave him the impression that he was at the North Pole, his imagination turning the white immensity of the clouds they were floating above into an endless field covered with a thick and fluffy blanket of snow, the plane a magical sleigh dashing through it. Riveting on a distant point in the snow-bound tundra, Lorin gave free rein to his imagination and memories, immersing into a state of contemplative apathy.

The fact that he hadn't been to Germany since he got out of jail gave him a feeling of melancholy that dressed all the memories from that period in a flamboyant and pleasant cloak, as it happens when we remember various adventures from our childhood holidays we'd love to go back to and live again. This analogy was even more veridical in Lorin's case, because he was only a child when he had gone to Germany, and the feeling of novelty and the spirit of adventure he experienced then could easily be relived, especially now that he was revisiting these places after all those years.

He had left then with a group of boys from Suceava, who knew about the route from other friends of theirs who were already there. In those days it was still illegal for Romanians to go to Germany, even though the communist wall had already fallen; at least now they could visit the neighboring countries, all of them ex-members of the Iron Curtain, situated a little closer to the West than Romania, closer to the lands that the boys dreamt of. Countries like Germany, the Netherlands, and France, about which they didn't really know much, but which they regarded as cows that needed to be milked. They had lived their entire lives, up to that point, in dire poverty, and were hungry not only for the riches of those places but also for information. Information about how the rest of the world lived and had fun, which had been kept from them by the communist regime of Ceausescu, the most drastic communist dictator ever, who isolated the country not only economically but also ideologically.

Raised without any access to foreign music or films, deprived of the most basic needs of a teenager, the young Romanians rushed into Western Europe after the revolution like veritable hordes of barbarians, taking by storm the much more peaceful and civilized locals, who hadn't seen such behavior before. Like dogs that had been kept in chains their entire lives, when the chain eventually broke, they swooped down upon the neighboring yards with all their might, making inroads into everything. This was done not out of malice but simply because of the regime of detention they had been put through by the communist fiends, who had turned them into beasts that had nothing to lose. They were people who had had everything taken from them and who now considered it normal to take back, by any means, everything that had been refused to them up to that point, even if the Western countries were not to blame for the way the Romanians had lived under the communist dictatorship.

Lorin and his friends had paid a trucker to take them to Poland, from where they took a train to the vicinity of the German border.

During nighttime, in the winter, they entered the upland forests that border the two states. None of the boys had been outside their country before, but they knew the route from some of their friends who had been there a couple of weeks earlier. They had given them vague instructions over the phone about how to cross the border by going through the mountains, the main reference point being the frontier road in the mountains. But they couldn't get too close to it or they risked being seen and shot by the border guards. The way through the mountains was very difficult, the thick fog obscuring their vision to such an extent that they could only see a couple of meters ahead of them. They were forced to walk down all the time to make sure they were walking parallel to the road and that they weren't going to lose their way. Several times they slipped on the slope, with the snow entering their every orifice and drenching their clothes every time; it was just like plunging in the ocean with their clothes on but their determination to reach the West pushed them forward and gave them wings, eventually bringing them to German soil.

Upon reaching the border town, they changed into the dry clothes they had in their satchels, threw away the wet ones, and took cabs to get to the railway station in a bigger town nearby. If they had gone to the station in the border town, they would have risked getting caught by the police because the bus and train stations along the border were always patrolled by the police in the period preceding the European Union. They were taking a huge risk anyway, because not only did the cab drivers get fined if they were caught transporting people who had crossed the border illegally but if, instead of taking them to their destination, they took them to a police station, they could benefit from tax exemption. So the chances of a cab driver taking them to their desired destination were rather slim. Nonetheless, their chances were greater than if they tried to take a train or a bus from there to the capital.

Having taken two cabs, the guys reached the station half an hour later without any trouble; they took the train to Berlin where the rest of their friends, who had gotten there a few weeks earlier, were waiting for them. One of the first things Lorin learnt in Germany was how to steal with an aluminum bag. The boys wrapped a plastic bag in aluminum foil bought from the market; after that, they covered the aluminum in thick adhesive tape so that the thin layers wouldn't break when they were forced. They put this bag in a shoulder bag, repeating the process until everyone had a bag lined with aluminum. This prevented the tags attached to clothes setting off the alarm when they exited the store. The guys decided they would only steal from the shops that didn't have surveillance cameras and they soon discovered that the stores inside the malls almost never had cameras, so they focused on those.

Their way of doing it was based on teamwork, three or four chaps for one mall, each with a shoulder bag lined with aluminum. They also took a larger bag where they would store all the merchandise stolen during the day. They entered the mall one by one, every one of them entering each store that had merchandise they considered of interest, and when the shoulder bag, which could not be very roomy so as to avoid attracting attention, got filled, they went out and moved the stolen goods into a bigger bag without any aluminum, then went back inside. Each of the guys entered each mall four or five times, filling up the bag with merchandise from every store.

In time, they became experts, getting used to stuffing more and more goods in their bags, learning new and improved ways of folding them and putting them into bags faster. They also started stealing without having to check whether they were being watched or not, observing everything that happened around them out of the corner of their eye. They would usually enter the store, look at the clothes, and go to a more secluded place to make a stack that, at the right time, when nobody was looking, they would slip quickly and with precision into the bag. They didn't risk being seen just by the shop assistants, but also by the undercover agents assigned to catch shoplifters. The agents didn't wear any uniforms and they spent their entire day pretending to look at the clothes or try them on. Likewise, the malls had agents in uniform, with guns and walkie-talkies, patrolling the corridors of the stores, ready to grab the likes of Lorin and his friends.

After two or three hours spent in a mall, the boys took various means of transport, the most frequently used being the U-Bahn, in order to get to other malls and repeat the action. Most of their clients were Turks. Lots of Turkish people were residents of Germany and especially Berlin, owning bazaars or fast-food chains. The Turks usually told them what they wanted to buy, and the Romanians tried to find exactly what they'd ordered to make sure they sold the merchandise.

Another problem was that of getting rid of the alarm systems on the clothes. Nobody would have bought from them if the alarms were still attached. The Romanians took the alarms off by setting their plastic cores on fire with a lighter and melting them, at which point the bleeping spring and the little balls fell through the hole made by the lighter; then they would dismember the two parts of the alarm and take off the nail which held them together. Going home to do that would have meant wasting time, so they decided to take off the alarms while they were still downtown and then go straight to their clients to sell them. The problem with that was that it was quite a process and gave out a pungent smell of burnt plastic, so they couldn't do it publicly, of course. The Romanians used the public toilets that were found at every turn in Berlin; they inserted coins to keep the restroom occupied while they hurried as quickly as they could to get the alarms off carefully as not to spoil the fabric. More than once their time expired before they could finish their job. The doors to the toilet opened and passers-by stared at the stack of clothes left on the floor and at the young people rushing to set the alarms on fire, with the smell of burnt plastic invading their nasal passages. The smell served to increase their disquietude at the unusual scene in a public restroom.

Another risk they were constantly exposing themselves to was public transportation; they were there illegally and the ticket collectors were obliged to call the cops if they met any Romanians. On top of that, they were carrying the bags wrapped in aluminum and the large bag full of stolen clothes with their alarms still on. The fact that they never bought tickets increased the risk of their getting caught; several times, they were forced to run away as fast as they could from ticket inspectors, the guards at the mall or even from the police. But to them, everything was an adventure at that young age and they didn't perceive the risks as being something negative; on the contrary, they saw it as a game where they had to be perpetually vigilant and one step ahead of everyone else.

The transition from shoplifting to bank robbery took place a few months later when they met some Romanians from Timisoara, who were making a living out of it and, after a discussion with them, Lorin and his friends decided to start doing the same thing. It was easier, there was more money involved, and less time was needed. At the suggestion of the guys from Timisoara, they decided to hold up the smaller branch banks in rural areas, not cities, because the security measures in the countryside were more lax. When he robbed his first bank, Lorin's heart was beating like crazy. With a ski mask on and armed with toy guns, the same as his friends, he entered the almost empty bank and started yelling at the top of his throat in a bad German: "Everybody get down! Nobody move! Give us the money and no one gets hurt!" An hour later, while counting their money, they couldn't believe how easy and fast everything had happened. In less than three minutes, they were out of the bank and jumping in the car they had stolen the previous night. However, they soon ran out of luck and one of the boys got caught pickpocketing in the subway, and he ratted on everyone else to the police.

After a short trial, Lorin was sentenced to seven years in prison, and so were his friends. The four years he spent in the German jail went by without any significant adventures, except for the few months when the Romanians started a genuine war behind the prison walls. When Lorin and his friends were incarcerated, the drug traffic in jail, the main way of making money inside, was controlled by the Turks. There were large numbers of Turkish people there and they had many relatives and friends who sent them everything they needed. At first, when they got in, there were few Romanians, but their numbers increased daily as more and more of them were coming to Germany in search of wealth. Many of the inmates were there just because they had crossed the border illegally, while others had committed various acts of violence or even murders.

Lorin and his gang were among the first Romanians in the prison, and their style had turned them into the leaders of all the Romanians living under the German roof. Observing that their numbers were increasing while the number of Turks was stagnating, it dawned on Lorin that they could take over the drug traffic from the Turkish inmates. This wasn't only due to the number of people, which was now almost even, but also because many of the jailed Romanians had already married German women or they had friends and relatives outside prison who could send them everything they needed to take over the traffic.

Before making any move against the Turks, he inquired about the exact quantities of drugs that could be smuggled in by the Romanians' relatives or acquaintances, and the result was the desired one. Together, they could cater for the whole prison, which was a small one, with everything they got sent from outside the prison.

He gathered all the Romanians in the yard and they agreed on a plan. They manufactured weapons for each of them from shards of glass sharpened on the metal frame of the bed and wrapped in cloths, used as handles, to tooth brushes melted and then sharpened at the end, and pieces of springs or metal bars taken from the jail furniture, all of them turned into lethal weapons. Lorin encouraged them, telling them that Stephen the Great and Vlad the Impaler would have been proud of their descendants and what they were about to do to the Turks. After that they threw T-shirts on the surveillance cameras in the corners of the yard, Lorin sent one of the Romanians, a giant man from Vaslui, over a meter and ninety centimeters tall and weighing a hundred and twenty kilograms, over to the Turks, as if to buy drugs. The Romanians all waited, shanks at the ready, prepared to swoop down on them at Lorin's signal. The man he had sent studied the merchandise and then he flung it in the Turk's face, telling him that it was calcimine from off the walls and not coke, then hit him in the chin, following the plan. When the other Turks dashed at the Romanian, Lorin and his army attacked them with all the speed they could master, starting a genuine carnage. They used the weapons they had forged against the Turkish inmates repeatedly, with an unexpected speed and violence that took the Turks by surprise. In less than a minute, the yard was a bloodbath. Many Turks had been stabbed in the throat, liver, or heart, and were in a pretty bad shape, while most of the Romanians hadn't suffered bad wounds with a few small exceptions.

After stabbing the leader of the Turks between his ribs, Lorin held him to the ground and put the shiv under his eye, its sharp tip touching his eyelid, and told him that from that moment on, they weren't allowed to sell any drugs in prison, and that if they tried to continue they would be executed, not just stabbed. Then, he cut deeply all over his face, to permanently remind them of what they were capable of. When he was taken down by a blow on the head with a tonfa, applied by one of the German guards, Lorin was still in a trance from the outburst of violence during the last minutes. After that, his whole body was covered with blows given by the German officers. After a few days in solitary confinement, he came back to join the other inmates, this time as the head of the most powerful gang in that prison.

The rest of the time in prison was quite pleasant. The Romanians were impressed by the conditions offered by the Germans, which included having a dentist, a TV in every room, a gym, and the food was even better than they had ever eaten in Romania. Four years later, when he was released, the Romanians still controlled the drug traffic inside and he had appointed a friend of his from Suceava as gang leader.

Lorin was reliving all these images and feelings as he stared blankly out of the window of the plane. Even though he had changed a lot since his days in the German prison, the feelings of power and control he used to have were now giving him goose bumps, and even if he didn't want to get imprisoned again, those feelings made waves somewhere in the subterraneous lakes of his being, deep and swampy lakes of the sort that he imagined Radu's universe was made of, although he was aware of the fact that the waters his friend bathed in were a lot deeper and darker than his, and the storms were much more violent.

Chapter 25

Cristina's interview was a lot briefer than she had expected. At the reception of the office building, she was greeted by a man who introduced himself as the manager of the company's sales division. About thirty-years-old, of Serbian origin, he was dressed in an expensive suit and generated an impression of self-confidence. He invited her to one of the top floors where the respective firm had its offices.

He commenced the interview by presenting her with a profile of the company and her future responsibilities, in case they decided to work together. The firm acted in the financial domain, organizing conferences for banks and insurance companies that paid a participation fee to listen to the strategies implemented by bigger or more successful banks. The most difficult burden was on the shoulders of the production department; they had to do a study of the financial market, come up with ideas for the topics to be tackled during the upcoming conferences, and, after agreeing on them, their job was to contact the directors of the respective departments from the most important banks, namely those who were in charge of the department the conference was going to focus on, and convince them to participate as speakers. The rest of the participants, the delegates, the bankers themselves, were those who paid to listen to what these heads of departments of the most successful banks had to say.

The position Cristina had applied for was in the sales department, the responsibility of this division being to contact as many banks as possible and persuade them to send delegates and pay to participate in the conference. Even though she had no experience with this kind of business, Cristina's intelligence, her pleasant ways, and the fact that she was a very good English speaker, recommended her for this position. This job could be a big step forward for her, mainly because it would be the first time she was hired by a foreign company. Also this sort of work in the financial domain seemed very interesting and getting this job would mean being a step closer to remaining in the city she had fallen in love with from the first moment.

The questions that the Serbian asked her were quite general, just to get a clearer image concerning her training and attitude. After he inquired about her studies and previous employers, the man asked her about her basic qualities and how she thought she could contribute to the well-being of the company, questions Cristina answered with some elegance and ease. She had the feeling that she had made a good impression on her future boss, but she knew that she could be wrong and his jovial attitude could be just a mask he wore every time he interviewed potential employees.

When the interview was over, the Serbian thanked her for participating and told her he would contact her again by the end of that week for an interview with the company director, something that Cristina interpreted as being a positive result. She thanked him back, shook his hand, and went out into Prague's hustle and bustle, full of an enthusiasm she hadn't felt in a long time. Being away from home, just with her man, and sensing that she was close to getting a well-paid job she was very pleased with, Cristina felt that she was starting to live her life on her own two feet, managing to make it on her own, far from the wing, a little too protective for her taste, of her intellectual parents. This self-confidence brought a smile on her lips while she was moved forward, stepping firmly through the crowd that formed along the causeways of Prague.

Lorin and Stefan landed in the Berlin airport and took a cab to the hotel where they had reserved a room. Stefan's shoot started the next day, and was going to last three days. They agreed they would go out to the renowned Berlin clubs only after the shoot was over, in order to be able to party properly.

Lorin spent most of the time while Stefan was working with an old friend of his he had met in the German prison, a guy from Timisoara who was already married to a German woman when he got arrested for armed robbery, and who remained in Berlin after he was released. He now had two kids with the German woman. Sorin was involved with a gang of Albanians, robbing pawnshops and jewelers, sometimes even pursuing other thieves and robbing them of their stolen goods. Having German papers, Sorin benefited from all the advantages offered by the German state, including kinder punishments in case he got caught than he would have gotten if he weren't married. Sorin had been a member of Lorin's gang in prison and had profited from the advantages surrounding the Romanian takeover of the drug traffic, but he had not actively participated in the operation against the Turks because he was arrested a couple of months after that action had taken place. He was very grateful to Lorin, and felt he somehow owed him.

In the three days he spent mostly with Sorin, Lorin walked through the familiar streets of Berlin full of melancholy, reliving the intensity of the sensations he had felt the first time he was here when he was just a teenager. He had been through so much since then, he had learnt so many lessons he couldn't have even imagined back then, that now, remembering the way he used to think and react, a smile lit up his features, and a sensation of self-love took him by surprise. He realized how much he had changed and how far he had come. Even if he hadn't entirely changed his way of being and seeing things, the baggage of experience he had accumulated had turned him into a more sophisticated and complex person than he would have been if he had lived his entire life in Romania.

One evening, Sorin took him to the tower near Alexanderplatz, the highest construction in Germany, an impressive structure where Lorin felt flattened by the speed with which the elevator lifted them several hundreds of meters in the air in just a few seconds. The view from this tower was overwhelming, stirring the admiration he had always felt towards this big European capital. From the tower he could see the whole city of Berlin, a vast expanse lit by billions of electrical fireflies, pumping life through its perfectly-structured arteries, with the efficiency characteristic of this nation.

Lorin appreciated the Germans very much, especially the Berliners, sensing the inner strength of these people, some kind of mental power he hadn't noticed in other nationalities. Also, he had heard that the Germans were a cold and inhospitable people, information that proved to be wrong, at least in the Berliners' case. He couldn't speak for the rest of Germany because he hadn't visited any other German cities. He found the inhabitants of this city very friendly, open-minded, and bright, but he was most impressed with that mental force he felt most of the people emitted, irrespective of their age or gender, which accounted for the fact that they had fought the rest of the world twice, considering themselves to be the superior race.

Even though Lorin didn't agree with the Nazi ideas, he understood exactly why these people regarded themselves as being superior to other nations and, in some respects, he agreed with that view. One of the main reasons that proved to him he wasn't wrong was the way in which Germany had reconstructed itself after World War II. Starting off with huge debts, a bombed-out country, decimated almost completely, regarded by the entire world as the number one public enemy, it became, just a couple of decades later, one of the top European countries, with a social and economic infrastructure any other state would have envied. And all this was due to their psychological strength and their manners, which Lorin appreciated and respected so much. If he were to choose a nation he respected the most, it would certainly be the German nation.

When Stefan finally finished the shoot, he invited Lorin to the underground clubs in Berlin he was already familiar with, having been invited by the porn crews he had previously worked with in Berlin. The mark that these clubs had left upon Stefan was very deep and he could hardly wait to show them to his friend and to enjoy the experiences offered by Berlin's nightlife together. He had always wanted that, to have his friends from back home with him when he was having fun in these places, where he felt like he was growing wings instead of the forever new faces he used to partying with, sharing nothing with them but the porn world.

"Lorin, my man, I'm going to take you to some clubs you won't believe exist, bro! The Germans are the best at clubbing. I don't think there are clubs as wicked as these ones anywhere else in the world, at least the underground ones. When I first went to some of these clubs, I was taken aback, it took me a while to get used to them. The atmosphere was too extreme, even for me!"

"Oh, really? I can hardly wait, I've never been to these clubs 'cause I was a kid when I was here for the first time. I had no idea about them, and since then I've never been back. Let's see what you're talking about, Stefan, my boy. I'm actually in the mood for one of those hardcore parties!"

"Bro, I think you can't get more hardcore than here. I talked to some DJs from London who mix everywhere on the globe and they said they'd never seen such extreme parties like these."

In the evening, they took a cab and Stefan gave the driver the address of the club. Lorin was taken aback when he saw where the cab driver had dropped them off. "Dude, this guy brought us to the wrong place. How the fuck could there be a club here?"

"Haha, wait until you see this, Lorin, my friend! The guy brought us to the right place, don't you worry!"

The cab had dropped them off in an industrial area, in front of a yard next to some disused factories from the second world war. Lorin saw no sign to indicate that a club existed somewhere near but he followed Stefan through the big rusty iron gates that opened into the factory yard. He noticed the immensity of the compound. There must have been few dozen factories there, perfectly in line, all of them rusty and with most of their windows broken. Lorin was more and more astonished by the place his friend brought him to and he couldn't make the connection between these former ammunition factories and the superclub he had been promised, but he followed him, somehow amused to see what his plan was. Stefan went along through the factories with a waggish smile on his thick lips, beckoning to his friend to follow him. He entered one of the main alleys, suddenly turned right, then left, increasing Lorin's curiosity.

"Stefan, mate, what the fuck are we doing here? This looks just like a horror movie setting. I expect to see a horde of zombies jumping out of these rusty factory buildings. Seriously now, where are we going?"

"Wait, dude, we'll get there in a minute and you'll see!" Stefan answered without losing his cunning smile.

After another couple of minutes of advancing through the center of the industrial compound, Lorin could hear some muffled noises that sounded like the bass rhythm of techno music. Perplexed, he followed Stefan until they stopped in front of the hall of one of the factories set in front of the compound. From the outside, it didn't look very different from the other shabby buildings, except the windows weren't broken but covered in black foil and there was a neon hanger dangling over the heavy iron gates of the factory.

"There you go, bro, we're here! How about this location?"

"Dude, are you barking mad? This is where the club is? But it looks like a dump, bro, have you ever been here?"

"Haha, wait until you see the interior!"

Lorin followed his friend somehow reluctantly, wondering if, by any chance, all these years of working in the porn industry had changed his friend's perceptions on life and the world in an unwanted way. Stefan used his fist to knock on the iron gates, which glided open and a gigantic bodyguard, steeped in steroids, over two meters tall and weighing a hundred and fifty kilograms of pure muscle, opened the heavy metal gate using only one hand, while scrutinizing the two Romanians. Seeing Stefan, he nodded and stepped aside to let them in, even though he looked Lorin up and down with a frown when he passed him by.

The girl selling tickets was almost naked, wearing nothing but phosphorescent pink underwear that glowed under the black light neon placed over the ticket office. If these things didn't seem strange enough to Lorin, the room they entered after paying for the tickets wasn't a club per se, but an antechamber, the dressing room where everybody had to leave at least part of their clothing, if not everything. Since it was summertime, the guys were wearing only a shirt and a pair of jeans, and Stefan took off his shirt, bustling Lorin to do the same, that ironic smile never leaving his face, not even for a second. Lorin realized that his friend's smile was probably due to the amazed expression that had been displayed on his face since the taxi left them in front of the factories. While he was reluctantly taking off his shirt, a group of seven to eight boys and girls entered the dressing room and hustled through another door. He guessed that was the door to the club, especially since they were almost completely naked; most of the girls were wearing heels, bikinis, undervests or bras. One of them had nothing on but her heels.

Stefan burst out laughing when he saw his friend's expression; the latter turned towards him inquiringly. He beckoned him to follow after taking the number from the dressing room and went through the door the group of young Germans had come through. They reached a dark vestibule where the music was much louder than in the dressing room, and when they entered the club per se, Lorin felt like he couldn't breathe and he had entered another dimension. After he waited for a couple of seconds in order to absorb the view, he turned to Stefan with the expression Stefanexpected him to have.

"Are you mad, dude? Where did you bring me to, bro? It's like Sodom and Gomorrah in here!"

"Yes, Lorin, my dear friend, Sodom and Gomorrah on amphetamines!" The actor chuckled. "Let's go to the bar and order some booze, so that you can calm down and get used to the atmosphere. You're looking around like some kind of a savage!"

The place looked nothing like the image Lorin had about clubs, even though he had been in many all over Europe. The club was, obviously, set in one of the halls where, half a century before, weaponry was made, and because of that, it was very high and broad. What Stefan hadn't told him was that it was an erotic club, not in the sense of a porn club or swingers' club, but a techno music club of the erotic sort. The bumper at the door only granted access to those who were dressed in an erotic fashion and even though they had come dressed normally, Stefan's appearance and the fact that the bodyguard knew him by sight had ensured their admittance. He certainly wouldn't have let Lorin in had he been alone or in different company.

These underground clubs in Berlin aren't considered the best in Europe only because of their lax policies and the orgies that happen inside. Mainly they are famous for their music. They have their own DJs, who mix techno songs with erotic rhythms, the result could turn on a nun. In this club, the DJ was standing on a balcony ten meters high, built especially for him on one side of the old factory. Behind him on the wall, there was a drawing of an aura that created a divine feeling, giving the impression that the music was played by angels. In fact, the whole factory had been organized in a way that resembled a church of lechery; the walls and the ceiling were covered in religious-erotic images, with decadent angels in various indecent postures, dragons with dozens of penises, and vicious demons.

Most people were partially or completely undressed, and what struck Lorin was the fact that they danced, talked, and drank like in any other club, without being distracted by their or other people's nudity. He noticed that there were more women than men in the club, probably a fairly logical administrative decision, and that most of the people present looked very good, like they'd been taken from the pages of adult magazines or from Stefan's movies. In spite of the fact that most of them were naked, there was a feeling of decency and common sense in the air, maybe precisely because of that, because the people weren't staring at each other's nakedness but they minded their own business, just like in any other club. For a moment, he tried to imagine what a club like this would look like in Romania and he burst out laughing, visualizing hordes of thugs drooling while staring at the naked dancing girls. Then he realized that in Romania no girls would dance naked except for the strippers and the prostitutes. A feeling of disgust at his own country took over him and, when he confessed to Stefan what was on his mind, the latter answered him in a casual tone.

"Well, why do you think I left that cesspool, bro? I was sick and tired of roughnecks and posers with empty stomachs. People abroad do exactly what they want, without any regard to what others think, and that's why they live better and have so much fun. Back home people gossip and judge your every move, like they're some sort of benchmark in morality when in fact they're a bunch of hypocrites who are dying of hunger. They play the morality card to hide their own frustrations and stupidity. Look here, see what a good life these people have and how happy they are and how hard they party, why the fuck would I want to go back to that shitty country? I'm glad you moved here too, brother. Maybe we can bring Radu boy here, too, in the future, 'cause that country is not for people like us, man. We deserve better, bro!"

He bought an ecstasy pill for each of them from one of the dealers in the club and, a bit later, when he wanted to go to the restroom, he noticed the same ironic smile on Stefan's face as he was showing him which way to go. A few moments later, he understood why: just outside the doors to the toilet, on both sides of the doors, there were two cages, each measuring almost four square meters, in which people were having sex. The floors of the cages were covered in mattresses, and in each cage, there were a few men and women having sex and masturbating. The gates to the cages were left open, and anyone who wished to participate in the orgy was welcome and, with the exception of a couple of voyeurs who were standing next to the cages and watching, the rest of the people weren't even paying attention to the cages, passing them by and casting only a furtive glance.

As he was going to the restroom, he noticed a gorgeous African-American woman, completely naked with the exception of her heels, who seemed very familiar and who smiled at him. At first he thought the X must have made some of his circuits connect in the wrong way, but then he realized that he really knew her, at least by sight. The woman was one of the most successful porn stars in Germany. Lorin felt completely swept off his feet by this place; he never wanted to leave this successful combination of sex, music, and drugs.

Although most of the people were quite okay, he noticed there were some weird characters there, too, but they seemed to be accepted by the rest without any problem. There was one man, around fifty-years-old, dressed in a Nazi uniform, with a Nazi helmet and boots and even a whip in his hand, but without any pants or underwear on. He was sitting on one sofa or another, whipping the girls over their asses as they were passing him by, or sometimes he even followed them around the club to smack them. The girls didn't seem to mind; what's more, they even made fun of the porno Nazi.

Another dingy character was a fat man with glasses, wearing nothing but sneakers and a metal belt around his waist. He approached the girls wearing heels and, lying flat on his back in front of them, asked them to step on him. The girls did it, but mercifully. At some point, however, Lorin noticed a tall blonde with typical Aryan features stepping ruthlessly on his genitals, provoking screams of joy and pain from the fat perv. He looked away quickly, not wanting to spoil the good spirits the place had inspired in him so far and told himself that in this kind of club, it was normal for such individuals to exist. Luckily, they were a small minority.

Back at the bar, while chatting with Stefan, he noticed that he was smiling at a woman behind him, and when he turned around, he saw a beautiful brunette, standing by a bar stool, with her back at the bar and facing the dance floor, looking intently at Stefan, smiling and licking her lips in a highly arousing way. Lorin turned to her for a fraction of a second, then back to Stefan, who couldn't take his eyes off her.

"What's the story, dude? Do you know her? Why is she looking at you like that?"

Stefan chuckled and told him to look at her again. When he turned to face her again and looked closely, he observed the detail he had missed the first time, which explained the intensity of the girl's reactions: in front of her chair, there was a man kneeling on the floor and giving her cunnilingus. The girl had already started quivering, feeling the thrill of the orgasm getting closer to the techno rhythm mixed by the resident DJ.

After pumping another XTC pill and snorting some speed offered on the bar by a girl Stefan had talked to for a few moments, the guys went out to get some air on the club's terrace, the former interior courtyard of the factory. The terrace was half covered; under the sun-blind, there were a couple of leather sofas and long tables where there was huddle upon huddle of young people, talking, smoking, snorting lines, or even having sex. The other half of the yard was uncovered, making way for the image of the shabby factories to complete the twilight scenery. Stefan saw two stunning girls on one of the sofas talking to a blond man, and he immediately went over and approached them, leaving Lorin at the table, a bit embarrassed, fixing a joint while he felt waves of energy generated by the combination of speed and XTC, the Berliner clubbers' favorite cocktail, because the pills aren't enough to keep you wired for hours in a row on the dance floor.

A few moments later, he noticed the blond guy got up from the girls' table and went to the entrance while Stefan motioned for him to join them. He introduced him to the girls, two superb German girls who had already started touching the mens' arms, pretending to be impressed by their tattoos and muscles. After a few lines of coke that one of them had taken out of her purse, they suggested they should go to another club, a bit smaller and less crowded, but equally extreme.

Twenty minutes later, they were all getting out of the cab in front of a suspicious-looking alleyway that opened into an inner courtyard, where there were some iron doors similar to those of the factory but smaller. They knocked on the door and an older biker with a leather vest and covered in tattoos took one look at them and immediately let them in. There was the same kind of dressing room as at the other club, where they left part of their clothing; after that, they reached a vestibule where another biker was guarding an iron door. He pulled the metal bar to let them in. When someone wanted to get out, he had to knock on that door and the biker let him out. The boys concluded that this system was meant to give the dealers time to get rid of the drugs in case they were visited by the cops.

Right after entering through the metal door, they started descending, the club being situated underground. This club was much darker than the previous one, being lit only by the black neon lights. Above the lights, there were paintings in fluorescent colors with an industrial-erotic theme, such as depictions of a woman out of whose vagina came a machine, or mechanical gadgets that, after a closer look, formed the image of a penis. They were all made with a lot of talent and they matched the ambience of the underground club perfectly. The music was very loud, you had to scream to get heard, and all of the existing objects were vibrating because of the volume of the music. Beds, sofas, and cages could be found here too, but what impressed Lorin the most was a suspended swing, about which Stefan, who had been there before, told him he would have the time of his life.

The swing was approximately two meters off the ground and, in order to get to it, you had to be pretty athletic, using the metal pole placed in front of the swing for precisely that purpose. The moment he got in the swing, Lorin understood why his friend had told him he would never feel better: the way you sat in the swing was as relaxing as possible. It was made out of metal pieces that blended perfectly together to create a position of total relaxation, just like an emperor's throne. The swing was covered in thick sponge cushions and bolted with chains from the ceiling.

Behind it, there was a cage for sex, and if you rocked it hard enough, you could get close to the DJ, to whom Lorin offered the joint he was smoking, taking it back a few see-saws later. Not only was his seat very comfortable, but also the fact that he was at a higher level than everybody else and looking down on them, truly gave him the feeling he had never felt better anywhere else.

Dazzled by all the sensations, Lorin hadn't even noticed that Stefan had disappeared with the two girls. He started scrutinizing the darkness of the club to locate them. From that height, he managed to see them on one of the beds; one of the girls had already started blowing Stefan while the other was caressing him and kissing him lecherously. Stefan looked in his direction and motioned him closer. Lorin jumped out of the swing and in two shakes of a lamb's tail, he was next to his friend, taking care of one of the girls.

Their sex scene lasted for an hour, and the sensation of having sex while being watched by strange eyes, even if it wasn't new to Stefan, was a completely novel experience for Lorin. He wouldn't have accepted being a part of it in other circumstances but the atmosphere of the clubs, pulsing with erotic energy, the ease with which his friend moved among women and the beauty of the two German girls, plus the drug consumption, made him relax completely and fully enjoy those unique moments.

When the orgy was over, they were invited to a private party by some club residents, mostly girls, who, along with the DJ and a couple of other friends, went to the mansion owned by one of the clubbers. The orgy continued for hours until everyone fell asleep, exhausted, in various awkward positions.

Next day, they were flying back to Prague, and while to Stefan, the events of the last couple of days seemed ordinary, they had a much stronger impact on Lorin. It was not only a positive one, given by the weird experience he'd been through, but also a negative one. He felt guilty towards Cristina and swore to himself he'd be a good boy for a long time thereafter. Stefan, who was dozing off in his plane seat, smiled sympathetically when Lorin expressed his disquietude, and while he was talking, fell asleep like a baby.

"Stefan, dude, only with you do I do stupid things like these. If Cristina knew, she would hate you with a passion, bro! Poor girl, waiting impatiently for me in Prague while I fuck women I've never seen before and I'm never going to see again! You're the only person that could ever make me do such things. Radu told me to beware if I ever moved to Prague 'cause you're the devil himself! Aren't you afraid that Jana's going to find out and get mad about the things you do with all these women? Don't you pity her for waiting at home, while you're screwing everything that wears a skirt?"

Then, realizing he was having a monologue, he smiled and pulled his cap over his face, adding: "You don't give a rat's ass about anyone else. It must be awesome to be like that!"

After that he fell asleep too, immersing himself in the images of what he had done in the last couple of days, with a satisfied look on his face, letting the waves of erotism that were still going through his body wash over him, making him jerk slowly from time to time.

Chapter 26

In the heart of the Carpathians, the routine and the monotony of a life spent in the middle of the forest had started to show their teeth in the relationship between Radu and Sophie. The latter, even if she loved the wilderness, had started to miss the clubs, pubs, malls, and beauty parlors more and more. In the Carpathians, the days went by slowly, without any major events, and Radu, when he wasn't with his dogs in the woods, did nothing but smoke weed, play games on his PlayStation, listen to music, and watch movies on DVD. And if this kind of living had pleased the Dutch girl at first, when she perceived this wilderness as some sort of a spiritual oasis, in the last few months, she had started to miss the hustle and bustle of the big cities, a busy schedule, and the responsibilities she had been used to. She missed her friends, Bo and Agnes, to whom she only spoke occasionally on the phone. She poured all this frustration down on Radu, he being the only person she knew here and, lately, the person she considered responsible for her unhappiness. The reproaches were being made more often, and the tension became more and more unbearable.

"You languish in the house all day long. When you're not in the wilderness with your dogs, you're lying on the sofa with a joint in your mouth, as if you needed constant relaxation! At first I liked this timeless life in the mountains, but for a while now I feel like I'm losing my mind from all of the inactivity! I want to go somewhere, see people, socialize, but you're the most antisocial person I've ever met! You only have two gears, an ultra-violent one, which scares the shit out of me, and a super-lazy one, which bores the hell out of me!"

Radu, who had moved to Poiana Tapului for that exact reason, to be as far as possible from the society he despised with every fiber of his being, was starting to feel the sharp blades the Dutch girl's barbs stirred in him sting his independent being: he had never stood for reproach from anybody. And the fact that Sophie was now raising a stink about these things, even though she had known how things were all along, intensified the irritation caused by the Dutch girl's attitude, adding to the baggage of negative feelings created by the fact that all he wanted was to be alone, surrounded only by his dogs, who loved him unconditionally. His answers were rather blunt. Sophie felt the iciness in his words and saw more and more clearly how everything that had been between them was falling apart at a rapid rate.

"Listen, Sophie, if you need the to-and-fro of civilization, this probably isn't the place for you and you should move back to The Hague. If you need a man you can take out to restaurants and clubs on a leash, I'm certainly not that guy. I moved here to have some peace and quiet and to be as far as possible from what civilization means to this world, rotten with greed, hypocrisy, and cowardice. If you miss it, maybe it's better if we say goodbye and take different paths, because now we're only managing to piss each other off and that's not what being together is all about."

Even though, after these tense moments passed, the feelings that the two of them had for each other found their way back into their hearts and breaking up wasn't something either of them wished for, layers of negative feelings had started to grow between the two of them, forming a wall they hit against more and more often.

One day, when Radu was returning from the woods with his three Staffordshire bull terriers, Atris, Drucilla, and Bullyson, on one of their walks on which Sophie joined him less and less, he noticed from afar that Sophie was talking to a man in front of the house, a man who, upon seeing Radu, made his farewells and went back to his mansion. He recognized him immediately. He was a guy from Bucharest who, in the last couple of years, had been building a mansion close to his, on the other side of the road, about two hundred meters uphill. He didn't particularly care for him; he had that arrogance he had seen in most of the people from Bucharest, and the fact that he had just talked to his girlfriend turned his resentment into pure hatred. Striding up to Sophie, who had already entered the yard, he addressed her in a brutal tone. The Dutch woman felt the wrath which had darkened his whole being, enhancing the horror she felt every time Radu's violence surfaced.

"What did you talk to that cocksucker about? What did he want from you? And why are you speaking to all the retards in front of my house?"

"Stop being such a freaking savage! He's no cocksucker, he's actually a nice man, and he's your neighbor! We were getting acquainted. He told me he recently moved here and that he has a pool in his yard, he invited me to take a swim whenever I feel like it. But he was very respectful and kind, so don't make such a fuss about it!"

"Oh, so I shouldn't make a fuss about it? Of course he was respectful and nice, since he wants to fuck you! I swear I'll break this retard's legs. This is a serious lack of respect towards me. He knows you're my woman and he invites you to his pool when I'm not around? Wow, he's got no idea what's coming to him!"

"If you do anything to him, I swear I'm never going to talk to you again. The man just came here and asked politely. Stop acting like one of your dogs! Nothing happened. I told him I have to talk to you first so stop reacting like this, please. You're scaring me!"

Radu made an effort to swallow his rage, but the image of the guy from Bucharest inviting his girlfriend to his pool tormented him, and he only just refrained from going over to his house and tackling him. The fact that the situation between him and Sophie had worsened lately didn't diminish the intensity of his hatred towards his neighbor, but he forced himself not to do anything about it, for the sake of the effort he was making to maintain whatever was left between the two of them, although it wasn't very clear to him why he was doing it.

A few days later, that same week, he had an unpleasant surprise. He usually took his dogs to the woods in three shifts, taking out the Staffie puppies first, then Cindy and Samson, and then Bronco. He did some light training with Bronco just to keep him in shape, even though he didn't want to let him fight again. Returning from the mountains with his favorite quadruped, he saw Sophie sunbathing in front of the yard, on a hillocky meadow, visible to all the passers-by. As if that wasn't enough, what made him lose his temper completely and got him in killing mode, was that next to her, squatting on his haunches, was the guy from Bucharest. The two of them seemed to be having a great time, laughing and gesticulating joyfully. Radu started to walk briskly, scenarios of what he was going do to his neighbor infesting his imagination at light speed. The two of them noticed him approaching, at which point the smile froze on their lips.

The man got up quickly and went off to his own yard but this time Radu addressed him. "Wait a minute, let's talk. Where are you running to? Wait a second, dude, I'm not going to do anything to you, I just want to talk!"

The man from Bucharest, who had reached the front of his house, answered him before entering the yard. "What's up, you wanker? Do you think I'm afraid of you? Why should I run away? Stop turning this place into a circus, you're not on your property now. You've terrorized this poor girl, too!"

Upon hearing these words, Radu's anger escalated and a black cloud covered his eyes. His universe was empty of everything except for his predator instinct, which dictated his reactions now. The same instinct stopped his hatred from taking over when he told him, in a somehow calm voice: "Well, then, come here and let's talk. Stop hiding behind the fence!"

"I'm not hiding. I told you I'm not afraid of you!"

That being said, the guy from Bucharest opened the gate to his yard and came out, followed by a friend of his, who had a Rottweiler weighing over sixty kilograms on a leash. They were both athletic, with well-developed muscles and a pretty high level of self-confidence as they approached him. A diabolic satisfaction imprinted on Radu's face when he saw them coming towards him because he knew that, had he done something to them in their own yard, he would have gotten into trouble. He was approaching them too and when the distance between them was less than twenty meters, he told them one more thing.

"What's the matter, you cocksucker? Do you want to fuck my woman? I'm glad you brought your friend along, now I can see that you're not afraid!"

He gave a short chuckle, and when he was only a couple of meters from them, he let Bronco off his leash, the dog sinking his teeth into the Rottweiler's neck that same second. After that, in two leaps, he was in front of the man from Bucharest. On the second jump, he landed with a powerful punch right in his chest, a move known in contact sports as the superman punch. The force of the blow would have been enough to make him lose his breath, but the speed added to Radu's jump made him fall flat on his back, unable to draw even a single breath of air.

Right after his friend fell to the ground, the second man from Bucharest threw a powerful hook aimed at Radu's chin, but the latter dodged it, anticipating the way in which he was going to be attacked. He bent down and went underneath the arm that missed his head by a few centimeters, and, at the same time, he threw an uppercut in his opponent's chin; the movement he had made earlier to duck, slightly to the left, offering him the perfect position for his right hand punch, the movement being continuous. Even though only less than five seconds had passed since he had released Bronco and let him fight the Rottweiler, the two men from Bucharest were now lying on the ground, one of them unable to breathe and making terrible rattling noises, and the other one losing his senses due to the punch he had received, which had dislocated his lower jaw and broken his cheek bone in three places.

In spite of the waves of adrenaline that were cascading inside his being and dictating he keep hitting the two of them, the fact that one of them wasn't even moving and, especially, the fact that Sophie was present, made him control himself, even though it required a superhuman effort on his part. He went towards the one who had invited Sophie to the pool and grabbed him by the neck with one hand, changing the key of his rattles:

"If I ever catch you talking to my woman again or even looking in her direction, I swear to you on everything I hold dear that I'll cut you in pieces!"

Even though he couldn't answer him, the look of horror in the man's eyes assured Radu that it would never happen again, so he let him go without hitting him again. Meanwhile, Bronco was shaking the Rottweiler, which was two times bigger than him. It was trying to cope with the pit bull's devilish bite but to no effect.

Radu turned to Sophie with an expression she had never seen on his face before, which made her blood freeze in her veins. "Get back inside, the circus here is over! Come on, take your things, and get in the house, do you hear me?"

Thunderstruck with fear, Sophie gathered her things quickly and was on her way to the house when she saw the brutal manner with which Bronco was shaking the other dog. She managed to say:
"Take your murderer off him. Can't you see he's killing the other dog, is that what you want?"

"Don't you worry about the dog, you just get inside and we'll talk afterwards!"

He let Bronco fight and escorted her to the gate, where he explained to her why he couldn't take Bronco off right away. "I can't take him off now because there's no one there to hold the Rottweiler. If I pull Bronco off now, the other one's going to keep attacking him. I have to let them fight until the Rottweiler retreats and then I'll be able to take Bronco. That's going to happen in a few minutes."

Just as he had predicted, in a few minutes, the Rottweiler couldn't stand the strength of Bronco's bite anymore and panicked because of the tenacity with which he was shaking him, while his bites seemed to be totally ineffective. He started pulling away instead of biting, trying to get out of his clutches and run, and then he started squealing. Only then did Radu get close and mount Bronco, holding his thighs in order to stop him from shaking his entire body, and with his elbows he blocked his shoulders with the same intention, while he grabbed the animal's collar and started squeezing it powerfully. This is the only way to make a pit bull let go of his clutch. He can't breathe because of the grasp on the collar and he lets go for a fraction of a second to inhale some air; at which point, the owner is able to pull him back. The thick wooden sticks introduced in the animal's mouth work too but only during the match, when the dogs are tired and don't have the same biting strength.

In a situation like this one, when Bronco was full of energy, Radu had no chance of unclutching his teeth with the stick; it would have broken. The uninformed had tried many ways of unclutching their pit bulls from their wrestling with other dogs such as splashing them with water, grabbing them by the testicles, or even kicking the dogs; all of them foolish methods that never worked, at least in the case of pit dogs.

After approximately half a minute, Bronco opened his snout for a fraction of a second, at which time Radu pulled him off his adversary, which ran away limping all the way to his yard. He patted Bronco on the back while praising him then he made towards his own yard, casting one last glance to the two guys from Bucharest, who were now trying to get up from the ground.

Back indoors, his anger boiled over the Dutch girl. "What the fuck were you doing, almost naked in front of the house? Is that why you went outside, so that your friend across the street could see you? If that's what you wanted, that's what you got, I hope you're satisfied!"

Sophie, who was crying, partially because of the shock and partially because she was angry, erupted: "You're an animal! How could you do that to the poor people? And to their dog, on top of that! I've never seen such a behavior before. I am absolutely astonished by it! How could you be like this? I don't want to be with you anymore. If this is what life beside you means, I'm better off without you!"

"I agree, I don't want to live with you either, if that's the way you react. As soon as you don't get enough attention, you go outside naked. I thought you were a different type of woman, but I see now that I was wrong! And you told that cocksucker that I'm terrorizing you? Have you no shame, when did I ever terrorize you? Since I met you, I've done nothing but try to act as nicely as possible to you, and you're complaining to strangers that I'm terrorizing you?"

Their fight continued until the afternoon, when each of them retreated to a different room. Sophie got herself a bottle of wine and started drinking in the yard by herself, while Radu lit joint after joint and played on his PlayStation, trying to take his mind off her. They met in the kitchen at some point but they didn't say a word to each other.

In the evening, around ten o'clock, when Radu had finally managed to calm down a bit, he heard the gate open and saw Sophie leaving, looking very sexy. Waves of anger washed over him again but he refrained from acting in any way; instead, he planned to get used to the fact that he was not going to be together with the woman he had fallen in love with without really knowing her. Despite the fact that his PlayStation game was very captivating, and in other circumstances he would have gotten completely lost in its atmosphere, his thoughts were constantly turning to Sophie, imagining different scenarios, each kinkier than the other. He felt a strange sensation of annoyance, combined with frustration and jealousy. This cocktail was turning his world upside down; he had never been in love before so he didn't know exactly how to react. But of one thing he was sure: between him and the Dutch woman, things were never going to work out again so he had to get used to the idea and act accordingly.

An hour later, he received a phone call from an acquaintance of his who was a bartender in one of the clubs in Sinaia, about a twenty-minute drive from Radu's house. "Hello, Radu, I'm afraid your girlfriend's here. She's quite drunk and she's dancing with a woodsman and they're smooching. I'm sorry to tell you this, I thought I'd call and let you know!"

"Thanks, Cornel, don't say anything to anyone. I'll be there soon!"

He got in the jeep and drove to Sinaia, heavy clouds of frustration enveloping his whole being. He was wondering how he had gotten into this situation and was mad at himself for letting his guard down for this woman, but none of that mattered now. He just wanted to see her one last time to tell her everything was over between them. He parked the car in front of the club and entered the club heavy-footed. He caught sight of Sophie after a few moments. Just as the bartender said, she was very drunk and dancing with her whole body pressed against a hefty man. He went straight to the man and put a hand on the woodsman's shoulder. The guy was head and shoulders above him and a lot broader in the shoulders. Radu looked into his eyes, trying to repress the feeling that made him want to dismember him on the spot, and told him to get lost in a voice he tried to keep calm.

The woodsman's first instinct was to knock the chip off his shoulders, but the demonic glow in the eyes of this stranger and the confidence he had approached him with, as well as the desperate gestures a few acquaintances of his were making behind Radu, changed his attitude and he left without a word. He went to the bar and watched the couple, asking himself what made him change his mind and refrain from hitting the stranger, as he would have done to anyone else bothering him. His friends approached him and told him in whispers that he did well by backing off and that no woman, not even one as beautiful as Sophie, deserved going to the hospital for.

Radu pulled the Dutch girl by the hand to a corner of the club and burst out: "What the fuck do you think you're doing here? This morning you are almost completely naked in front of the house for those wankers to see you, now you're dancing completely wasted with a woodsman who would have raped you, together with his friends, if I hadn't come here. You're totally out of your mind! You know what? It's all over between us! You've humiliated me and made me angry enough for an entire lifetime. I've had it! I thought you were a different kind of woman, but I was wrong!

"At the first sign of trouble, you run into the arms of other men. I've met women like you before! From this moment on, there's nothing left between us. Come, get your stuff and don't you dare contact me again! The last piece of advice I'm giving you is that you get the hell out of here, unless group rape is your plan for this evening!"

He turned around and left and Sophie followed him quickly, realizing that Radu was probably right, and that the way in which she was used to acting was probably very different from the way the locals acted. They would see her as a sure victim, especially since she was drunk.

Back home, she went to lie down on the couch but Radu cut that short. "I told you to pack your things and go away. Did you think I was kidding? You have your own house close by, go home, and leave me alone!"

Furious, Sophie started packing her things while smashing everything in her way, and a quarter of an hour later, she was walking out of Radu's gate. As the effects of the alcohol started to wear off, the realization of the way she had acted suddenly became much clearer. She didn't even know why she had acted like that. She assumed it was because she wanted to give Radu a lesson, to get back at him for the monotony of the past few months of her life, hoping he would somehow change and accept going out more and doing things she wanted; instead, she had only managed to make a fool of herself and lose the man she loved.

During the two weeks she remained in Poiana, she tried to contact Radu a couple of times but he refused politely. Back in The Hague, after a few other failed attempts to get back together with Radu, and a few months of waiting, she decided to sell the mansion in the Carpathians. She could never go back there; all the memories disturbed her in too brutal a manner. She decided she had to bury the whole "Romania" chapter and everything it meant, starting with the man who managed to make her feel the way no other man had ever made her feel, both when he had lifted her to the peak of happiness and when he had lowered her into the deep abyss of despair.

Chapter 27

Back in Prague, Stefan decided to take a break from filming in order to spend more time with Jana and bandage the wounds inflicted on her by his line of work. They decided to take a short vacation to Karlovy Vary, the most renown spa town in the Czech Republic, situated in western Bohemia at the foot of the Metalliferous Mountains.

On their way to Karlovy Vary, they discussed the break-up between Radu and Sophie, and while Stefan was, obviously, on his friend's side, asserting that the way in which he acted was quite legitimate and being very disappointed with the Dutch woman's behavior, Jana saw the issue in a different light. She agreed with Sophie, saying that she understood her perfectly and that she herself couldn't have lived with such a violent man as Radu either, and that the way in which she acted around other men was a cry for help. Cristina, however, saw things more like the guys did, and even if Radu wasn't her favorite person, her typically Romanian way of seeing things, more conservatively, made her agree with Radu, and towards Sophie she felt a slight disdain, the same kind that she always felt when it came to floozies.

After their first day at the resort, during which they fully benefited from what this remarkable town had to offer, Stefan and Jana went back to their hotel room, feeling exhausted. She was the first one to take a shower; meanwhile, the Romanian flung himself onto the double bed and turned on the TV. A few minutes later, Jana entered the room, completely naked, and the sparkle in her eye brought a smile to Stefan's face. Without saying a word, she climbed on the bed, mounted him, and sat on his face, shaking her pelvis with synchronized moves. Her lover's face with its Mephistophelian features appearing from between her legs was one of her favorite images, getting her extremely wet every time she imagined it. A few moments later, the people in the neighboring rooms became the auditory witnesses of an orgasm of an intensity they would have all liked to experience, but not all women were so lucky as to have a partner with Stefan's sex-appeal or, especially, one who possessed his techniques.

While his woman was still trembling, he turned her around and penetrated her, kissing her lips and her neck wildly, intoxicated by the scent of her pheromones invading his nostrils. Sex with Jana was in no way similar to having sex with any other woman, whether at work or in his private life. While his moves were generally robotic and brutish, without him getting too close to the women, kissing or caressing them during sex, the tenderness he felt while possessing Jana made him feel somehow addicted to her, turning him on every time he thought about her. The combination between the irresistible sexual attraction he felt towards her and his respect for her nature, augmented by all the experiences that they had shared and that had cemented their relationship, made Stefan wish to settle down and be a one-woman man, and forget about his easygoing way with women. The way in which she responded to the intensity of his actions, the way in which she enjoyed everything he had to offer, and the sensation that she gave him when she whispered in his ear, with complete satisfaction, "You're a beast!" made the Romanian draw away from the paths he had previously taken. Now he wished to be with her only. Feeling that this uplifted him and made him rise above the vulgarity he despised more and more, even though, until then, it had been his characteristic feature, to which he had felt very attached.

Lying in the hotel bed in Karlovy Vary, encompassed by satisfied exhaustion, they lit up a joint while a small portion of their brain was paying attention to the images rushing by on the TV screen.

Suddenly, Stefan noticed something that caught his attention, and he asked her to translate the message for him, as his knowledge of Czech language wasn't advanced enough for him to understand everything spoken around him. One of the biggest TV channels in the Czech Republic was offering the viewers the opportunity to come up with ideas for a show; the most interesting idea would be chosen and implemented.

Jana teased him: "If you have any ideas for a TV show, send it to them, but I don't know if they'd be interested in the life of a porn actor!"

"Oh, shut up. Don't you realize how cool it would be if we had our own TV show? You would make a perfect presenter, you're very photogenic and telegenic, and everybody likes you with your typically Czech features and your constantly smiling nature. I've noticed this about you. Everybody gives positive feedback upon first meeting you, your style makes you very likeable. Don't you see how ugly most of the TV presenters are? You would sweep the viewers off their feet!"

"I'm not sure I'd like to be on TV anyway, so that the whole country could see me. And what show would you have me host? Tell me, what do you have in mind?"

"Well, I'm not sure yet, but we could come up with an idea! If we had our own TV show, I would be able to retire from the porn industry, plus, it would be awesome if we could do something together!"

Stefan became obsessed with this idea, and he tried to come up with various alternatives of TV shows that had never been done, but would be successful with the viewers. In less than ten minutes, he exclaimed with the voice of an enthusiastic child upon seeing the ocean for the first time: "Got it! I know the theme of a show and I'm sure it would be a real hit in this country!"

"Tell me, what do you have in mind?" Jana asked him, amused by her lover's childish enthusiasm.

"The Czech Republic is one of the most dog-loving countries. I've read that it is among the most highly-rated countries when it comes to the number of dogs per one hundred inhabitants, and I've noticed that the most loved breeds here are those of the bull type, such as the pit bull, the amstaff, the bull terrier or the Staffordshire bull terrier. Here, each of these breeds has its own club that organizes swiftness trials and dog shows specifically designed for them. I think that a TV show about these breeds would enjoy a real success! Especially with you as a hostess!"

"To be honest, I expected you to come up with a lousier idea, but this thing might actually work! I've noticed that the owners of these dogs are more fanatical than the owners of other breeds of dogs, and that they are inveterate defenders of their quadrupeds against the attacks of the media, and of society in general. Giving them the opportunity to express their beliefs and to advertise these breeds in order to change public opinion might be a pretty good idea, and many people may be interested in watching such a show, not only the dog breeders. Now, I don't know what the network would think about this idea, they might find it brutal-"

"They'd have no reason to find it brutal. The main purpose of the show would be demonstrating the true character of these dogs and the fact that everything depends on the way they are bred. The show could give advice to old and new breeders alike. We could invite some of them on set to talk about these breeds, we could go to various kennels, film champions and their cubs, as well as dog shows. I think this is a very interesting topic, especially in this country where most people are dog lovers.

"Oh, and I have another idea. We could bring to Europe some of the sports specifically designed for these breeds, which are very popular in America, as they test the physical and mental qualities of the dogs without letting them fight. Weight pulling, for example, where the dogs are hitched to a cart that's loaded with different weights and set on tracks, and they have to pull the cart for a few meters. That's a sport where pit bulls win all the time, even against larger dogs. Or high jumping, where a graded wooden platform is placed vertically and the dogs jump higher and higher to catch a collar that is lifted on the platform with a cord. There's another sport, called tug-of-war, where two dogs face each other, each of them is given an end of a rope to pull, and the one which manages to pull the opponent towards him wins.

"All these sports were made especially for these dogs' qualities, and even though I'm not a breeder myself, I've always been surrounded by this type of dogs because of my friends, and I know enough about them to make me appreciate them very much. Plus, I have Radu to help me if need be. He knows everything there is to know about these breeds! I'd take care of the logistics and you'd be the hostess of the show, how about that?"

"It sounds like an interesting idea, Stefan, what can I say... but who knows if I'd be appropriate as a TV presenter. Maybe the network will agree with your idea, but not with me hosting the show."

"I can't see why not. They could train you how to speak in front of a camera, and that would be it! Anyway, I'm sure there would be a lot of sponsors interested in this show, companies that produce special equipment for these dogs, such as harnesses, collars, special leashes, chucks, and treadmills for dogs. There are also clothing companies that use the names of these breeds and manufacture products with this theme. I'm sure that the sponsors would fight for a chance to have a billboard in our studio! Furthermore, it's an original idea; such a show has never been done, not in the Czech Republic anyway!"

"Okay, listen. Why don't we make a draft of the idea and send it to the TV network to see whether or not they're interested in it. You should make a blueprint, a plan, in English, and I'll translate it into Czech and when it's done, we'll send it!"

Stefan was very enthusiastic about the idea and couldn't get the plan out of his head. If it were to become a reality, it would mean a huge step forward for him and his girlfriend. That week, after conducting some thorough online research, he planned the framework of his future TV show, adding all the advantages of this project to this short presentation. Jana translated everything into

Czech and sent the document to the respective network, but without the same childish enthusiasm that her lover had. Even though she would be very pleased to see this project come to life, the fact that neither of them had any experience in showbiz made her a bit skeptical about its outcome.

Before receiving an answer from the network, Stefan had to interrupt his relaxation time alongside Jana for a troublesome job. The plants grown by his cousin had reached their maturity, they had already been cut and left upside down to dry, and now the buds had to be harvested, the most difficult operation in the whole growing cycle. The boy couldn't manage such a workload by himself, and, moreover, Stefan and Lorin wanted to supervise the process and participate actively in it. Then they could ensure the improvement of the quality of the buds by carefully cutting off the leaves and weighing the quantity of skunk that they would get at the end of the process. It took them an entire afternoon and the whole night. Only by morning did they manage to finish cutting the thousands of buds off the plants that measured almost two meters.

Meanwhile, the boys chatted, and suddenly, Costin made a confession that took the two friends aback: "Guys, do you know what I did last week? I inhaled some heroin through aluminum foil. I had such a good time, I can hardly wait to do it again!"

Stefan and Lorin stopped cutting off the buds simultaneously and looked at each other. Then Stefan erupted. "What have you done? You did heroin? Are you an idiot, how could you get such a thing inside your body? But where did you get it, who did you snort it with?"

Costinel, who had been caught off-guard by his cousin's reaction, answered half-heartedly: "I did it with some guys I met from Constanta, but don't worry, I didn't tell them about my job. I told them that I work in construction and that I live in Karlin with other workers. They're gypsy pickpockets married to Czech gypsies here, they have kids. In the evening, when they come home from stealing, they prepare some heroin in aluminum foil to chill out a bit and I took some with them. I met them in a bar where I heard them speak Romanian so I wedged in. They're good guys!"

"You little idiot, you deserve to be kicked in the head. You're lucky you're my cousin and I love you. But if you ever use some of that shit again, our friendship is over. We close this house, sell the equipment and that's that. How could you do heroin, man? That's the silliest thing ever invented. It turns you into a dry potato! Not only does it destroy all your internal organs but it also creates physical addiction, and the way it makes you high is the most awful possible!

"I tried it myself a couple of times to see what the fuss was all about and I couldn't believe how bad I felt! What kind of drug is that? It makes you unable or unwilling to move, you're hot as hell, your brain barely functions at all; what the fuck did you like about that shit? When I take something, I want it to lift me up so I either take coke, 'cause it gives me that feeling of well-being and satisfaction, or LSD in case I want to take a trip into my subconscious or transfer myself into different dimensions. If I go out to clubs, I take an XTC or MDMA to get me in the mood for dancing and socializing, but under no circumstances do I use crappy heroin that turns me into a stuffed animal! It's the drug of the weak, the beggars, and the people with no will power. You do as you please, but if you want us to be in business together, or at least have some kind of contact with me, this has been the first and the last time you've done this, do you understand?"

Lorin chipped in too, only to underline their attitude towards this drug and to convince the boy to refrain from trying it again.

"We never get into business with junkies. You'll have to choose between staying in the growing business with us and taking heroin, 'cause we're not paying you to use this shit. Even if you're not shooting it in your veins yet, that's the next step after using the aluminum foil because after you take it like this for a couple of times, it stops having an effect. At the first sign that you didn't stop doing heroin, it's over. The business is over, we close this here and we send you home. We brought you here to make money, not to become a junkie. And what were you doing, hanging out with those darn pickpockets? Don't you know we've fought against gypsies all our lives, in Galati and wherever we met them? Now you have an entourage of gyppo pickpockets who are heroin junkies on top of that?

"Honestly, you disappointed me. I didn't expect such a thing from you, and if you weren't Stefan's cousin, I would break a couple of your bones for having invested all that money in this house just so that you can make a mockery of it, jeopardizing everything so that you can break your veins with a couple of poor excuses for human beings! Think about what you want to do, but if you want to remain here and keep growing, you must never see those people and you must never touch that crap again, okay?"

The boy felt like hiding his face in shame and felt very guilty, knowing the kind of trust and money that his cousin had invested to bring him here and make things hum, and now he felt like he had disappointed him and he had ruined everything with his carelessness. If he could have predicted the guys' reaction, he would have never told them what he did, but he thought they would be impressed with the fact that he was integrating into the foreign lifestyle. He now understood that he had done so in the worst manner possible and that he had to change his behavior quickly, unless he wanted to be sent back home. He apologized, promised never to meet the three gypsies again and never to touch heroin. After that he remained quiet until the work was finished.

The guys weighed the merchandise. There were almost ten kilograms and a half of it, everything over ten kilos was split between them for personal use and the rest was carefully packed in several layers of plastic that Lorin took in order to sell in Italy. Thenceforth, Costin's job was to throw away the leftovers from the plants along with the dirt from the pots. The pots would be filled with fresh dirt and he would plant new seedlings for the future cycle.

The next evening, Lorin was in Turin, where his jail mate was waiting for him along with two other friends, who were also dealers and wanted to invest. Lorin had specified that he couldn't give them anything on credit, and that he could only bring them the merchandise if they were going to buy all ten kilograms at once, so the other dealers were needed to raise the necessary cash. Back in Prague, he split the money with Stefan, and put aside Radu's share, to give it to him when they met. Little did they know that this was going to happen sooner than they expected.

One morning a few days later, the intercom in Jana's apartment rang, and a man's voice asked in English for Stefan to come downstairs. Looking out of the window, he saw five Harley Davidson motorcycles parked in front of the stairs, and some well-built, tattooed bikers, all of them in leather vests with the same symbols, waiting in front of his apartment building. He put his gun under his belt and went downstairs, curious about what the bikers wanted from him. He realized that they didn't come in peace, judging by their menacing attitude and the way they approached him. One of them was broad-backed like a bull, a skinhead sporting a long ginger beard. On his chest Stefan noticed the patch that recommended him as the president of this group of bikers.

The man approached him until there were only a few centimeters between them, and told him in a throaty voice that sounded more like a bark: "We have a big problem. You've stolen some clients from us and our business, you Romanian! You deserve to be executed on the spot but I prefer to think that you simply didn't know they were our people or else you wouldn't have trespassed on our territory!"

Although he had come downstairs in a pretty good mood, black clouds of anger darkened his core and he barked at the Czech bikers, while flapping his jacket a little so that they could notice the gun he was carrying: "I don't know who you think you're talking to, but this ain't the tone you should adopt when you address me. And if something happens to me, you, your club and your families are gonna go up in flames, so stop threatening me or you'll end up harming yourselves. We didn't know we were dealing on your territory. I can't possibly know where all the cokeheads in Prague buy their stuff from, but we can work something out.

"I'm not alone in this business, I have some partners, I will talk to them and then we'll come to your club to see how to deal with this. But if you want us to work something out and remain friends, stop coming to my place 'cause you're scaring my woman! By the end of the week, we'll look for you and we'll find a way to solve this."

The biker nodded and got on his motorcycle, followed by the other members of their gang and they were off like a shot, deafening the passers-by. Without knowing it, the guys had stepped on this gang's territory, taking away some of their clients. But the money from this business was too good to give up just because they had trodden on someone's toes. The situation had to be solved in a different manner.

Chapter 28

The motorcycle gang that had accosted Stefan was called the Iron Dragons and it was the Prague branch chartered by an American motorcycle club. Like many other motorcycle clubs, it had been founded after World War II by former soldiers, who were thrill-seekers. The banality of everyday life was hard to bear for people who had lived every day of their lives as if it were the last, always surrounded by the specter of death, and counting exclusively on their brothers-in-arms. This coming to terms with imminent death, which meant they put a smaller price on life than people who hadn't been on the battlefield, and the intensity of the relationships formed between them in the trenches when their lives depended greatly on the help they could offer each other, had given birth to this brotherhood, which transcended friendship or even blood ties. Fellowship and the need for thrills were the reasons for the founding of these motorcycle clubs, most of them based in America.

This was also the case of the Iron Dragons, who had named their club using a metaphor for their Harley Davidson motorcycles, the flames coming out of the exhaust pipes of these metallic monsters enhancing the similarity between them. If the initial purpose of the club had been to celebrate the fellowship of these men, in just a few decades it had become one of the most powerful and dangerous gangs in the States. This was due to the large number of members, which turned the club into a redoubtable force, their brutal ways and, most importantly, their need for a large sum of money to keep the whole outfit going. The original members of the club, who had founded it in order to celebrate their friendship and not because they wanted it to become a fierce criminal organization, were now either dead or had been removed from their leading positions by the younger, more ambitious, bloodthirsty generations. Their rivalry with other outlaw motorcycle clubs had led to many territorial disputes, which had often ended in a bloodbath.

In the last decades, they had branched out to Europe in order to diversify the profit sources, and the chartered clubs in countries like Sweden, the Netherlands, and Germany were just as violent and fierce as the ones in the States. But in the Czech Republic, things were a bit different. The peaceful nature of the Czechs made their outlaw world equally peaceful. The guys from Iron Dragons had barely any competition in their business, and territorial disputes were totally nonexistent. While the chartered clubs in other countries were made up entirely of inveterate outlaws, the one in Prague had members who were mechanics or motorcycle enthusiasts, who had never been involved in violent acts or illegal operations before entering the Iron Dragons, as well as criminals. The main source of money for the club was the women; they owned several brothels in Prague and dealt with trafficking prostitutes. Most of the time, they brought them over from the poor countries in Eastern Europe and sent them to countries with a more prosperous economy in the West. Besides prostitution, the club made money from drug trafficking, especially cocaine. The Romanians were the first people to ever mess with their business when they took over some of the bikers' clients, albeit unknowingly.

Lorin called Radu, telling him that some issues had come up and that his presence in Prague was needed. The next day, Radu flew in to the capital of the Czech Republic, after asking Irinel, who had returned to Poiana a few weeks before from his latest trip to South America, to take care of the dogs. When he got to Stefan's apartment, his friends filled him in on the situation.

"Dude, we've taken some clients away from them, the most important being the guy who owns the gay club downtown. He has already bought a few kilos from us, which he used to buy from these bearded fuckers. We have to bring in some determined people, ready for anything 'cause these bikers are wicked. There are a lot of them, and they're on their own territory. I think the best way would be for you to call your mates in London, those who rob and torture other gangs over there. Tell them to come over here!"

"I'll call them, but we need to pay them for their trouble 'cause nobody does anything for free. I think I should ask for five guys and we'll pay them a grand each; this way they'll take the deal. What's more, we could keep using them if they offered to stay. We could give them some coke to push in the clubs because if we sell it by the gram, we can get twice as much as we get when we place a kilo. This way we could have our own mini army here in case we have any more problems with the fucking bikers, or with any other assholes. And these guys are dead serious; they'd do anything for the right sum of money. I trust them because we had many operations together while we were inside and I've seen what they're capable of."

Radu called Faur, one of his friends in London, and told him that he had a job for him and four other guys, that they were each going to earn a thousand euro, and that they could go back to England in two days.

The very next day, the five guys were landing at the airport in Prague, and an hour later, they were in Stefan's living room. The eight Romanians gathered around the table and Radu filled them in. He told them they'd have to go to the bikers' club the next day and solve the problem. Then he presented them with the second part of the proposal.

"If you're tired of England and you want to stay here for a while, there's a cow to milk for everyone here. My buddy Stefan has connections in many clubs; if you want, he can get you in to make some money. We'll give you the stuff for fifty euro and you could get eighty, or even more if you sell it to the tourists. The clubs are open every day of the week here and you could easily push a few dozen grams a day, more at weekends. Also, there'd be more of us this way. You see how we're bumping against others and we need some backup."

"Bro, to be honest, I'm sick of torturing people for a few coins, and I'm especially tired of going after Romanians. There aren't the same opportunities for making money that there used to be in London. A lot of the people we used to rob are in jail now, and those who aren't in jail can barely make it on their own. And it's getting harder and harder to make money cloning cards nowadays. So a change would be welcome. We could see how things work here in Prague, especially since you have these sweet deals. So much the better. We need to keep a low profile in London for a while, especially since we have a bone to pick with a lot of people there and the cops are all over us. I, for one, want to move here but I can't speak for the rest of the guys. I don't know their plans."

Except for one guy who had a girlfriend in London, the other four agreed to move to Prague for a while and see how the business worked. They partied together for the rest of the evening at Stefan's place, which gave him and Lorin the chance to get to know their future partners better. They got along wonderfully, all of them having the same background and many things in common.

The next evening, after having contacted the bikers, they were invited to one of their brothels situated in the old town center, near the Charles Bridge, on an antique lane, paved and lit only by street lamps. A girl in a short transparent dress opened the door when they rang the bell, and invited them in with a big smile on her lips, although the guys were able to detect the anxiety hidden under that friendly mask. After they went down a few stairs and passed through the foyer, they entered the club's main room, which had many sofas arranged in the shape of a U around the assorted tables. The walls were painted a blood red and the windows were covered in black foil so the clients would lose track of time and, without being able to tell whether it was day or night, lose themselves in the sensuality of the girls who worked for the bikers. There were no clocks of any kind in the club either, their absence having the same purpose.

On the right side of the main room, there was the bar, approximately ten meters long, behind which a topless barmaid was smiling at them. The girls were sitting on the couches, dressed as provocatively as possible. Some of them were entertaining the customers sitting at the tables when the guys came in. Where the bar ended, a long hallway began, intersected by another hallway at some point. On each side of the two corridors, were the rooms where the girls worked, a total of ten rooms, each of them fitted, apart from the double bed and two bedside tables, with their own toilet and shower. Some of them were also furnished with whirlpool bathtubs, the price for visiting those rooms being slightly higher than for the others.

The club was open 24/7, the girls worked eight-hour shifts, and they were paid half of what they made in a shift. By working for the club and not on their own, the girls had a much better flow of clients, and they also benefited from the protection offered by the motorcycle gang.

The girl who had opened the entrance door for them led them through the semi-dark corridors of the brothel and invited them into one of the rooms at the back, which the bikers used as an office. The room was equipped with leather sofas, a heavy wooden table, a pool table, a computer, a TV set, and a vending machine. There were ten bikers in the room and Stefan recognized the president of the club and the four sidekicks who had visited him a few days before. They motioned them to sit down around the wooden table and then they also sat down. Radu and the president of the club sat on opposite ends of the table, and it became obvious to those present who the leader of each group was. Before starting to speak, Radu noticed with utter satisfaction that an expression of anxiety had appeared on the faces of some of the men dressed in leather, which showed that they felt intimidated by the presence of the Romanians, whose level of brutality could easily be perceived by those with a keen sense for such things. Those who didn't show any signs of anxiety, such as the president of the club, tried to remain calm, but each of the Romanians in that room could sense the fear the Czechs felt, their predatory reflexes signaling them when someone was intimidated or scared in their presence. Without further ado, Radu cut to the chase, looking directly into the bright blue eyes of the club's president – the red-bearded skinhead.

"Guys, here's the deal. I understand we've taken some of your clients. We didn't know that and we didn't do it on purpose, but we all have to eat. We didn't force anyone, they called us, and everybody has the right to buy goods from wherever they like. And, since we have a better and cheaper product than yours, the only thing you can do is to upgrade. How long did you think you could make it without any real competition?"

While he was talking, Radu analyzed the Czechs' features, noticing their increasing nervousness and the glances they were exchanging. He continued.

"We have an offer to make you so that everybody is happy. We can give you guys the goods at the same price we sell it to the others, namely thirty per gram. As you probably know, the merchandise is very good, definitely the best in Prague, and you can cut it and sell it further, especially in other towns, because I know you have clients all over the Czech Republic. I don't know the price you paid for it before, and I don't care, but I know for sure that the quality-quantity ratio couldn't have been better than what we're offering you. Now, there are only two alternatives: you either agree to it, in which case we remain friends and we do business together; or you don't, in which case, let the war begin! We're prepared for either alternative. It's up to you how you choose to proceed, but I can promise you one thing. Irrespective of your decision, we won't leave this place and we won't downplay our business!"

The bikers left the table and went to a corner of the room, sitting on some couches to discuss their further actions. The Romanians waited for the Czechs' decision quite tensely, each of them ready to attack in case of a negative decision.

A few minutes later, they came back at the table, and the president addressed Radu. "Okay, we'll do business together, but only if you agree on twenty five! If the merchandise remains top notch and you sell it to us for this price, we'll need five or six kilograms a month. Can you manage to get us this quantity?"

Radu, who had known that this was going to be the Czechs' decision even before they knew it themselves, answered him with a sparkle in his eye. "Twenty seven and we've got a deal! You tell us in advance how much you need, and we handle it. One more thing before we shake on it. We're also going to sell in some clubs, and if you want to keep this friendship, you won't sell a thing in those places where you see us dealing. Okay?"

"Well, we don't deal in clubs anyway. We sell wholesale to our people. We need a kilo now, to see how it goes. Can you bring us the stuff?"

Radu turned to Stefan and Lorin, who both gave him almost imperceptible nods. And with that, Radu stood and shook the biker's hand, and Lorin took off. Half an hour later, he returned, carrying a bag with a kilogram of coke, which the bikers paid for in full after they tested the quality of the product.

In order to celebrate their latest connection, the bikers invited the Romanians to party at the brothel the whole night, everything being on the house. After a few hours of drinking, Radu launched into one of his anarchistic tirades, as he did almost every time he snorted coke. The guys who had come from London, even if they didn't fully understand the meaning of his words, were very impressed with the way he formulated his ideas and they had the feeling that they somehow agreed with him.

"If we could turn back time a few centuries, I'm convinced we'd be surprised by the way people used to fight back then. I'm sure it had nothing to do with the way they're portrayed in the movies. We can only assume how they fought, according to the standards we have nowadays, which are limited now that fighting is just a hobby for a small percentage of the population. But in those times, their lives depended on the way they moved, and battles were men's main occupation. And, given the fact that they learnt the art of war since they were kids and they spent their whole lives perfecting it, I think their moves and their efficiency in battle would impress us as much as, let's say, a close encounter with an alien.

"I believe that people have forgotten about the extraordinary things that our minds and our bodies are capable of, because of the apathetic comfort offered by the present-day civilization. Never finding ourselves in extreme situations, hiding behind our false moral values to mask our cowardice, never taking risks, evolution has led to the loss of the warrior reflexes and the survival instincts we were once endowed with. It has all been replaced by the reflexes necessary for integrating into this capitalist society, governed by petty principles. The taxpayers first pay their dues to the state, only then do they eat. They never enjoy the present because they are constantly worrying about the future. That's exactly how the government wants them to be. And people get used to being controlled and become addicted to the chains that become so familiar to them. They take the information delivered to them by those who control themfor granted, and completely lose touch with the warrior inside them, because this characteristic is not agreeable to the social and moral values that we are kept in line with."

The party continued until noon the next day. The eight Romanians left the premises feeling very satisfied, concluding that these bikers were nice guys and very pleased with the fact that their numbers had increased. They were delighted with their new business, which was going to augment their profit considerably.

Chapter 29

A few days after the party at the bikers' brothel, Stefan called his cousin to see how things were going at the plantation. Much to his surprise, he discovered that Costin's phone was switched off, in spite of the fact that he had expressly told him never to switch it off in case an emergency occurred.

Slightly flustered, he got into the car and drove to the house outside Prague. He entered the residential area but when he turned down the street where their rented house was, he shuddered. A couple of police vehicles were parked in front of the house and the yard was full of cops who were taking pots along with the plants from inside the house. Stefan gulped nervously and kept on driving without slowing down. He called Lorin and Radu to break the tragic news, while a vague feeling of guilt engulfed him; after all, he was the one who had brought the boy to Prague.

Later on, they found out what had happened. Costin had been out for several hours, even though the boys had told him not to do so, and while he was gone, the tube connected to the air purifier came off, having been glued to the respective engine with adhesive tape. Thus, the stench of weed from the plantation went out through the chimney without being purified, intoxicating the whole area with skunk miasma. After a few hours, during which the inhabitants of the neighborhood were besieged by the scent of marijuana, someone called the cops, who immediately discovered the plantation. They staged an ambush in order to catch the culprit red-handed. This happened a few hours later when Costin arrived home, eager to go to bed. Except that he was only able to do so after ten hours of questioning concerning the plantation, and under police arrest. The boy kept his word. He didn't give them the names of the others; instead, he told them that the entire operation was his and nobody had helped him. After a few months, he was tried and convicted to three years in prison, but he would get out on probation after a year and a half.

Even though Stefan felt responsible for what had happened to his cousin, he didn't let himself get too affected by it, blaming Costin for not minding his advice and leaving home for more than a couple of hours, something that the boys had forbidden him upon his arrival in Prague. The fact that he was now receiving calls from Romania almost daily from his aunt, Costin's mother, who was asking for news about her son, didn't help the situation and only aggravated his anger at his cousin's insubordination and the financial loss.

Luckily for him, he received some news that made him forget about his troubles almost entirely and filled his heart with joy and hope. The TV network had contacted Jana, telling her that they were interested in their idea. They wanted to meet with them for a more detailed discussion about the possibility of producing the show.

Upon their arrival at the network headquarters, Jana and Stefan were taken to the director's office, where he was waiting along with several heads of departments. The network's chief executive made a good impression on them as he was very open-minded and agreeable. He told them that their idea for a TV show was among the finalists, along with a cooking show, where two chefs were going to show the viewers how to cook various goodies. Ondrej Majdak, the chief executive, told them frankly that he was more interested in the other option because it was less risky. On the other hand, he admitted that cooking shows weren't something new while a show about fighting dogs hadn't been done before so he was giving Jana and Stefan the opportunity to convince him that their show had potential. While Jana was a bit more reserved and less convinced by the aces up their sleeve, which could turn their idea into a winner, Stefan participated in the dialogue and, after approximately an hour of highlighting the pros and cons, it seemed that he had persuaded the staff that this show was going to have the desired impact upon the viewers.

A week later, the young couple received a phone call from Ondrej, announcing that they had decided to endorse their idea and that shooting for the pilot episode was going to start in a few days. The interesting and innovative idea, along with Jana's pleasant physical appearance and her outgoing, smiling personality, had convinced the staff that this was a project worth investing in. Furthermore, they suggested that Stefan should participate more actively in the show, and not only off-stage. They found him to be very telegenic and wanted him to promote the show as a couple's business, the youth being the ones who were usually breeding dogs such as these. He suggested that Stefan take some Czech language classes, in order to participate in interviews and discussions on the set. Stefan started taking intensive Czech classes immediately, taking a break, which he hoped could become permanent, from the porn industry.

That month they shot the pilot episode, and a few weeks later, it was broadcast. The ratings exceeded even their most optimistic expectations. As a result of the positive feedback, Stefan's show got the confirmation that it was going to be produced by the television network and broadcast weekly, for half an hour, on Thursday afternoon, with two re-runs, one of them on Thursday night, the other on Sunday night. It was the first time that Jana felt truly proud of her man. Up until then, she had only been attracted to him like a moth to a flame, but without ever feeling satisfied with his accomplishments or his nature. But now, she felt like he had risen from his own ashes, like the Phoenix, leaving the porn shootings and drug trafficking behind, focusing on Czech language studies and, mainly, on the show, towards which he had paternal feelings, being prouder of it than he had ever been of anything before.

He hardly saw his Romanian friends, leaving the whole business in Lorin's hands, as the latter had always wanted. The fact that he had his mini army again, as he did when he was in the German prison many years before, gave Lorin great satisfaction, which couldn't even be matched by the doubling of their funds in the last couple of months. He had brought two more guys over from the London team to work with them in Prague, and Irinel had started bringing two kilograms of coke paste from Peru instead of one, which they processed into eight kilograms of powder to cover the increasing demand for their product.

Radu, in order to take his mind off Sophie, had found a new hobby, which kept him pretty busy: building a pool in his basement where the plantation had been for years. He received the news of Costin's arrest with sorrow, lapsing into a sarcastic smile as he realized that his decision to dismantle the plantation had been taken because of his relationship with the Dutch girl, which was now over, and the money invested in the house in Prague was now lost. But, consistent with his pragmatic way of looking at things, he concluded that everything happens for a reason and that every experience, especially the negative ones, teaches something. The lesson here was one he had already learnt, namely, don't change anything for anyone, and, most of all, don't fix it if it ain't broken!

The people working at his indoor pool, brought in from the village, were in his basement for more than ten hours a day, and in less than a month, the pool was ready. Radu was beside himself with joy. He'd been dreaming about having his own pool for a long time, and now that the dream had come true, he decided to equip it as best as he could. He bought a surround audio system, a few couches, chairs and tables, all of them suitable for a humid environment. The only sources of light in the room were red neon lights, which he had ordered online. He managed to create a very relaxing atmosphere, maybe too relaxing for people who weren't used to Radu's dark, underground style. They would probably have found this ambience demonic, with its red lights filtered by the steams coming from the water and creating, along with the darkness of the room, the impression of a swamp in hell, where you expected a dragon, or some other mythological creature with negative connotations, to appear.

Radu spent most of his time in this room, listening to music and smoking while lounging on a sofa, immersing into the depths of his own being, and feeling as if this devilish pool he had built was a portal to other worlds. He was in a universe of his own, where he submerged into his subconscious and touched the abyss, which had lately become his main playmate, in which he could find himself, and where he could find answers to all of his questions.

But he wasn't able to enjoy this state of dark melancholy for long. Something happened that affected him more than all the problems in the last years combined: one morning, when he went to feed his dogs and take them for their daily walk in the woods, he noticed that old Samson wouldn't get out of his house. He went inside his enclosure and saw his old friend gasping for air, barely breathing. When he tried to pull him up and help him get to his feet, the dog whimpered softly but couldn't move at all. Panicking, Radu immediately took him in his arms, put him on the back seat of his jeep, and headed straight for the vet. The latter told him that Samson was suffering from kidney failure and that, given his old age, his chances of recovery were slim to none. He suggested he be euthanized. Radu wouldn't even hear about it.

"This dog is a gladiator; he's been fighting all his life and I will let him fight until the end. If he dies, then that's that, we all have to die sometime, but I will let him leave this world as he came into it, fighting!"

The doctor gave him some shots to help him with the pain and to diminish the effects of the renal failure. He told Radu there was nothing more he could do, and that, should the dog make it through the night, he could bring him again the next day to continue the treatment.

Radu could barely drive home because of the tears obstructing his vision. He felt as if something was breaking inside of him every time Samson whimpered on the back seat. Back home, he lay a mattress on the ground for him to lie on and sat down next to him, petting him gently on the head and whispering words of encouragement to him, his husky voice drowning in a stream of tears. The dog was asleep because of the sedatives administered by the veterinarian but he still whimpered in his sleep from time to time. Radu only left him to go to the toilet, returning to lie by his side and pat him gently.

He felt that an entire era was ending. He had had this dog since he was very young and they had been through many hardships together, one of which was when he and his parents were attacked by the Carpathian shepherd in the mountains, and Samson had saved their lives. Everything he had ever achieved in life, every life-changing experience, happened with loyal Samson by his side, and the fact that he was now in pain and his days were numbered caused Radu more suffering than any person ever could.

Radu kept himself awake all night next to old Samson as if his wakefulness were somehow contributing to the dog's recovery. At the crack of dawn, he fell into an agitated sleep for half an hour, and when he woke up, jumping to his feet, his four-legged friend had already left this world.

Chapter 30

In the following months, Stefan learnt the Czech language almost perfectly, even though this Slavic language is pretty hard to learn for speakers of Romance languages. He went to classes three times a week, and Jana talked to him almost exclusively in Czech, helping him understand the complicated grammar of her native tongue. They had become one of those *à la mode* couples in Prague, their weekly appearance in a TV show bringing them fame in the Czech capital. Several local tabloids presented them as one of the sexiest Prague couples. People recognized them on the street, and the fact that Stefan had been a porn actor was no drawback, as he had first expected it to be; on the contrary, the Czechs had the chance to amaze him once again with their liberal, open-minded way of thinking. Not only did they not write or say a single malicious thing about his past, but the fact that he had starred in several porn productions actually increased his fame and the viewers' appreciation. The show had an increasing female audience thanks to the animal magnetism he generated, and, since he had started making an appearance in the show, his movie sales had increased.

After burying Samson in the heart of the Carpathian forest, in a little glade that had been the dog's favorite place and where they had spent many hours together, Radu sank into a state of apathetic melancholy, spending long hours in his dark underground pool room. Now he walked the dogs in two shifts, he first took Bronco with his mother Cindy, and in the second shift, he took Bullyson, Drucilla and Atris, the three Staffies, who were growing up fast and rapidly approaching maturity. He spoke to his friends less and less, as they were up to their eyebrows in their activities in Prague. Money was steady and there was more every day, as Lorin and his guys were extending the parameters of their business and getting new clients. But, even though things were going well financially speaking, this idleness had started to get on his nerves. The lack of adrenaline and conflict, which he needed to put out his inner fire, occasionally gave him feelings of anxiety he couldn't fully refute with the help of weed, which he smoked in larger and larger quantities. Radu needed some action but he didn't know which action would give him the greatest satisfaction.

One day he received a phone call from Joker's owner, who requested a return match regardless of the sum of money invested. Upon Radu's refusal, the guy from Bucharest tried a series of tactics to make him change his mind. He even proposed that they have the match without any witnesses or bets, solely in the presence of the owners. Radu explained to him that he had given up the pit bull fights, and suggested he tell the other breeders to get their mind off any matches against Bronco because he was never going to fight again.

Even though he made this decision according to what he had wanted for a while, the logic behind the decision was becoming more and more shaky. And that wasn't only because he missed the ring fights and the adrenaline rush given by his dog' s victories more and more, but because he knew that Bronco had at least a few more years of fighting in him and there was no dog that could defeat him, at least not in Romania or the neighboring countries. And it wasn't all about the considerable amounts of money he knew he could earn if he let the dog fight again. Firstly, it was about the fact that all his life, he had wanted to have the perfect ring dog; now that he did, he had no matches, which induced him a vague sense of frustration. In spite of the fact that he hadn't changed his decision not to get involved in fights anymore, he started training Bronco more and more intensely, so that both he and his dog could get rid of the negative energy that had accumulated because of the lack of activity and confrontation.

Meanwhile, Lorin and his boys had become one of the most feared gangs in Prague, known as "the Romanian Mafia." Their brutal behavior and the ease with which they resorted to violence had ensured their rapid climb up the hierarchical ladder of Prague's underworld. They had taken over clients from several clubs and had gotten into conflicts with various dealers, disputes that were always solved in the same manner, promptly and brutally. Lorin's spirits were high, leading a very good, money-making business and having as acolytes an army of loyal soldiers, capable and always ready for anything.

Less than six months after her employment in the firm, which acted in the financial domain, Cristina got promoted from the sales department to production. This was not only due to the large number of clients she had brought to the firm but mainly because of her professionalism and deep understanding of the ins and outs of the business. In the new department, not only did her salary double but she also gained more freedom. She was now the one who came up with the ideas for conferences after careful market research, and the responsibility of choosing the conference venues was also hers. With this promotion came more than just a new status. She also had the opportunity to travel more, her presence at the conferences she organized being a must. The chosen venues were five-star hotels in the big European capitals, in order to create a bonus attraction for those who paid large amounts of money to participate.

The evening they found out about her promotion, Lorin invited her out to celebrate. After a romantic dinner in a floating restaurant on a luxury ship across Vltava River, the two of them decided to go to a club to celebrate the good news, especially since it was a Friday night. Since they had come to Prague, things had started going great for them, both of them stepping up in their expertise. In this jovial mood, they entered the club, which belonged to one of Stefan's acquaintances, and where two of the boys from London were working. They sat at the table they had previously reserved and ordered a bottle of rum on the rocks, being occasionally joined for a drink by the two dealers who were working for him. After two or three hours of partying, spirits were pretty high. The party was very good;

the only ones missing were Stefan and Jana, who couldn't join them because they were filming the next morning.

Lorin's attention was caught by five Ukrainians at a table a distance from theirs; they were in an advanced state of intoxication and they were louder than the rest of the people in the club. Lorin didn't care much for this but decided not to ruin the cheerfulness and the party organized for the woman he loved with all his heart from the moment he first met her years before. He decided to ignore them, despite the fact that his instinct was dictating he go to their table and make them aware of the fact that they were disturbing everyone around them. He continued to drink in the company of his lover, snorting lines of coke from time to time, planning, together with Cristina, how to proceed further and where to go on their vacation, which was quickly approaching.

At some point, Cristina left the table to go to the rest room and Lorin's eyes followed her, smitten with the love he felt for this wonderful woman, who brightened his life and whose accomplishments he was now so proud of. He smiled as he watched her steps, slightly tangle-footed because of the glasses of rum the girl wasn't very used to, when, suddenly, in a blink of an eye, his serenity and affection turned into feelings at the opposite pole of his spiritual barometer. One of the noisy Ukrainians was at the bar, which Cristina had to pass by in order to get to the rest room, and the man, who was in his thirties, bulky and a skinhead, stopped her, grabbing her by the arm with his rough hand.

Lorin jumped up like a spring and went towards him at the speed of sound, motioning the other Romanians to stand by. Lorin grabbed the Ukrainian, who, meanwhile, had let Cristina out of his clutches upon seeing her prompt reaction, by the shoulder and turned him so that they could face each other. Growling through his teeth, which were gnashing with hatred, he said: "If you ever lay your hand on my woman again, I'll cut it off, you cocksucker!"

Without replying, the Ukrainian flashed a smile then threw a powerful hook, which was meant to smash the Romanian's jaw. Lorin, who was expecting this kind of reaction and who was as tense as a fully stretched spring, repelled the blow with his left arm and, after his forearm had stopped the right hook, he grazed his hand behind his adversary's arm, thus blocking his chances of moving. At the same time, he drew back his right arm, taking a full swing for a tremendous punch to the hulk's jaw. The Ukrainian took a step back, his right arm still blocked by Lorin's grip, but he didn't fall. His firm jaw and the perfect balance he displayed impressed the Romanian. Three more hooks to the chin were needed for the bumper to fall.

As he watched him fall flat on his back and the thrills of satisfaction started running through his body, he felt a blow in the head and his ears immediately clogged; at first, he couldn't understand what had happened. One of his enemy's friends had hit him over the head with a champagne bottle, which instantly broke. In that moment, he saw the two Romanians jump next to him like two tigers, attacking the other Ukrainians. But he didn't have time to turn around and see who had attacked him and with what, because he noticed, out of the corner of his eye, that the one he had sent down on the floor had jumped to his feet and now had a pocket knife in his hand. He repelled his thrust with his forearm, but he got a deep cut in the process and he didn't get the chance to do what he usually did every time he got attacked with a knife: take off his coat or his shirt and wrap it around his left forearm in order to deflect the impact of the blade.

The Ukrainian, who was hopping mad, was attacking him violently, moving towards him throwing knife blows all the while, constantly aiming at the Romanian's stomach. Lorin jumped backwards a few times in order to avoid being stabbed with the knife; he was hit once, his shirt was slit and impregnated with blood in a few seconds. While he was stepping back, he drew out the switch blade he always carried around in his pocket. With an evil look frozen on his face, seething with hatred towards this man who had molested his girlfriend, he managed to cut him pretty deep while he was trying his best to inflict some other wounds on him. The Ukrainian, upon seeing that the Romanian had drawn out a knife, attacked him even more angrily, charging him with all the strength and speed he could muster.

Lorin, already used to the rhythm of the moves that protected him from the enemy's blade, jumped to one side with a virtuosity similar to Maradona's roll-outs, and the moment his adversary was parallel to him, he plunged the knife between his ribs, pulling the knife a lot to the left as soon as he felt that he had touched a muscle, in order to avoid penetrating too deep or touching any vital organs. As in all the other fights he had taken part in, he wanted to inflict serious injuries on his opponents but not fatal ones. Thus, he administered a pretty deep cut, approximately twenty centimeters long, which ploughed into the Ukrainian's ribs.

No sooner had he pulled his bloody knife out of his enemy's body, ready to plunge it again, this time into his shoulder, than he felt the cold barrel of a gun against his temple and heard someone screaming in Czech. As if he was just recovered from a trance, he noticed the police crew with their guns ready to fire, the cops having been alerted by the club's bodyguards, who wouldn't dare take action in such a large conflict without the cops' backup. The three Romanians and five Ukrainians were handcuffed, put in the police vans, and, after a short while in hospital under the officers' watch, moved to jail to await trial; except for the one slit by Lorin, who needed more complex surgery and a longer recovery period.

Lorin tried not to let himself get depressed by this turn of events, being used to life behind bars and taking things for granted. He admitted to himself that if one is a criminal, it's just normal that one would occasionally do prison. If he was a bit worried, it was about the way their cocaine business would progress and who would be its boss in the future.

There was yet something else that gave him even more trouble: the fact that he had disappointed Cristina again. He hadn't kept his promise to her that never again would he put her in the situation where she would be on her own, waiting for him to finish his sentence. However, the fact that this time his reaction was caused by his need to protect her gave him some peace of mind, and he hoped his woman would not be angry with him and would wait for him as she had done in the years he was imprisoned in Germany.

He met Costin in prison, who was beside himself with joy that he had somebody familiar around, somebody who could protect him from those who had already tried to abuse him. The boy showed him a Romanian full of tattoos, a thief whose gang was with him, and who had beaten him several times, and probably abused him in ways he preferred not to mention. Right away, Lorin and his two friends grabbed the fellow and gave him and his gang a serious pounding, not just to take vengeance for the boy's abuse but also to show the other Romanians in the Czech prison who the new leaders were and what they were capable of.

Unfortunately, they were in deeper trouble than with the other Romanians, and the cause of that trouble was the Ukrainians with whom they had locked horns. They were their fellow inmates and the gang of Ukrainians in prison was much larger than that of the Romanians. Lorin didn't know to what extent he could count on the other Romanians, except for his two friends. He immediately confiscated a few daggers crafted by other Romanians, saying that they would need them and telling everybody to be ready to fight, just in case the Ukrainians were planning any acts of revenge. The next day, Cristina came to visit, she being the only one who was allowed to pay visits for the time being. Lorin used the opportunity to transmit a message to Radu and Stefan, knowing that the meeting would last only a few minutes.

"Listen, baby, I know I promised I would never make you go through this and I'm sorry to put you in this situation again, but you were there, you saw how it happened and you know there was no other solution. Don't worry, they won't keep me long. In a few months, maximum a year, I'll be home; the witnesses saw it was self-defense. You'll manage to get by with the money we have in the account and Stefan will give you my monthly share of the business, plus, you have your new job now so you wouldn't have had money trouble anyway.

"Hey, I have a message that I want you to deliver to Stefan, please, remember everything I tell you: someone has to take over the business and Radu is in Romania, Stefan is super busy with his show, so the only person who could do this is Irinel. The boy has demonstrated countless times that he is trustworthy, that he has balls and he's a man of character, and he's not at all stupid. He wanted to be more involved, anyway, now is his chance. Tell Radu to bring him here, introduce him to the boys, and explain to him exactly what he has to do."

"And don't you think these guys might try to take the business from him? I mean, Irinel is a little more than a child while these other guys of yours are inveterate criminals who would sell their own mother for the right amount of money-"

"No, baby, they would have no way of doing that. They'd have nowhere to buy merchandise from if they stepped on our toes, and even if we suppose they might get the merchandise from some place else, they wouldn't have access to the clubs where they need to sell it. Stefan would settle it with the clubs' owners, and they would kick their asses out in no time at all. Besides, they respect Radu too much to try to do anything against him, and I know they'd rather be our friends than our foes."

After they talked for some more minutes, the visit was over and Cristina let her man resume his activities in prison while she could hardly stop her tears from falling. The pain caused by the idea that the person she loved most was confined and the thought of the ordeal she imagined he had to experience overwhelmed her, adding to the anxiety caused by the fact that she would be on her own and in a foreign country for the next few years.

A wave of loathing at her own weakness struck her hard. She wiped her tears with the back of her hand, and her Romanian character, typical of a people who had experienced numerous hardships in their long history, made her swallow her sadness and take things as they came. Her man was hard as a rock and time spent in jail was nothing more than a break for him. As far as she was concerned, she could do worse. She was living in one of the most beautiful cities in the world and doing a job for which a lot of people might envy her. She focused on the trips to other countries occasioned by the conferences she would organize, and on the new friends she had made at her work place. She decided she would visit Lorin in prison as often as she could; she was thinking of all this while she was going through the prison gates with a firm, sure-footed gait.

Back from the visit and finding himself in the room full of other inmates, Lorin noticed that the Ukrainians they had fought in the club, together with their compatriots, were talking to one another in a closed circle, and that they were casting him fleeting but meaningful glances when their eyes met. It was clear to him now that the Ukrainians were going to hit soon, and he started to get ready both physically and mentally in order to cope with it. He worked out more often and took cold showers, to prepare his body for the shock in case he got stabbed. It was crucial to avoid passing out in order to be able to keep fighting despite the inflicted wounds.

In the evening, on the TV in the cell, Stefan's show was being broadcast. He was wearing his Mephistophelian smile on the set while he was playing with a bull terrier champion, brought to the studio by his proud owner, along with all the cups and prizes he had won at the beauty competitions they had participated in. As he watched Stefan's show and sharpened his shiv on the metallic edge of his bed, he nostalgically remembered Radu's words, spoken at the New Year's party, and he smiled sarcastically, realizing how much truth there was in them.

"We're all fine now, we're among friends, we can't ask for anything more, but tomorrow we may be in jail or taken from this world. This life is exactly like a fighting ring, brothers, and we're the dogs who do their best to survive and to win. And you often win and have the impression that you're someone, but then life hits you so hard that it puts you in a tight corner, and it takes way longer to get up than it does to fall down. On the other hand, there are times when you're down on the ground and you're so angry you feel like killing everyone, and suddenly you see a weakness in your opponent and that twinkle of hope gives you strength to get up and fight more fiercely than you did at the beginning. We're nothing more than dogs fighting for every inch won in this pit that is life, where there can only be winners and losers. Draws are not accepted, brothers, not while you have a pair of balls!"

-------------END OF PART ONE-------------